COLIN WILSON is one of the most prolific, versatile and popular English writers at work today. He was born in Leicester in 1931, and left school at the age of sixteen. After years spent working in a wool warehouse, a laboratory, a plastics factory and a coffee bar, his first book *The Outsider* was published in 1956. It received outstanding critical acclaim and was an immediate bestseller. Since then he has written many books on philosophy, the occult, crime and sexual deviance, plus a host of successful novels which have won him an international reputation. His work has been translated into Spanish, French, Swedish, Dutch and Japanese. He is, according to *The Times Literary Supplement*, among the most discussed English authors in Moscow's university circles. In addition to his literary career, Colin Wilson is also a well-known television personality, broadcaster, and journalist.

D1806436

Also by Colin Wilson

Non-Fiction

The Outsider
Religion and the Rebel
The Age of Defeat
Encyclopaedia of Murder (with Pat Pitman)
The Strength to Dream
Rasputin and the Fall of the Romanovs
The Brandy of the Damned (Essays on Music)
Beyond the Outsider
Eagle and Earwig (Essays on Books and Writers)
Sex and the Intelligent Teenager
Introduction to the New Existentialism
Poetry Mysticism
A Casebook of Murder
Shaw – A Study of his Work
The Occult
New Pathways in Psychology
Order of Assassins

Fiction

Ritual in the Dark
Adrift in Soho
The Schoolgirl Murder Case
The Philosopher's Stone
The Mind Parasites
The Killer
The God and the Labyrinth
The Glass Cage
The World of Violence
Necessary Doubt
Man Without a Shadow
The Black Room
The Space Vampires

Autobiography

Voyage to a Beginning

Colin Wilson

Origins of the Sexual Impulse

PANTHER
GRANADA PUBLISHING
London Toronto Sydney New York

Published by Granada Publishing Limited
in Panther Books 1966
Reprinted 1970, 1978

ISBN 0 586 02127 2

First published in Great Britain by
Arthur Barker Ltd 1963
Copyright © Colin Wilson 1963

Granada Publishing Limited
Frogmore, St Albans, Herts AL2 2NF
and
3 Upper James Street, London W1R 4BP
1221 Avenue of the Americas, New York, NY 10020 USA
117 York Street, Sydney, NSW 2000, Australia
100 Skyway Avenue, Toronto, Ontario, Canada M9W 3A6
Trio City, Coventry Street, Johannesburg 2001, South Africa
CML Centre, Queen & Wyndham, Auckland 1, New Zealand

Made and printed in Great Britain by
C. Nicholls & Company Ltd
The Philips Park Press, Manchester
Set in Monotype Garamond

DEDICATION

To Professor G. Wilson Knight

At about the same time I realized that
what my instincts most desired to attain
was precisely the reverse of what
Schopenhauer's instincts wanted, that is
to say, *a justification of life*, even where
it was most terrible, most equivocal
and most false; to this end, I had the
formula *Dionysian* to hand.
NIETZSCHE, *The Will to Power*, 1005

Nothing is easier than to judge what has
substance and quality; to comprehend
it is harder.
HEGEL

ACKNOWLEDGMENTS

I would like to acknowledge the generous help of G. Wilson Knight, who has never received due acknowledgment for his work on D. H. Lawrence, although his discoveries were later publicized and exploited by others. I would also like to acknowledge the co-operation of certain friends and correspondents who have allowed me to quote from letters, private journals and other unpublished material. For stimulating discussions on phenomenology and existential psychology, and for many invaluable suggestions, I wish to offer my thanks to Professor D. T. Murphy, recently of Wake Forest, N. Carolina, without whose initial suggestions this book would certainly never have been written.

I also wish to express my grateful acknowledgments to the following publishers for their permission to quote copyright material:

Crest Publishers for Nelson Algren's *Walk on the Wild Side*; The London Encyclopedic Press for Magnus Hirschfeld's *Sexual Anomalies and Perversions*; Charles C. Thomas (Illinois) for Paul de River's *Crime and the Sexual Psychopath* and *The Sexual Criminal*, and for James Melvin Reinhardt's *Sex Perversions and Sex Crimes*; Vision Press for Stekel's *Sexual Aberrations*; Martinus Nijhof (The Hague) for Herbert Spiegelberg's *The Phenomenological Movement*; Basic Books (New York) for *Existence*; Heinemann Medical Books for Berg's *The Sadist* and Havelock Ellis' *Psychology of Sex*; Medical Publications for Camps' *Medical and Scientific Investigations in the Christie Case*; Harcourt Brace for Beckhardt's *The Violators*; The Bodley Head for Joyce's *Ulysses*; Nonsuch Press for Geoffrey Keynes' *Works of William Blake*; Macdonald & Co. for Powys' *Glastonbury Romance* and *Autobiography*.

I wish to thank various friends and correspondents, including Philip de Bruyn and Frank Mitchell, for allowing me to quote from books that have not (at the time of writing) been published. Finally, I wish to acknowledge the help of my wife Joy in preparing the manuscript and the index; also of my daughter Sally, who carefully read the manuscript but unfortunately, owing to her age (eighteen months), was unable to understand it.

Colin Wilson

CONTENTS

INTRODUCTORY NOTE: A DEFINITION OF AIMS

THIS book is a kind of Siamese twin of another volume, on which I have been working simultaneously: *An Outline of a New Existentialism*. Its scope is less wide than that of its twin; in fact, it should be a sub-heading of the total discussion. But the subject of sex and of existential psychology demands space; to treat it adequately would demand that I expand the parent book to a thousand pages. I have preferred to take the other risk: of repeating some ideas on "the New Existentialism" in this volume.

I should begin, then, by making a general statement of purpose. For about two years now, it has become apparent to me that all my work, since the publication of my first book (*The Outsider*), has been an attack on the same problem: the creation of a new existentialism.

To the general reader this may sound technical and of limited interest. What is existentialism? – an obscure modern philosophy developed by a few French and German thinkers, with far less general application to society than the ideas of Dewey or Bertrand Russell.

But this is a false definition. Existentialism is an *approach* to any kind of knowledge; although it began as a revolt in philosophy, it has already extended its sphere to psychology. In due course, it may well reach all the sciences. The present book is mainly concerned with its impact on psychology, and particularly on the theory of sex.

In an early chapter of *An Outline of a New Existentialism*, called "What is happening to modern science", I argue that modern science is moving away from the purely analytical approach that has been its characteristic since Newton and Descartes. The scientist knows he cannot find the "life" in a body by vivisection. In the nineteenth century he was inclined to say: In that case, life does not concern me as a scientist. If the "binding principle" could not be isolated, then it had to be ignored. This was reasonable. What was worse was the tendency to deny the necessity for any binding principle. Freud at least never went this far; he posited a binding principle called the libido, but then concentrated his attention upon analysing its effects. The libido stayed in the background, like a titled sponsor or a sleeping-partner in a business; if anyone objected that Freud was analysing life out of existence, he only had to gesture towards his "mystical premise" as evidence that he also recognized basic forces.

The present book is concerned mainly with the post-Freudian revolt against a totally analytical approach, and with raising the question of whether the methods of Gestalt psychology and of Husserl's phenomenology (see Chapter III) can be applied to the psychology of sex.

On another level, this book is a more personal approach to sex. I have treated the problem of sex on three previous occasions: in my novel *Ritual in the Dark*, in a chapter of *The Strength to Dream*, and in the essay "The Study of Murder" that introduces my *Encyclopaedia of Murder*. The present book is an attempt to give a certain unity to these speculations, and to carry them to their limits. Inevitably, some of the ideas of these earlier books are re-stated here; for readers who notice the repetitions, I offer an apology.

A word on the "new existentialism". It may be asked: Why a new existentialism? What is wrong with the old one? The answer is that the old one is fairly recently deceased (I would offer 1950 as the approximate date of its collapse), and must now be counted as dead as nineteenth-century romanticism. Before the end of this volume, I shall try to explain why I consider sex to be a valid approach to a new existentialism.

A comment about the method of this book may save the reader from some confusion. There are two ways of writing an analytical book on any subject. One is to define all your terms with scientific precision in the first chapter, and then stick closely to these definitions throughout. The other is to rely on your reader's instinct and common sense. All originators in philosophy are forced to rely on the second method (because so much of their work depends on intuition). That is why Plato, Hume, Berkeley, and Nietzsche are so much more readable than Aristotle, Kant, Hegel and Heidegger; they do not overburden the text with too much definition, and they are in closer touch with the reader. Aristotle is certainly more precise than Plato, but it is difficult to imagine anyone reading him for pleasure. Any professional writer – that is, any writer who is concerned about direct communication with the reader – will certainly be inclined to prefer the "intuition" method, and avoid overburdening the text with definitions.

In the present book, definitions are not excluded, but they are kept to a minimum. I have made a great deal of use of inverted commas to indicate that words or phrases are being used in a certain limited sense (i.e. "nature", "perversion", "life-force"), but have avoided circumlocutions to make this sense obvious.

It might be convenient, therefore, if I stated at this point some of the book's underlying assumptions. The first is connected with my use of the word "nature". In a certain sense, this book might be summarized as "an indictment of nature". We tend to define the word "perversion" in an *ethical* sense (as opposed to a practical sense – meaning "inconvenient for society"). That is to say, we think of it as having an "absolute" meaning – signifying "against God" or "against nature". This is the intuitive meaning we attach to the word, and I have accepted it: perversion is an act that man commits of his own free will against nature. "Nature" is here considered as having a quite definite purpose in mind in devising the human machine; perversion is to oppose nature's purpose. The meaning might be made clearer by means of a parallel. If a man bought a farm tractor, and used it for driving long distance at fifty miles an hour, he could hardly complain if the machine broke down. If he complained to the manufacturers about this, they would reply: "You are responsible. The machine was never intended for such treatment." (De Sade thinks of "perversion" as a defect of the mechanism due to misuse – a kind of general loosening of all the parts, the outcome of "satiation".) If the man could reply: "On the contrary, the machine is also full of mechanical defects", then the onus would be on him to prove the manufacturers responsible.

The point of this book is that, if we think in these terms, then the "manufacturer" is undoubtedly responsible for sexual perversion. It can be regarded as a mechanical defect, due to bad design in the sexual mechanism.

But this pleasantly simple conclusion is partly the outcome of accepting the "intuitive" definition of perversion – an act of free-will against nature. But man is not wholly a creature of free-will, neither is nature a divine mechanic, mass-producing cheap working models. This conception is a product of an older and vaguer system of ideas, with a fully conscious and omnipotent God in his heaven, and man, a fallen angel, on earth. We are nowadays aware that man possesses some free-will, but not as much as he used to believe, and that he might be regarded as a co-partner in the business of evolution rather than as a mere manufactured product. Therefore, subtler realities underlie these simple words "man", "nature", and "perversion". In the same way, we sometimes speak of "indicting society" for an injustice committed against an individual, although we realize that society is a mass of individuals and therefore cannot be indicted. Neither can "nature" be indicted, for nature does not exist as something completely separate from man; rather, man might be regarded as nature's instrument of evolution. It is not a simple matter of blaming the manufacturer for a mechanical defect in the machine, for in this case, the machine is to some extent its own manufacturer.

If I had begun this book with an analysis of the body-mind relationship and the man-nature relationship in the manner of C. D. Broad, and then attempted to analyse sexual perversion with a battery of metaphysical terminology, I doubt whether the book would have got written. But it is important that the reader should take full account of the inverted commas around words like "nature" and "perversion", and recognize that they may conceal *double entendres* that the necessities of the discourse make it impossible to indicate.

CHAPTER I

GENERAL DISCUSSION OF
SEXUAL ABERRATION

Statement of central problem of book: what part does sex play in man's total being? Views of Tolstoy and Gide. Freud and Gurdjieff. Aldous Huxley and sex. Noyes and the "karezza". D. H. Lawrence and sodomy.

It will be convenient to begin by stating the question with which this book is centrally concerned: What part does sex play in man's total being?

This immediately involves two more questions. The first – and most immediate – is about the nature of the sexual impulse. The second is: What is meant by "man's total being"? If any kind of a satisfactory answer can be provided to the first question, it may be possible to use it to shed light on the second.

The most obvious statement about the sexual impulse is that here is a point where man and "nature" have two different aims. The aim of nature appears to be procreation. The aim of the individual is to achieve the fullest possible satisfaction in the sexual orgasm.

It is true that man's purposes and nature's seldom correspond exactly. Nature requires that a man should take as much interest in food as will keep him alive and healthy. This is not sufficient for most civilized men; their interest in food goes beyond anything that nature requires; some are even capable of eating themselves to death. Still, on the whole, most men keep within the bounds of "what nature requires". The same is true of the needs for drink, sleep and exercise.

In the sexual impulse, the gap between man's purpose and nature's seems unusually wide. This is the reason why there are more perversions of the sexual urge than of any other human preservative impulse.

But here, the first problem occurs. A perversion is usually defined as "an unnatural act". The word "unnatural" is easy enough to understand when man feels a strong instinct for what is natural. No one, for example, doubts that the eating of excreta is unnatural, since what has once been rejected by the body can hardly provide nourishment for the body. But where nature has separated its own purposes from man's as widely as in the case of sex, how are we to judge what is natural?

Tolstoy's Definition of Normality

To some extent common sense is helpful. The essence of the common-sense view of sex was stated by Tolstoy in the novel *The Kreutzer Sonata*. Basically, this is a kind of Wesleyan tract against sexual licence. The wife murderer, Podsnichev, feels that modern society has plunged into a kind of sexual insanity. This is because the increase in leisure has given man far too much surplus energy, which he uses in a feverish pursuit of pleasure. In the natural course of things, neither man nor wife has energy for much sexual indulgence; she is worn out by childbearing, he by his daily labour; his interest in sex is limited. But the aristocracy (particularly the "cultured" aristocracy) spend their days with thoughts of sex – which, in its more innocent stages, is disguised as romance. Podsnichev's jealousy of his wife began when she played Beethoven's Ninth Sonata for piano and violin with a young aristocrat; this kind of cultural dilettantism, Tolstoy implies, is only another excuse for relationships that can drift into adultery.

Tolstoy concluded that the only "normal" sex is sex directed specifically to producing children. All indulgence for pleasure – even between man and wife – is "abnormal", i.e. somehow unnatural.

This view has at least the merit of consistency. It goes a stage beyond St. Paul, and the teaching of the Catholic Church on birth control. It is, in fact, a basically religious view. It declares that man's own inclinations have no part in the definition of "normality"; a "higher" view must be taken, even if it runs counter to desires that men count as "wholly natural".

There would be very few of us who would be prepared to go as far as Tolstoy in defining what is "normal". Most writers on sex, from Ellis and Krafft-Ebing onwards, have been inclined to define sexual normality as "any sexual activity that leads ultimately to the act of reproduction". This view produces certain contradictions. It states that all sex is normal if ejaculation finally takes place in the vagina, no matter what unusual practices may have led up to it. Consequently, a man who withdraws before he has an orgasm, or who wears a preventative, is more "abnormal" than a man who likes to beat his wife to increase his sexual excitement, or a man who rapes a girl after knocking her unconscious. But the main objection to the view is that it offends logic by defining abnormality in terms of the *end* rather than the means. After all, the end of most sexual activity is an orgasm; surely it is the means by which it is procured that counts in judging "abnormality"? The "sexologist" view of abnormality is a convenient working rule, that appears to be accurate only because most men who reach an orgasm inside a woman achieve sexual excitement in the usual way.

Gide's Corydon

Gide, who made no secret of his pederasty, wrote four dialogues between a sexually "normal" narrator and his homosexual friend Corydon, in which he attempted a philosophical justification of homosexuality. But the book is more than an argument in favour of uranism. Gide himself said frequently that he regarded it as his most important book, and he was too intelligent a man to make such a statement merely because the work justified one of his favourite indulgences. In fact, the questions it raises go far beyond the question of whether homosexuality is "natural" or "reprehensible".

Gide points out that, in animals, sexual attraction is usually due to the smell of the female on heat. It might therefore be regarded as entirely "physical" and natural. Even so, Gide contends, it would not be true to say that the male animal feels no sexual urge except when he smells oestrum; most animals overflow with sexual desire, and may attempt to induce an orgasm by mounting another male animal, or rubbing themselves against any convenient object (the leg of a human being, for example). Nevertheless, the odour of oestrum has the effect of uniting and directing the animal's sexual instincts.

Man also overflows with sexual desire, but in his case there is no smell of oestrum to unite the instincts and direct them towards the female at any particular moment. The stimulus that unites his instincts is purely mental. This is the reason for the wide variations in the type of stimulus – in other words, for "perversions". The "normal" man is excited by the sight of a naked woman; but he need not be particularly abnormal if he prefers a very fat or a very skinny woman, or a middle-aged "motherly" woman. He may not be especially abnormal if he is more excited by the sight of a woman in her underwear, or a woman with long hair down her back.

Gide argues that therefore it is in no way abnormal for a man to prefer a boy, or another man. It is true that exclusively homosexual intercourse would not people the earth. But Gide takes care to mention several cases of "manly" homosexuals who have produced families. He seems to imply that it would not be an undesirable state of affairs if every single man and woman had homosexual inclinations, provided they also did their duty of producing families.

All this raises questions of immense interest and deep implication. I have suggested, in "A Study of Murder", that the sexual desires in children are "undifferentiated"; that is to say, they are no more than the need for stimulation of the sexual member, as simple as the desire for food. At an early age, the sexual appetite is "hypnotized" by some object, so that the object becomes associated with sexual satisfaction. The object may be some fetich – a crutch, a nightcap, an apron; it may be the child's own sexual parts or those of another child of the same sex. Luckily, for most men the "object" that hypnotizes the imagination is the opposite sex.

One basic fact should be noted here: that sexual desire, in its simplest form, is *a demand of the sexual organ*, associated with it in exactly the same way that magnetism is associated with a magnet. The difference is that the sexual organs might be compared rather to an electromagnet, that may be either completely "dead" or magnetized. It is a kind of static electricity of the sexual organ, which the organ wishes to discharge. We may know very little of the "dynamo" that produces the sexual electricity, but the electricity is undeniable. In discussing the part played by the imagination in sex, we should not lose sight of the real existence of this genuine physical component. A man whose thoughts are a long way from sex may be surprised when the loins accidentally press against something and he feels a tingling as the "electricity" is discharged.

At this stage it is possible to make only one clear generalization about the sexual instinct: that it works on a deeper level than any other human impulse – even, perhaps, that of self-preservation. On the whole, man can understand his tastes and desires. If he wants money, or social position, or fame, or even if his dominant urge is a desire to collect paintings or old books, he can trace the need back to its source, and understand how it became dominant in his scale of values. The sexual urge is the most difficult of all to assimilate into the consciousness; a man may think he understands it, and then be thrown completely off balance when it takes him by surprise. Shaw's *Man and Superman*, for example, shows that even a man dominated by the need to be a world-reformer can be hurled, against all his better judgement, into sexual union with a woman for whom he has little personal respect. As he embraces Ann, Tanner exclaims: "The Life Force enchants me; I have the whole world in my arms when I clasp you", and "The Life Force. I am in the grip of the Life Force." Romain Rolland makes the same point in *Jean Christophe*, when he points out that Christophe's parents have nothing in common, and that, in fact, the father has no idea of why he threw away a promising career to marry a little servant girl: "But what did that matter to the unknown force which had thrown him in with the little blonde servant? He had played his part . . ." [in fathering a man of genius].

But I have no wish, at this stage, even to attempt to offer generalizations about "evolution"; all that I wish to emphasize is the actual *power* of the impulse, and its ability to override conscious checks. Hirschfeld cites an interesting case of a thirty-five-year-old doctor, who had been subject to fits of somnambulism and epilepsy since childhood, and who was charged with committing an indecent sexual act with a thirteen-year-old schoolgirl. The doctor was treating the girl for eczema, which covered her whole body:

"He sat on the settee, drawing the child's head down to him; during this act, her whole body approached his and induced in him sexual excitement accompanied by an erection. He now pressed the child closer to himself. Of the rest of his actions, the defendant had no clear recollection. When he came to himself, he was sitting on the settee, with the child, now in tears, standing between his legs. . . . His mind did not clear until he reached his flat. . . ."

During his "blackout", the doctor had induced an orgasm by rubbing his sexual member against the child's body. Hirschfeld mentions that the doctor was greatly depressed at the time, and was in a state of exhaustion due to overwork.

At first sight, it might seem that the blackout story, and the emphasis on his depression, are both lame attempts to excuse an act that was completely conscious. This may, of course, be so. But certain facts should be taken into account. The first is that human consciousness is peculiarly limited. Although all human beings have an immense reservoir of memory, our actual awareness of the everyday world is relatively narrow and dull. For reasons best known to the evolutionary force, man is not allowed access to his unconscious storehouse of knowledge and memory, except on rare occasions. (Elsewhere, I have compared human consciousness to a horse that is blinkered in the traffic, because too much "consciousness" would only hinder its efficiency.) Human beings wilfully limit their own consciousness, for single-mindedness and a broad consciousness are incompatible, and most men need to be single-minded for survival. Now for the most part, "nature" seems to have no objection when man dispenses with his sense of wonder and curiosity. It does not insist that a man's senses should be as broad and intense as those of a child. But where the sexual impulse is concerned, nature is more stern. If, in a state of exhaustion or depression, a man attempts to dispense with his sexual appetite, it is likely to boomerang back on him in a way that may shatter him. The sexual impulse is the favourite child of nature; no matter how great the demands on a man's energy, the sex impulse must have its share.*

It is therefore interesting to observe that many sexual crimes involving "blackouts" or uncontrollable impulses are committed by men in a state of exhaustion or depression.† And the claim that the conscious will could break down or be completely dominated by the sudden eruption of an urge from the subconscious may not be summarily dismissed as an attempt to evade the consequences of the act.

At this point it is possible to make the following generalizations about human sexuality:

(a) As with animals, it has a definite physical component – the desire of the sexual parts to achieve an orgasm – a "tingling" of sexual "electricity" that wishes to be discharged.

(b) Although they may be influenced by smells, the human sexual urges are not united by the stimulus of a smell, as are those of animals. The component that unites and directs the

*This is confirmed by a story I heard from a soldier who helped to "liberate" a German prison camp in 1945. Far from killing the sexual appetite, the state of semi-starvation seemed to intensify it, and male and female prisoners hurled themselves together like animals. It is only fair to add that I have heard this story hotly denied – although not by anyone who was actually present at a "liberation".

Krafft-Ebing writes that the libido of consumptives is abnormally powerful.

†See, for example, the case of Robert Irwin, cited in Quentin Reynolds's *Courtroom* and in Frederic Wertham's *Show of Violence*, as well as in my own *Age of Defeat*, p. 36. Irwin actually attempted to amputate his penis, in order to reserve his full energies for an exercise of the imagination that he called "visualizing". He later committed a treble murder, whose main motive was jealousy.

human sexual impulses is purely mental or imaginative, although it is usually strongly tied to sensual impressions.

(c) Of all human instincts and desires, the sexual instinct is the one that most transcends man's *conscious* awareness of himself and his purposes. It is almost as if man carried a "separate self" around with him of which he is usually ignorant.

Freud and Gurdjieff

So far, no psychologist or philosopher has produced a unifying view of the sexual impulses. Freud's contribution was mainly to emphasize that the sexual energy (which he called the libido) is one of the deepest and most powerful of man's subconscious forces. When he first made this statement – around the turn of the century – it produced something of a furore, since the previous century had been an age of social idealism, and nineteenth-century man preferred to think that his deepest urges were of a more creditable nature – towards knowledge and social betterment, for example. Since then, twentieth-century man has been far more aware of the sexual impulse, until he now sees it reflected around him in most of the activities of his everyday life. Freudians would claim that psycho-analysis is partly responsible for this increased awareness, but this is debatable. What is certain is that if no Freud had existed to assert the supremacy of the sexual impulse, the notion would have developed of itself out of the "mental climate" of the twentieth century.

Among modern philosophers, I can think of only one who has made any attempt at a unifying sex theory – George Gurdjieff. Even so, there is very little information on the subject in the writings of Gurdjieff's followers.

Gurdjieff declared that man has seven "centres" that control his various functions. There is an instinctive centre, an intellectual centre, an emotional centre, a moving centre (which is concerned with the body's motions) and a sexual centre; there are also two "higher centres". Each of these centres works on a different kind of energy. Unfortunately, human beings tend to mix up the energy of the various centres, and may use emotional energy to drive the intellect, instinctive energy to drive the emotions, intellectual or emotional energy to drive the sexual centre, and so on. And apparently all the centres tend to steal energy from the sexual centre, and use it for their own purposes. (Gurdjieff would say that Robert Irwin used his sexual energy to drive his intellect and emotions.) They then "give back" useless energy of their own to the sexual centre, so that the sexual centre is frequently forced to work on emotional, or even intellectual energy. Gurdjieff told Ouspensky: "It is a very great thing when the sexual centre works with its own energy."

Now these remarks on the "centres" may strike some readers as completely unscientific. In fact, Gurdjieff attempted to create, not merely a philosophical system, but a religion; various rituals and dances were an important part of his "system", and there are also semi-mythological statements that most people are inclined to take with a pinch of salt. There is no "scientific evidence" for the centres. And yet, whether Gurdjieff's general remarks on the centres are true or not, no one can deny that there is a feeling of truth about his statement that "it is a very great thing when the sex centre works with its own energy". And this, at least, is worth careful consideration.*

No one, for example, who reads *Lady Chatterley's Lover*, can doubt that part of the motive power of the book is Lawrence's feeling of *social* underprivilege, and that he identifies himself with the gamekeeper who makes love to a "lady". These social feelings are not only emotional; they are *negatively* emotional. (Gurdjieff declares that the negative emotions – fear, hatred, disgust – are completely useless in the economy of the "human machine", mere excreta.) The sexual emotion of the book is consequently impure.

In the same way, no one can read the memoirs of Casanova without becoming aware of the same impurity of motive. For

*A brief account of Gurdjieff's ideas will be found in my *Outsider*, pp. 263–70. The best simple account is Kenneth Walker's *Study of Gurdjieff's Teaching* (Cape, 1957).

all his excellence as a writer, Casanova emerges as a vain and weak man, concerned largely with the effect he can make on other people. Consequently, it is hard to believe that it was the sheer energy of the sexual centre that drove him to spend his life in seduction; it seems more likely that it was some will to power, to convince himself of his own importance.*

Huxley on Sex

Are there examples in literature of the sexual centre working with its own energy? I can think of none; and the reason may be that when sex is written about, it is mixed with the energy of the intellectual or emotional centre. The true sexual energies make a self-enclosed circuit; the man who experienced this circuit would feel no urge to write about it. There are, however, a few interesting examples that seem to come close to describing the sexual centre working with its own energy. The work of Aldous Huxley contains several of these. His novel *Antic Hay* is concerned largely with describing "inauthentic" sexual encounters, wanton promiscuity that is basically futile and unsatisfying; but there is, by contrast, one single completely "satisfying" encounter. Gumbril is having an innocent affair with a girl named Emily, with whom he is in love. After a concert when the music leaves them both feeling emotionally cleansed, they go to bed together:

"Very gently, he began caressing her shoulder, her long slender arm, drawing his finger tips lightly and slowly over her smooth skin; slowly, from her neck, over her shoulder, lingeringly round the elbow to her hand. . . . Through the silk of her shift, he learned her curving side, her smooth straight back and the ridges of her spine. . . . Under the smock, he learned her warm body, lightly, slowly caressing. He knew her, his fingers, he felt, could build her up, a warm and curving statue in the darkness. He did not desire her; to desire would have been to break the enchantment. He let himself sink deeper and deeper into his dark stupor of happiness. She was asleep in his arms; and soon, he too was asleep."

*See Chapter II.

This lyrical, almost mystical description of sexual emotion is interestingly unlike the usual sexual encounters in Huxley; more typical is one in *Point Counter Point*, described by Lucy Tantamount in a letter to Walter; she explains how she picked up an Italian and drove with him to a hotel:

"He came at me as though he were going to kill me, with clenched teeth. I shut my eyes, like a Christian martyr in front of a lion. Martyrdom's exciting. Letting oneself be hurt, humiliated, used like a doormat – queer. I like it. . . . Beautifully savage he looked, a Red Indian. And as savage as his looks. The marks are still there, where he bit me on the neck. I shall have to wear a scarf for days. Where did I see that statue of Marsyas being skinned? His face was like that. I dug my nails into his arm so that the blood came. . . ."

In *The Genius and The Goddess* there is another description that is evidently supposed to invoke the perfect sexual encounter, but this time it is largely verbalized: "That night of the twenty-third of April, we were in the Other World, she and I, in the dark, wordless heaven of nakedness and touch and fusion. And what revelations in that heaven, what Pentecosts! The visitations of her caresses were like sudden angels . . ." etc. In this case, the intercourse is completed; but its description is less convincing than the description in *Antic Hay* where the two fall asleep.

In the Appendix of *Adonis and the Alphabet*,* Huxley raises an interesting question that throws some light on the scene in *Antic Hay*. He writes about John Humphrey Noyes, the founder of the Oneida Community in the United States, and of Noyes' theories of "male continence". Noyles' Oneida Community was an experiment in what he called "Bible communism", a simple "share-and-share-alike" community, whose most curious feature was its sexual communism. Noyes believed that the exclusive possession of one man by one woman is evil; in the Oneida community, women were communal. This could have led to some embarrassments – for example, the perpetual pregnancy of most of the women. To

*Called in America *Tomorrow and Tomorrow and Tomorrow*.

ɔvercome this, Noyes advocated the system of *karezza* ("the idea that the amative functions of the sexual organs could be separated from the propagative"); the man should simply restrain himself from reaching an orgasm. This, Noyes claimed, was far more satisfying than the usual sex, culminating in an orgasm. His aims in the community were "Perfectionist Christianity" and the propagation of the idea of the *karezza* and complex marriage.

High claims have been made for the method of *karezza* by its various devotees; certain writers have taken it even further than Noyes, suggesting that a newly married couple should allow their desires to reach a point of high tension without reaching the stage of copulation. When, after a long period of preparation, the male finally inserts into the female – but without permitting himself any movement that might lead to orgasm – it is asserted that the couple will experience an intensity of sexual emotion beyond anything obtainable in ordinary sexual intercourse; one description declares that they may even experience a sensation of hovering in the air.

It is obvious that Huxley was describing something very like this in *Antic Hay*; and the approval with which he speaks of the *karezza* in the appendix of *Adonis and the Alphabet* may confirm this.

It seems possible, then, that Noyes had hit upon a method of allowing the sexual centre to work with its own energy. The insistence upon perfect relaxation, upon complete control of the desire to reach orgasm, would insure that the sexual energies are unadulterated by the energy of the emotional or intellectual centre. The sexual act, unless led up to by a long period of anticipation, is almost certain to be involved with emotions and thoughts connected with other matters. The length of time involved in the *karezza* would allow the sexual energy to "run pure", to separate itself from other types of energy.

Gurdjieff, then, contradicts Gide, and suggests that there *is* such a thing as "sexual normality" – when the sexual centre works with its own energy. He implies that, when this happens, all desire for promiscuity would vanish, since the man and the woman would become for one another the embodiment of the male and female principle; no other sexual partner could offer more than this.

"Inauthenticity" in the Sexual Impulse

Even at this early stage, it is necessary to attempt some broader generalization about the relation of the sexual impulse to "human nature", for the terms of the discussion are already revealing themselves as too limited. Generally speaking, it may be said that the basic activity of all living organisms is the discharging of various forms of tension, and that the act of discharge leads to a temporary "broadening" of consciousness. A starving man, for example, feels a physical tension which is discharged by the act of eating; and the discharge of the tension is accompanied by a sense of affirmation of "life". This affirmation would not be experienced in the same degree if the man fed at two-hourly intervals, allowing no time for the tension of hunger to build up.

Tensions may be released in various ways and on various levels: physically, by eating, drinking, smoking a cigarette; emotionally, by listening to music, seeing a film, reading a romantic novel; intellectually, by doing mathematics or a cross-word puzzle. All games aim at releasing tension by a process of building it up and allowing it to relax again (but it should be noticed that a game that released only the tension that it built up would be a bad game; its act of release should also involve emotions that were unreleased before the game began).

Some of these releases involve only a soothing of the nerves; others may involve a definite heightening of consciousness.

I have pointed out elsewhere that it is relatively easy to achieve "heightened consciousness" through the body – through sex or other forms of physical relief; it is fairly easy to achieve it through the emotions. The most difficult to achieve is heightened intellectual consciousness. Most men have been "carried out of themselves" by the sexual orgasm; a large percentage have experienced release through strong emotion; the number who have known the intensity of an Einstein or a

Newton must be very small indeed.

And yet this need for release, for heightened consciousness, is one of the most basic human strivings. The inference to be drawn from this is that, whatever the ultimate purposes of the evolutionary force that drives man, heightened consciousness surely plays some important part in them? Eliot may write gloomily that human life appears to have no other meaning than "birth, copulation, and death", but he is leaving out of account the equally basic factor of the need for a more intense consciousness that dominates all human activity. The strange thing is that we never take this need of ours into account; we regard it as an unimportant freak in human activity. No man wakes in the morning and wonders: "Shall I have a moment of heightened consciousness today?" He thinks only of what has to be done, not of the state of consciousness that will accompany the doing. If he is a working man, tied to a routine job that affords him little personal satisfaction, he may occasionally feel that life is completely futile. "I work to eat, and I eat to keep up my strength to work." He would not dream of taking into account the occasional moments of "expansiveness" that might come to him over a pint of beer, or because it is a pleasant spring day, or for no reason at all. Human beings take their consciousness and its states for granted.

I am trying to point out that the things human beings normally think of as their "aims" are superficial, and it does not take a philosopher to discover that most of them are futile. But then, in the same way, all games are futile, since they involve a great deal of effort, but nothing is profoundly changed by their result. It is the states of consciousness that are achieved *en route* that give them their purpose and meaning.

The sexual impulse, then, has an important factor in common with all the other human impulses. It is not somehow unique, belonging to a different order. Although a man may have less understanding and control of his sexual impulses than of, say, his desire for financial security, this is not to say that he is a puppet, a slave in the hands of a force that is completely inscrutable. The sexual urge is unlike most human desires in only one important respect: it is by far the shortest and easiest route to "release of tension" and heightened consciousness. It satisfies both man's purpose and nature's.

Before leaving this point, it is instructive to compare the following three quotations:

"An exquisite pleasure had invaded my senses, but individual, detached, with no suggestion of its origin. And at once, the vicissitudes of life had become indifferent to me, its disasters innocuous, its brevity illusory – this new sensation having had on me the effect which love has of filling me with a precious essence; or rather, this essence was not in me, it was myself. I had ceased now to feel mediocre, accidental, mortal. . . ."

". . . a refreshing laughter rose in me, and suddenly the forgotten notes of the piano came back to me again. It soared aloft like a soap bubble, reflecting the whole world in miniature on its rainbow surface, and then softly burst. . . . The golden trail was blazed, and I was reminded of the eternal, and of Mozart and the stars. For an hour, I could breathe once more and live and face existence, without the need to suffer torment, fear or shame."

". . . all of a sudden a mysterious change came over my senses. I entered a plane of being where nothing mattered save the infusion of joy brewed within my body. What had begun as a delicious distension of my innermost roots became a glowing tingle which *now* had reached that state of absolute security, confidence, and reliance not found elsewhere in conscious life. With the deep hot sweetness thus established and well on its way to the ultimate convulsion, I felt I could slow down in order to prolong the glow."

The first of these descriptions is from Proust; it is Marcel speaking of the strange moment of "remembrance of things past" brought about by the taste of a cake soaked in tea. The second is from Hesse's *Steppenwolf*, describing a moment of release that comes through drinking a glass of wine. The third is from Nabokov's *Lolita*, and occurs in the passage where Humbert cautiously masturbates by rubbing his erect penis against Lolita (who is unaware of what is going on). The similarity in the language is striking. It might be emphasized by a second quotation from *Steppenwolf*, this time describing an extension of consciousness due to erotic ecstasy:

"Now, at the magic touch of Eros, the source of [memory] was opened up and flowed in plenty. For moments together my heart stood still between delight and sorrow to find how rich was the gallery of my life, and how thronged the soul of the wretched Steppenwolf with high eternal stars and constellations."

It is true that the affirmation of the sexual impulse need not communicate itself to the intellect in this way, or even to the emotions; it may be no more than a physical warmth and relaxation. But it should be borne in mind that such experiences as the one described above can be counted among the highest type of sexual experience.

D. H. Lawrence and Sodomy

The passage from Nabokov raises again the basic question about "abnormality", as does the whole of *Lolita*. If the highest kind of sexual experience can be gained by such a means, is it possible to call the means "inauthentic"? This question opens up the whole problem of "sexual aberration". Here again it is instructive to consider cases.

D. H. Lawrence is normally regarded as the high-priest of a mystical sexual "normality". And yet Professor Wilson Knight has pointed out, in a brilliant essay, that Lawrence placed a great deal of emphasis on the act of sodomy. In *Lady Chatterley's Lover* most of the early sexual encounters are "normal". But towards the end of Chapter 16, Mellors takes Constance Chatterley "in the Italian manner". Lawrence is careful not to be *too* explicit, but a number of early references in the book lead up to the final act. She is "a little frightened, but let him have his way", and the sensuality burns out "the shames, the deepest, oldest shames, in the most secret places", and the sensual flame "pressed through her bowels and breast". Lawrence leaves no room for doubt that he considered this act to be somehow a deeper consummation than "normal" sex (although, of course, there is never any suggestion that he regarded it as a substitute for normal sex). In the same way, *Women in Love* leads up to a strange scene between Ursula and Birkin (in the chapter "Excurse") where the exact physical details are vague, except that Ursula kneels in front of Birkin, and causes him to reach orgasm by exploring with her fingers at "the back of the loins" to "the quick of the mystery of darkness". Lawrence makes it clear that he is not speaking of the phallus, for he repeats the word "back" several times, and comments that Ursula had thought "there was no source deeper than the phallic source" until she had this experience. Lawrence reveals that Birkin has already possessed Ursula "in the Italian manner", but now Ursula has learned how to satisfy Birkin most deeply. Later, he remarks that "with perfect fine finger tips of reality she would touch the reality in him". Lawrence's meaning is underlined in a poem, "Manifesto", where he writes:

"I want her to touch me at last, ah, on the root and quick of my darkness. . . ."

Birkin's act of sodomy with Ursula is also described in terms of the "root of her darkness".

Professor Wilson Knight makes it very clear that Lawrence attached great importance to this final act, and he offers full documentation in his essay.*

It is true that there is no need to seek complicated psychological explanations for a phenomenon that might well have a physical basis. The anal regions, after all, share some of the erotic sensitivity of the genitals. Professor Knight failed to note the passage in Mrs. Bloom's monologue where she mentions that her lover "made me spend the 2nd time tickling me behind with his finger" and describes the intensity of her sexual satisfaction. Hirschfeld mentions two sister prostitutes who specialized in performing an act of simultaneous genital and anal stimulation on their clients. Hirschfeld adds: "According to Freud, the evacuation of the bowels and the passing of

*"Lawrence, Joyce and Powys", *Essays in Criticism*, Oct. 1961.

urine is also accompanied by similar pleasurable sensations", but he points out that certain peoples do not practise kissing, and that therefore the lips are not included among the "erogeneous zones" by these peoples. Hirschfeld also mentions a prostitute who sometimes performed fellatio on her customers while inserting a silk handkerchief into the rectum, and withdrawing the handkerchief at the moment of orgasm; she claimed that this produced an intensity of sexual experience beyond "normal intercourse".

It is therefore hardly necessary to speculate how Lawrence's "normal" sexuality managed to drift towards anal eroticism. (Wilson Knight even cites passages from Powys's *Glastonbury Romance* to argue a connection between the anal regions and mystical ecstasy.) No one who has read *Women in Love* or *Lady Chatterley's Lover* with sympathy can fail to regard the "anal scenes" as a more-or-less logical development of what preceded them. No doubt it would have seemed equally logical if the act had been one of mutual oral stimulation. One must say, then, either that these "consummations" are "normal", or that Lawrence's sexual mysticism is somehow basically at fault. I am not at present concerned to argue either view; only to point out that the borderline between apparent normality and "abnormality" is very thin.

On the other hand, a case cited by Paul de River in his volume *The Sexual Criminal* (Chapter Six) is instructive. De River writes of a moronic school guard who murdered three small girls (whose ages ranged between seven and nine) and committed acts of sodomy and of "normal" intercourse on all three. The school guard was married but he had developed an obsessional feeling that only the tight vagina of a child could bring him the deepest sexual satisfaction. Having lured the children to a secluded spot with a promise to show them rabbits, he took them away one by one and strangled them, committing a double act of violation upon two of them. But when questioned afterwards, he admitted that he had experienced the greatest pleasure with the elder of the three. Here the confusion of his desires becomes apparent. He imagines that he can achieve the deepest satisfaction only with a very young girl, but in fact, he prefers the child who is nearest to woman-hood. At first sight, the case might be used as an argument against the idea that the deepest sexual consummation should be pursued as an aim in itself, but the man's confusion spoils the argument, proving that he had no idea of what he really wanted. In fact, the case is rather a support of Lawrence's view that certain developments of the normal act of sexual intercourse are not "unnatural". The guard's "unnaturalness" arose out of his confusion, his misreading of his desires. There is no such confusion in Lawrence; even his opponents have to admit that there is a powerful interior logic in the development of his sexual mysticism.

However, this juxtaposition of Lawrence and Paul de River's school guard makes it apparent that Tolstoy's theory of sex is the only one that offers a consistent statement about abnormality. Lawrence and the caretaker may be two extremes, but there is only a difference in degree; both felt that sex "ought" to lead to some ultimately satisfying consummation, beyond the bare act of "natural intercourse".

This view, it should be noted, is implicit in our attitude of increased tolerance towards books dealing with sex. When such books as *Ulysses*, *The Well of Loneliness*, *Lolita*, *Lady Chatterley's Lover*, can be openly published, it means that we are willing to accept that the acts they describe are not wholly "unnatural". Tolstoy would have condemned them all, as he condemned Maupassant's *Bel Ami*, as "dirty books"; for by his definition, any kind of emphasis on the pleasure of sex is "abnormal". By this standard, *Lady Chatterley's Lover* is as abnormal as *The Well of Loneliness* or Angus Wilson's *Hemlock and After*.

And yet there are few of us who can accept Tolstoy's view as a solution. Tolstoy would imply that, if one day human-kind reaches a stage of god-like perfection, sex will have dis-appeared, except as an occasional act of "duty" (to reproduce). It is difficult to feel that Tolstoy has arrived at a balanced vision of the part played by sex in man's total being.

In the following chapters I wish to investigate this problem of the rôle of sex by considering the part that sex has played in the lives of various men and women, and the theories of sex that are implicit in their attitudes.

CHAPTER II

PROMISCUITY AND THE CASANOVA IMPULSE

Gurdjieff's psychology of sex. Mann and Faustus. *Casanova, Frank Harris and* My Life and Loves. *Henry Miller. The case of "M". The Strange case of Artsybashev. Female Sexuality.*

A CONVENIENT starting point for the discussion of "abnormality" is the question of how far promiscuity is unnatural. Tolstoy certainly regarded it as a sexual disorder, as reprehensible, if not as rare, as bestiality or sadism. I have already commented that Gurdjieff's view of the "sexual centre" seems to imply a one-man one-woman view of "natural sex", not unlike Lawrence's. But it is an interesting fact that Gurdjieff himself was known as something of a Don Juan. In *God is my Adventure*, Rom Landau mentions the stories about Gurdjieff's "immorality" with his female disciples; he goes on to tell a story about a woman who was sitting in a restaurant when she experienced suddenly an intense sensual excitement, as if someone had "pierced her sexual centre"; looking round, she found that Gurdjieff was sitting with his eyes fixed on her.*

Whether or not Gurdjieff possessed this curious power of stimulating a woman at a distance, the Don Juan legends about him undoubtedly have their basis in fact, and several of his illegitimate children are alive in America.†

The contradiction implied here is of great interest. Gurdjieff made several statements about the sex centre. It is the highest of the five centres, and works with a finer energy. There are

*Many of the stories about Gurdjieff credit him with strange psychic powers, and Ouspensky declares that he had personal experience of Gurdjieff's telepathic abilities. (*In Search of the Miraculous,* pp. 262 et seq.)

†This was probably one of the reasons why Lawrence decided against becoming Gurdjieff's pupil at Fontainebleau.

only two other centres above it: the "higher emotional" and "higher thinking" centre; and the higher emotional centre works with the same energy as the sex centre, implying that it is on the same level.

Gurdjieff's main interest was the study of the "human machine" and its workings, and he concluded that the "human factory" is planned for a very large output, but that it never reaches more than a fraction of "full production" because human beings are short-sightedly interested only in their own needs and desires, and never explore their potentialities. To express it by a different simile, one might say that the human machine is like a four-engined aeroplane which never flies on more than one engine. Admittedly, the sexual orgasm often brings man a feeling of great power – as if all four engines began to work momentarily – but it vanishes in a few seconds. Gurdjieff also maintains that the states of "higher consciousness" experienced by the mystics are the result of the working of the two "higher centres"; but most human beings spend their lives completely unaware that they possess higher centres.

Whether we are inclined to accept Gurdjieff's psychology or not, it cannot be denied that human beings experience occasional moments of "insight", of certitude and confidence about "life" in general, that imply that our normal state of everyday consciousness is a poor, barren half-ration. This makes an excellent starting point for the study of sex.

But now the contradiction in Gurdjieff's views becomes apparent. "Normality" means the sexual centre working "authentically" with its own energy. This brings to mind a vision of some ideal, Lawrencian relationship in which a man and woman are somehow perfectly satisfying to one another. On the other hand, "abnormality" begins when one partner regards the other as a mere passive instrument of pleasure; it can lead to the type of sex murder described by Paul de River. But this impersonality lies at the root of Don Juanism. It is hard to imagine a perfectly balanced man – strong, un-neurotic, possessing a "real" centre of gravity, a deep knowledge of his own being, an "essential" personality – pursuing a career of enthusiastic seduction. Either Gurdjieff's view of the sex centre is more paradoxical than it appears to be, or he was a less integrated personality than he pretended to be. The second question is hardly relevant in this context; but the first is worth keeping in mind.

The urge to sexual promiscuity is generally regarded as a disease when it reaches a certain point of "loss of control"; in women, this point is called nymphomania, in men, satyriasis. Sexologists have pointed out that nymphomania is frequently due to "frigidity" in women; because the woman fails to gain any deep satisfaction from the sexual experience, she tends to repeat it as often as possible in an attempt to achieve satisfaction. The records to which I have been given access in preparing this book included the following interesting case:

"X, a man in his early twenties, had experienced a nervous breakdown after living for six months with a girl whom he claimed to be a nymphomaniac. The woman, who was Jewish, and worked as a journalist, was several years his senior. She was not only incapable of fidelity to X, but appeared to take pleasure in freely describing her infidelities to him. She seemed to feel that he ought to experience a vicarious pleasure in listening to her descriptions, and often became sexually excited as she dwelt on the details. X remembered particularly an experience she claimed to have had at a party. She had gone into an empty cloakroom to get her coat; there, she bent down to adjust her suspender. As she was doing so, a man entered the room behind her and stood watching her. She could see only his trousers and shoes, with her back to him. After a few moments, the man raised her dress from behind, and inserted his penis. He reached orgasm, and then left the cloakroom without speaking to her. She thought he was drunk. During all this time, *she had not looked at his face*, and was sure she would be unable to recognize him if she met him again."

Here it is obvious that the girl took pleasure in the anonymity of the encounter. Her bending position emphasized her animality; the man was as anonymous as a stray dog.

It is observable that in this case the girl did not mention

whether she experienced an orgasm; it seems probable that she did not, and that she conformed to the pattern of "frigid nymphomaniacs".

It would be a mistake, though, to regard all nymphomaniacs as slow to reach orgasm. Mr. Rexroth, the American poet, has related a case that disproves the idea. The girl in question was arrested and charged with prostitution; the police were unable to prove their case because the girl never took money for her services, and she came before a psychiatric board, of which Mr. Rexroth was a member. She told how, on the day she was married, she and her husband spent several hours in bed in a hotel room on Park Avenue. Immediately after this, she went out and allowed herself to be "picked up" by a man in Central Park; she accompanied him to a hotel room, and intercourse took place. She picked up several more men before she returned to her husband. Later, when her husband was at work, she made a habit of going to bed with strangers picked up on the streets. Her last client was a detective who "framed" her by putting marked money into her handbag and then arresting her.

The board asked her if her original experience with her husband was so unsatisfactory that she felt impelled to seek satisfaction elsewhere. She replied: "Oh no. I enjoyed it so much that I wanted to do it again immediately." She insisted that she experienced an orgasm with every man, and was completely satisfied, but that the desire would re-form an hour later. The board regarded her as an unusual case of insatiable sexual appetite.

Both these cases emphasize the element of *impersonality* which seems to be so important in sex. Thomas Mann discusses this in his novel *Doktor Faustus*. After the marriage of his sister, Adrian Leverkuhn talks about "the domestication of sex" by the Church. The relation between lovers is based upon strangeness; therefore, it is hardly accurate to say that "these twain shall be one flesh", for this would be the end of strangeness. Leverkuhn argues that the lust of one flesh for another is not mere sensuality, but love, for "the flesh is normally inoffensive to itself only. With another's it will have nothing to do." The breakdown of this resistance in sexual union is a phenomenon "for which sensuality is only an empty word".

Mann has here touched upon an important and profound problem. But it should be observed that the resistance to alien flesh is part of civilized conditioning. It is the civilized man who cannot eat off someone else's plate or wear somebody else's trousers. Babies and animals are usually indifferent to such questions. The more civilized a man becomes, the more his basic response to other human beings is the *noli me tangere* – don't touch me – that Lawrence was so fond of quoting. "The more things a man is ashamed of, the more respectable he is"; says Shaw's Tanner. One of the most basic of the "psychological horrors" in Orwell's *Nineteen Eighty-four* is the idea of men being continually observed, even on the lavatory.* When Joyce's *Ulysses* was first published, many people found that one of its most disgusting passages is the one in which Mrs Bloom spits chewed seed cake into her husband's mouth in an act of love-making.

All this suggests an important idea: that civilization conditions us to a dislike of the alien "other" flesh, and that sex is an important act of de-conditioning. Many children and adolescents find the idea of sex disgusting, and this disgust later becomes an important part of its fascination. A simple act like kissing with the tongue seems at once nauseating and desirable, a symbol of the strange, poisonous, and shocking world of sex. So at an early stage sex is associated with the idea of violating one's natural fastidiousness, the desire not to be "touched", the dislike of dirt and of alien flesh. The stronger this fastidiousness, the more sex is likely to be associated with "sin". This idea must be brought up later, particularly in the discussion of sadism.†

*In Russia, I noticed that many public lavatories are mere boards with holes in them, where men squat side by side, their trousers around their ankles.

†It might be noted here that the need for "alien-ness" – the illusion of the inviolability of the other person, upon which all sexual desire depends – has an interesting extreme in the abnormality known as "auto-

It seems probable, then, that many cases of nymphomania involve a revolt against civilized conditioning; this seems particularly obvious in the case of the girl who allowed herself to be "used" as she bent down to adjust her suspender. Promiscuity – at least in women – may be an escape, a revolt against the complexity of civilization.

Male and female promiscuity have one thing in common: the impersonality of the sexual object. The first thing that strikes readers of books like Casanova's *Memoirs* or Frank Harris's *My Life and Loves* is the complete selfishness of the authors. Even when they assure the reader that they were deeply attached to some particular woman, the woman in question never makes a deep impression on the reader.

I am not, of course, suggesting that these books are of equal literary merit. Casanova's *Memoirs* are a masterpiece, and it is not surprising that some critics have actually believed they were written by Stendhal. (Recent research has established their authenticity beyond all doubt.) Frank Harris's book is not particularly well written, and some of its later volumes (in the "banned" Paris edition) are undoubtedly written by "ghosts".

But when the reader thinks back on either of these books, it is not *people* he remembers, but certain events. Casanova cannot actually be called a pervert, but his memoirs seem to con-

---

eroticism". (This should be distinguished from onanism, in which self-stimulation occurs when the mind is fixed upon some sexual object – probably a fantasy of a member of the opposite sex. The auto-erotic is excited by the sight of *his own body*.) In auto-eroticism, the body of the subject takes on the illusory alien-ness that normally makes "the other" desirable. Some years ago, I learned of an interesting case that occurred at Nottingham. The young man lived alone in a dirty cottage, afraid of the strength of his own sexual desires. A latent homosexual, he could be excited to orgasm by the mere sight of a pair of riding breeches, and used to travel on buses near riding schools to catch a glimpse of them. But he was most excited by the sight of his own body seen in the mirror, and so had destroyed all mirrors in the cottage. He was "taken in hand" by a practising homosexual who heard of his difficulties, and the auto-erotic impulse was directed outward – towards other male bodies. This may have been as "abnormal" as auto-eroticism, but at least the subject ceased to have guilt feelings about it, and became reconciled to his tendencies.

tain every typically sexual fantasy dreamed up by mankind. I am not asserting that they are necessarily untrue; in fact, I would guess that Casanova was a curiously truthful man.*This only makes the *Memoirs* an even more interesting study for the sexual psychologist.

Casanova's first love affair occurred in his teens, but his first sexual experience is not with one woman, but with two; he sleeps between the sisters, and takes the maidenhood of both within half an hour. A few chapters later, he repeats this feat – with another pair of sisters, of course (Vol. 1, Chapter Ten). In the third volume occurs an affair that is completely typical of Casanova; at a card party he sits by the fire, talking to a young girl who is recently out of a convent. The talk turns to sex, and Casanova shocks her by showing her his sexual member. He then takes hold of her hand, and uses it to masturbate himself. Later, upon a promise of marriage, the girl becomes his mistress. It is typical of Casanova that he cannot even remember her Christian name, and refers to her as "Mlle. de la Meure".

This example illustrates as well as any the "wish-fulfilment" aspect of Casanova – the stories that sound as if they had been invented solely to get an advance out of some publisher of pornographic literature. (In fact, the *Memoirs* were never published in Casanova's lifetime, or even finished.)

Casanova is very seldom scorned by the women upon whom his choice falls. When this actually happens (Vol. 3, Chapter Six) Casanova resorts to cunning. The girl has taken another lover, who impregnates her. She approaches Casanova to ask his help in procuring an abortion. Casanova persuades her of the efficacy of a certain specific, mixed with fresh semen, and offers his help in the "operation". The gullible girl actually allows him to possess her several times in the course of performing the experiment. She is finally forced to go into a convent to have the baby. In the course of the same volume, Casanova succeeds in taking the maidenhead of a young married woman (whose husband is either shy or impotent),

*All references that follow are to the Elek edition of the *Memoirs,* in Arthur Machen's translation, 6 vols., 1959–60.

and has a sexual orgy with three girls which (with unusual reticence) he declines to describe. He also becomes a factory owner, and sleeps with most of his work-girls, but this is too unimportant to describe at length, and he mentions it only *en passant*.

Frank Harris's volumes have much the same pattern – in fact, their style seems at times to echo Casanova. He also lays considerable emphasis on the taking of maidenheads and the love of innocent girls. He seems to be slightly less discriminating than Casanova. The latter seems to enjoy living in all its aspects – particularly luxurious living and polite society; he gives the impression that he thinks of many things besides sex. Harris never ceases to think of sex, and never looks at any young girl without speculating what she would be like in bed.

But Harris and Casanova have one point in common: both are crooks. Their autobiographies have a curiously plausible surface. They frequently tell stories against themselves; they also tell stories that seem to have very little point and which sound all the more true for having no point. But they also leave no doubt in the reader's mind that they are accomplished confidence men. Both spent their lives trying to impress society, to get themselves accepted on their own valuation. Casanova, the son of an actor, gave himself an impressive title, but he does not trouble to deceive the reader about his title or his origins. Both had lives of considerable difficulty, and were periodically denounced as tricksters. And in both of them the air of honesty and straightforwardness is an engaging mannerism. (Shaw describes Harris as a loud-mouthed buccaneer with a Rabelaisian turn of speech, but you would not guess this from Harris's own autobiographical writings.)

All this enables the reader to understand the basis of the "seduction mania" that possessed both of them. Both had difficult beginnings; both were brilliant young men who were socially unacceptable, in an age that attached great importance to such things. Their attitude to society was defensive; they were "upstarts" who mixed smoothly with their social superiors, but always with a consciousness of deception. They never felt a basic "adjustment" to society – the kind of adjustment reached by such men as Beethoven and Shaw, who were accepted on their own terms. In fact, both Harris and Casanova were talented enough to demand such acceptance; but they started on the wrong foot; they started by deceiving, and could never cease to feel themselves deceivers.*

So sexual conquest became the basis of self-respect in both Harris and Casanova. Cultured society might throw them into the psychological attitude of the liar, but as successful lovers they could feel themselves supermen. Significantly enough, both ended their lives in poverty and bitterness. Casanova finally returned to Venice (from which he had fled many years before) as a spy and political informer. He died at Dux in Poland, as the librarian of Count Waldstein. He spent his last years writing *Memoirs*, resenting imagined insults, and mourning for the passing of the "age of chevaliers". The younger generation regarded him as a quaint old man, completely out of date. Harris also died in poverty and obscurity in the south of France. Both wrote their famous memoirs in their eclipse, when they had little left but memories of sexual conquest. These conquests, as related in their books, are probably largely true, although probably "improved". In writing of them, they could again feel strong and virile. (Both lay emphasis on the number of times they were able to satisfy a woman in one night.)

If Harris and Casanova are taken as typical of the Don Juan temperament, then it would seem that there is a world of difference between the motivation to promiscuity in men and women. In the woman it may be due to a perverse kind of rebelliousness, an almost self-destructive urge, the need to defy society with an obscene gesture. In men, it seems to be simpler: a straightforward will to power. Far from being a sign

---

*Shaw was one of the few men with whom Harris seems to have behaved naturally. This was probably because Shaw always treated him frankly as a buccaneer. Feeling no need for a basic pretence, Harris also felt no temptation to try to impose on Shaw or practise any kind of dishonesty with him.

of strength, Don Juanism may indicate a lack of basic self-belief. The men who feel unable to assert themselves among men, do so among women. The unusual or talented man, who is still not unusual enough to make his mark as a creator, a thinker, a soldier, turns to sexual conquest to achieve self-respect. Among men of genuine talent, Don Juanism is frequently an early stage, before more serious work claims their energy.*

But the main thing to be learned from a consideration of Casanova and Harris is that the Don Juan temperament is often accompanied by habitual mendacity and criminal tendencies. Shaw has an interesting account of his fellow socialist Edward Aveling, who was one of the models for Louis Dubedat in *The Doctor's Dilemma*. Aveling was a convinced socialist who, according to Shaw, would have gone to the stake for his convictions. But where women and money were concerned, he was completely immoral. He coached female students for science examinations, seduced the pretty ones and swindled the less attractive. He lived with Eleanor Marx for many years; then, when his wife finally divorced him, married someone else, and encouraged Eleanor to commit suicide (which she did). Aveling was a small, curiously reptilian man, and Shaw was intrigued by the combination of Shelleyan idealism and total shamelessness where women were concerned. (The combination may not be as odd as it sounds; Shelley's ideas on women did not favour monogamy or fidelity; Aveling was a whole-

*James Joyce, for example. In an early "autobiographical" poem, "The Holy Office", he writes:

> And for each maiden, shy and nervous
> I do a similar kind service . . .
> At night when close in bed she lies
> And feels my hand between her thighs
> My little love in light attire
> Knows the soft flame that is desire.

This is undoubtedly wishful thinking on Joyce's part. Although Joyce claimed to be a formidable seducer of innocence, his exploits involved mainly prostitutes, and *Stephen Hero* makes no secret of his frustrations as a would-be Casanova. This "great lover" affectation disappeared with the writing of *A Portrait of the Artist*, and never reappeared in later work.

hearted disciple of Shelley, and died reciting the *Prometheus Unbound*.)

But to speak of the combination of mendacity and Don Juanism is perhaps imprecise. It would be more accurate to say that there is a certain type of man of talent whose self-confidence is below the level of his vitality. The ideal combination is, of course, talent united with self-belief, as in Beethoven, Shakespeare, Shaw. Perhaps the most extreme example of talent without self-belief is the case of T. E. Lawrence, whose inferiority feeling affected even his sense of sexual capability. Casanova and Harris are less extreme cases.

Equally interesting from this point of view are the writings of Henry Miller.

Henry Miller

Miller is an altogether more complex personality than Casanova or Harris, as well as being a better writer. The first qualities that strike the reader in books like *The Tropic of Capricorn* and *The Rosy Crucifixion* are the depth of the intuitions and the remarkable command of language. It is true that Miller is not a sustained thinker; nevertheless, he brings to his autobiographical writings a kind of inspired penetration that compares with D. H. Lawrence.

It would be pleasant to be able to declare that Miller is a writer who can be taken as seriously as Lawrence; unfortunately this is impossible, since Miller does not take himself all that seriously.* For many years to come, he will remain an embarrassment to literary critics. For his work is seventy-five per cent serious and thoughtful writing, and twenty-five per cent unashamed pornography.

Until the publication of the two *Tropics* in America, Miller had to live off the American and English tourists who go to Paris to buy "dirty books". There seems little doubt that his first book, *The Tropic of Cancer*, was written with that market in view, and that Miller decided to pour some of his serious

---

*Although many sound critics – Sir Herbert Read, for example – would not hesitate to place him beside Lawrence.

writing – for which he had so far discovered no market –into a book that was bound to have a wide circulation.

It is impossible to say whether Miller might have made a better writer if he had not started by writing pornography. He is not a pornographer by vocation; he does not write about sex because he is obsessed by it. So much of his work gives the impression that he is laughing at himself – and at the reader – as he recounts some preposterous sexual exploit. His sense of humour reminds one of the comic and near-obscene postcards that used to be sold at Brighton and Blackpool; he enjoys emphasizing the indignities connected with the sexual and excretory functions.

His most important books so far are the two *Tropics* and *The Rosy Crucifixion* in three volumes (*Sexus*, *Nexus*, and *Plexus*). Miller considers this latter his masterpiece. All are auto-biographical, and concerned very largely with Miller's sexual exploits. These cover an even wider range than those of Casanova – or at least, are told in more detail. *The Tropic of Cancer* is the most lyrical and least readable; the language seems to have been inspired by Rimbaud and Lautréamont; it has very little story, but what little there is concerns the lives of a few American exiles living in Paris. *Capricorn* is an altogether better book, and tells about Miller's earlier American period. The narrative is less static, and the language less pretentious. One interesting point is immediately observable. Unlike most "autobiographers", Miller is not in the least concerned to present himself in a dignified light. It is almost as if he had decided that, if he was going to write a dirty book and tell all kinds of lies, he might as well go the whole hog and present himself in as unflattering a light as possible. Harris and Casanova tell stories against themselves; Miller does nothing else. If he were less innocent and buoyant, one might suspect him of a kind of Dostoevskian craving for self-humiliation and public confession. In fact, one soon comes to suspect that these "confessions" are only another way of "giving the reader his money's worth" – and incidentally, of laughing at him. One feels that he would cheerfully write in a scene in which he has sexual intercourse with an elephant, if he thought it would amuse the reader. As it is, he details endless infidelities to his wife, various episodes in which he is shown as borrowing, cadging or stealing, and a great many undignified stories involving excrement. Typical of these "confessions" is an episode in *The Tropic of Capricorn* in which his wife is lying ill in bed. A female neighbour comes in to attend to her, and bends over the bed in her nightdress. Miller stands behind the neighbour, lifts the nightdress, and while they both continue to speak comfortingly to the wife, has sexual intercourse with the neighbour.

And yet while he represents himself as completely cynical about sex and money, Miller obviously has social passion, and a dislike of cruelty, and he spends a great deal of time explaining to the reader what is wrong with Western civilization. For this reason, *The Rosy Crucifixion* is a literary curiosity. It is interspersed with detailed descriptions of the sexual act – often involving more than one woman – and various rapes and orgies. But the author seems to want to puzzle the reader by creating two distinct and incompatible Henry Millers. There is Miller the avid reader, the lover of books and ideas, whose dialectic is often as passionate as Dostoevsky's, whose interest in human beings and their problems is inexhaustible. Then there is Miller the scrounger, whose chief motivation seems to be the desire for a quick, undignified "poke", and who refers to his sexual member as his "pecker".

Miller himself denies that his work was intended to be pornographic, and although he has admitted that some of the exploits he recounts are not wholly true, claims that *The Rosy Crucifixion* is an honest attempt to tell "the whole truth". This sounds plausible enough until one opens the book, and reads some preposterous account of intercourse, told largely in four-letter words. "We went into a blind f——, with the cab lurching and careening, our teeth knocking, tongues bitten, and the juice pouring from her like hot soup", etc. "She had two or three orgasms, and then sank back exhausted, smiling up at me weakly like a trapped doe."

In Miller, then, the Don Juanism is even more complicated than in Harris or Casanova. They were only out to glorify themselves; Miller's intention appears to be the reverse.

But the general thesis that applies to Harris and Casanova applies also to Miller. His talent exceeds his self-belief – and therefore his seriousness as an artist. This lack of self-confidence is almost synonymous with mendacity, just as the fierce arrogance of a Beethoven is synonymous with aggressive truthfulness. The effect of reading Miller in large doses is curious. He is an exciting thinker, always faithful to his intuitions; when speaking about writers with whom he sympathizes – Rimbaud, for example – he can be a superb literary critic; there are times when ideas pour on to the paper in a breathless jumble of words. He is always a "man-alive", like Lawrence, and there are times when the vitality and the intensity of thought become so perfectly fused that the reader is overwhelmed by a sensation of his greatness. And yet the effect of reading long sections of his books is strangely depressing; their moral air is dead – damp and slightly rotten, like the air in a tomb. There is a weary, exhausted lack of self-respect, a sense of defeat, more oppressive than in Sartre or Joyce. The book has a low moral ceiling, and the reader gets cramped keeping his head bowed and his knees bent. There is a Thomas-Wolfe-ian vitality about the whole thing, but no real poetry, no idealism, nothing heroic or tragic; in short, no greatness. Even Rabelais seems religious and idealistic compared to Miller. At his worst, when uninspired by sex or people, his tone is almost nihilistic; *The Air-Conditioned Nightmare*, for example – an attack on America – is a bitter, bored, carping book that has none of the qualities of his best work.

The point of these lengthy discussions of Harris, Casanova, and Miller is to try to show the relation between Don Juanism and the failure of values. These writers, taken in large doses, produce an indefinable oppression in the sensitive reader. There is movement and colour in their pages, but it is the movement and colour of a merry-go-round. Ultimately, their vision of life is nihilistic; it is all "sound and fury, signifying

nothing". The works of idealistic writers – poets and philosophers – move towards climaxes that attempt to make life
appear meaningful. There are plenty of climaxes in Casanova
and in Miller, but they are only satisfactions of ordinary human
appetites, and they leave nothing behind. Since they view life
as nothing more than a procession of their desires and biological processes, they naturally have no more moral sense "than a
fox in a poultry farm". Boredom is to be expected from life –
unless distractions can be found. Minor deceptions come to
them as naturally as to children who lie to get out of trouble.
They are basically too good-natured, too well-satisfied with
life, to become dangerous criminals; and yet their moral
nihilism is the basis of all criminality. (This is a point that will
recur in later chapters.) If their appetites were as brutal as those
of a Kürten or Gilles de Rais, there would be no reason why
they should not satisfy them. There seems to be nothing in the
life of Casanova which is not summarized by Eliot in the harsh
lines:

> Those who sharpen the tooth of the dog, meaning
> Death
> Those who glitter with the glory of the hummingbird, meaning
> Death
> Those who sit in the stye of contentment, meaning
> Death
> Those who suffer the ecstasy of the animals, meaning
> Death.*

This is Casanova's life in four lines: sex, good food, personal
vanity, and resentment; its summary: death. (This is brought
home powerfully in Arthur Schnitzler's novel *Casanova's Home-
coming*, an imaginary "addition" to the *Memoirs*, which shows
Casanova in old age, disillusioned, ugly, on the point of
becoming a police spy.)

One more example will help to make these issues clearer. I
quote from an unpublished autobiographical manuscript in my
possession.† Its portrait of the ex-officer "M" is an excellent

*T. S. Eliot, "Marina", *Collected Poems*, p. 113.
†With the author's permission; for obvious reasons, no names are given.

analysis of a type of "Don Juan" whom I have not mentioned so far.

"M is an ex-guards officer who, at the time when I first knew him, was in his middle twenties. He had been to a public school, then to Sandhurst, but had only spent two years in the army, having decided to go into his father's business. He was good looking and athletically built, and a heavy drinker. He enjoyed playing with revolvers, frequently talked of his army experiences (when he had been a member of the occupation forces in Germany) and often said that he wished the Russians would start a war so that he could fight. He thought that peacetime was demoralizing, and had the typical army officer's contempt of civilians, regarding them as sloppy and undisciplined. He held a kind of mystique of power, which emerged constantly in his conversation – especially when drunk – and admired Hitler as a 'strong man'. In spite of his talk about physical violence and discipline, he was by no means unintelligent; his bookshelf showed a wide range of interests, and when I engaged with him in arguments or discussions, the acuteness of his reasoning powers often surprised me. Nevertheless, he affected to feel contempt for all 'intellectuals', although this was inconsistent with his friendliness towards me."

[There follow several more paragraphs expounding "M's" power-philosophy; I omit these as not relevant here.]

". . . But all this emerged most clearly in his attitude to sex. His experience with women has been very wide, and he claimed that the number of women he had slept with was equal to the number of months that had passed since his fourteenth birthday (roughly 140). These included two mistresses whom he had supported in Germany. M had many theories and beliefs about sex. For example, he often claimed that he found masturbation more satisfactory than intercourse with a woman because 'it could be controlled more exactly'. He set great store by his sexual prowess; he believed that if a man can have a second orgasm soon after the first, he can carry on making love for the rest of the night with no real difficulty; he had often proved this, he said, by having as many as ten orgasms in a night. Although he talked a great deal about sex – indeed, this and the 'will to power' were his favourite subjects – his interest in it seemed curiously experimental; I do not think I can accuse him of ever talking 'filth' for its own sake. . . .

"These two obsessions [sex and the will to power] came together in a story that immediately struck me as being of great interest, and which I give here as accurately as I can remember it.

"M gave a birthday party for his mistress at a hotel. Among the guests were an art student who had a reputation as a nymphomaniac, and an old army acquaintance of M's. This man was a giant, whom M described as having 'the body of a Greek god'. Towards the end of the evening he approached M and explained that the art student wanted to sleep with him; unfortunately, neither had a room that would be convenient for this purpose. M had taken a double room in the hotel, which contained two single beds; he immediately offered to let his friend use one of the beds.

"The party ended, and M and his mistress retired. She was very drunk. M made love to her, and she immediately fell into a deep sleep. Ten minutes later, M's friend entered the room with the nymphomaniac; they undressed in the dark and climbed into bed. M lay awake, listening, and soon heard the girl making sounds that indicated she was not satisfied with her lover. M finally asked 'Is anything the matter?' The girl replied that she was still unsatisfied, and that the man had fallen asleep. M asked 'Can I help?', and the girl said yes. They switched on the light; the army officer was persuaded to get out of bed, and M climbed on to the girl and made love to her. Watching them, the army officer became excited, and as soon as M had finished, made love to her himself. M stood watching them, and later commented to me on the beauty of the sight. He said: 'It was so beautiful that I forgot to be excited. They were simply two beautiful animals.' He added that he was particularly interested to observe the lamplight reflected on the man's sexual member, and said: 'You don't realize it's shiny when you're doing it yourself.'

"By this time a feeling of rivalry had developed between the two men; as soon as one finished, the other began again. The girl seemed to be insatiable. However, towards dawn, the army officer lay down on the other bed (in which M's mistress was still asleep) and began to snore. M said: 'I was determined not to be beaten.' He continued to make love to the girl until she protested that she was sore. M then mustered all his energy for a final orgasm. After this, he crossed to the sink and washed his hands and genitals. He said: 'I looked at the roomful of prostrate bodies. And suddenly I felt myself THE VICTOR.' I cannot describe the satisfaction with which he said the last words. M went on to say that he then rolled the officer off his own bed on to the floor and slept until late the next day."

The author of this account later supplemented his narrative with the following comments:

"M was in no way creative: he did not attempt to express himself through writing or painting, and I think he had no interest in music. He struck me as permanently unsatisfied, and often left his father's firm to take other jobs. He had been engaged several times, but on each occasion had been unable to restrain his appetite for other women, so that his fiancées always ended by throwing him over. He liked reading books describing physical feats of endurance, like the Kon-Tiki expedition, the ascent of Everest, Scott's journey to the South Pole, etc. He became in quick succession a policeman, a whaler, and a Canadian mounted policeman. I think he suffered from boredom."

These details add up to an interesting portrait of the typical Don Juan figure. Because they are recounted in the third person, it is possible to gain a franker and less biased insight than in the cases of Casanova, Miller and Harris, who may take a very different view of themselves from that of their contemporaries. Here it can be seen plainly that the intense interest in sex is a substitute for other creative outlets. There is the physical energy and strength, and an attitude towards war and other forms of aggression that might be inaccurately called

Nietzschean. But it is also apparent that the usual outlets of the physically healthy man – sports, strenuous hobbies – are not able to satisfy him. His social background ensures that his various employments should not involve too much physical effort; but he might be happier as a coal miner or a farm hand. His "mystique of power" demands an outlet, and finds it in the urge to dominate other men, and in sexual "feats". In fact, the absorption in sex and the aggressiveness are the only available outlets for the will to power.

"M's" character could hardly be called "abnormal", but it is of great interest because it lies on the threshold of the abnormal. And it can be seen that here is a case of a man who is not well adapted for life in mid-twentieth-century Europe, although he might have made a highly satisfactory career in the army two hundred years ago. Like Casanova, Harris and Miller, he finds it difficult to discover a place for himself in society; but the profession of "adventure" is not open to man in our time, and he is forced to accept poor substitutes in becoming a policeman, whaler, etc. Unlike Casanova, he has no criminal leaning – this would not accord with his desire for leadership and his aggressiveness – but neither has he, apparently, any creative bent. He possesses great energy, and his lack of creative outlets forces most of it into the channel of his interest in sex. The episode with the officer and the nymphomaniac provides outlet for both his chief urges: the developed sexual interest and the aggression towards other men. Sexual encounters involving more than two partners are sometimes referred to as "pluralism" by psychologists, and it is frequently cited as a minor perversion; it can therefore be seen that, in this case, the "perversion" is a simple result of the frustration of creative energy.

There is a final interesting footnote to the case of "M"; although it may seem to have little relevance to the problems of sex, its significance will appear later in the discussion of "existential values". Apropos "M's" will to power, the author of the manuscript adds:

"We argued one day about his wholly physical attitude

towards life. I objected to the repetitiveness of his experience,
and said that a hundred experiences of sex could teach you no
more than one. He said this was not true – that each experience
is subtly different from all the others. I said: 'But what is the
good of learning something if you forget it the next day?' I
cannot quote his reply exactly, but it surprised me. He said
that each thing 'learned' is somehow telegraphed to the infinite – he may have said to God – so that nothing is ever lost.
It is therefore not the business of human beings to store and
correlate all their experience; their business is only to seek new
experience, and what they learn from it is preserved in some
eternal filing system."

It can be seen that "M" differs from the usual Don Juan
type in one important respect: that he feels a certain need for
logical consistency. This is a point worth noting. Don Juans
are seldom thinkers; and this holds true generally for all kinds
of sexual perverts. Each experience is "sufficient unto the
moment". But for men or women with a developed instinct for
"meaning" in life, too much casual sexual experience can produce a suicidal sense of futility.

The Strange Case of Artsybashev

This is nowhere more obvious than in the literary career of
Michael Artsybashev, the Russian writer who died in 1927, and
whose novels present a developed philosophy of Don Juanism.
Artsybashev achieved enormous fame in 1906 with the publication of *Sanin*, whose Ibsen-like hero preaches total *laissez faire*;
he loathes big words and pompous ideals even more than
Hemingway's heroes, and also believes in enjoying life without
making yourself miserable. His attitude is expressed in the
words of the old song:

> I eat when I'm hungry
> I drink when I'm dry
> And if whisky don't get me
> I'll live till I die.

He casually helps himself to the virginity of his best friend's
lady-love; the friend commits suicide; when Sanin is asked to

make a speech over the grave he only comments "One fool less in the world". There is a strong incest theme, and it is obvious that if the censor had allowed it, Artsybashev would have enjoyed developing this into an affair between Sanin and his sister. But although *Sanin* has several suicides, it is a cheerful and happy book.

In his next novel, *The Millionaire*, gloomy clouds have descended. There is a scene in it in which the bored millionaire hero casually possesses a girl by offering her a vast sum for her services; but the atmosphere of futility is overpowering. The millionaire is bored, disappointed, and ends by committing suicide. It reads like Dostoevsky without the religious mysticism. The misery and stupidity of human nature are presented with great power, but there is no compensation; and sex, which in *Sanin* possessed a lyrical quality, is now sordid and meaningless.

Artsybashev's last major novel was *On the Brink* (translated as *The Breaking Point*), and it now shows the moral collapse in its final stages. The message of the book seems to be "Everybody wants sex; it is the only reality underlying human existence". The artist-hero of the book is a Don Juan who argues that the delight of sex lies in conquest, and that marriage is usually cowardice; the book is a series of seductions, quarrels, duels, picnics, and intellectual arguments about suicide. But again, the whole atmosphere is dull and grey. The artist agrees that it is necessary to be cruel to be a Don Juan, but he shrugs his shoulders and accepts the necessity. There is no sign that the author condemns him. And the engineer Naumov preaches that all life is a confidence trick, and that the only dignified way out is suicide. Sex may be the final reality, but it is basically as futile as everything else. Artsybashev hammers home his idea that sex is the "basic reality" by showing how two of the characters almost drive one another to suicide in their love hate relationship; but at the end of the book the man flings the woman on the bed, possesses her, and then discovers that he has now lost all interest in her. *On the Brink* ends with an epidemic of suicides.

But it is interesting to trace the downward curve in Artsybashev's work (which resembles in many ways that of Maupassant). First of all, casual sex is glorified in an almost mystical way, as in the passage from Blake quoted on page 90. Then it slowly degenerates into a vicious Don Juanism, which in turn passes into suicidal despair and self-destruction.

What is more serious is that Artsybashev's own work steadily degenerated; *Sanin* is a good novel; *On the Brink* is incredibly bad and pointless; its movement resembles the jerking of a dead frog's leg when galvanized.

His death in 1927 – exiled from Russia by the Bolsheviks – seemed a strangely overdue catastrophe.

Female Sexuality

I have already commented that this book is written from the "male" point of view, for the obvious reason that the author is male, and finds it impossible to make the mental "act of sympathy" that would make the book more comprehensive. It is true that many women writers have produced brilliant and informative books on female sexuality – like Simone de Beauvoir's *Second Sex* and Sophie Lazarsfeld's *Woman's Experience of the Male*. But this present book is not an attempt at an "encyclopaedia of sex"; it is an attempt to explore the subject intuitively in the light of existential psychology, and using a phenomenological method. The following chapter will make clear why this confines the author strictly to "his own" point of view (i.e. as a male).

But although this approach means that it is impossible to treat the central problems of this book from the "female" viewpoint, it is nevertheless interesting to consider the question: how far does woman's attitude to sex in general differ from the man's? Stekel, for example, has declared that masochism is usually an important component in female sexuality, and this leads him to connect masochism and homosexuality. Most men would be inclined to accept this notion, since the male idea of the satisfactory woman is often of a submissive, easily dominated girl. On the other hand, Joyce's portrait of

Mrs. Bloom has often been praised (by women as well as men) for its insight into female psychology, and Mrs. Bloom appears to have not the slightest sign of masochism in her make-up. Her thoughts form an interesting contrast with those of her husband because they never become abstract or speculative; they remain "down to earth", anti-metaphysical. And this may be the reason that women acclaim Joyce's insight into female psychology. For the poles of the feminine mentality are more "personal" than those of the male. The woman is at once more romantic and more down-to-earth than the man; the male is given to abstraction and also to physical brutality. In Mrs. Bloom's life these poles are represented by her husband, always speculative and intellectual, and her lover Boylan, who walks round her bedroom without his trousers and makes love with a lack of finesse that disgusts her.

But if woman's attitude to sex is always more "personal" than the man's, it does not follow that this attitude has a necessary component of masochism. Consider, for example, the following case, cited by Reik:

"A young girl in a day-dream or fantasy, imagines herself on a table in a butcher's shop waiting to be butchered. Occasionally, as she lies nude . . . an employee comes by and touches her body. The touch gives her a pleasant sensation. Finally the butcher comes in with his knife, presses his hands over her nude body before starting to cut her up. Then before applying the knife, he puts a finger into her vagina. At that instant she has an orgasm."*

But it should be noted that the actual cutting up formed no part of the fantasy; the climax came with the insertion of the finger. The girl had been indulging in this fantasy since she was small. Her position on the butcher's slab symbolized helplessness, complete submission to the male – possibly because she would have felt guilt at the idea of being in any way a willing partner in the act. The insertion of the finger is close enough to the insertion of the penis to make this a more-

*Quoted in Sex Perversions and Sex Crimes by J. M. Reinhardt, p. 143.

or-less normal fantasy of a sexually frustrated girl who day-dreams of an all-conquering male. When the case is examined closely, the "perverse" element disappears, and the masochism is seen to be a magnification of the naturally passive rôle of the woman by frustration. If a "perversion" develops from habitual indulgence in this kind of fantasy, then it is a result of conditioning by frustration.

It is important not to allow such cases as this to lead us to the conclusion that the woman's receptivity is actually an embryonic masochism; there is no more reason for this con-clusion than for assuming that the active rôle of the male is a form of sadism. In neither case is *pain* necessarily involved.

What does seem likely is that the male attitude to sex leads to "perversion" more easily than the female attitude, since it is less personal. Again, Joyce has caught this difference with extraordinary dramatic force in the "Nausicaa" chapter of *Ulysses*. This is the chapter written in the language of romantic novelettes, since it is seen through the eyes of Gertie Mac-dowell. She sees Bloom watching her on the beach, and imagines that he is a "dark romantic stranger"; her thoughts then run on romance and marriage. Once, she recalls the physical aspect of sex when she remembers a lodger who used to masturbate in the bed, but her mind hastily thrusts this into the background. She then allows Bloom to see up her dress by leaning backwards – but still thinking of him in romantic terms. Joyce's viewpoint then switches to Bloom, who is cautiously masturbating, and whose thoughts are completely devoid of romanticism. The contrast is abrupt and brutal, and it makes clear a certain basic difference between the male and female attitudes to sex in a way that could hardly be achieved by whole volumes of discussion. For Bloom, sex is physical and cerebral; for Gertie, it is largely emotional. The final chapter of the book – Mrs. Bloom's monologue – only drives home this difference between male and female. Mrs. Bloom is twenty years older than Gertie Macdowell, and has none of her romantic delusions (although she shares her taste for romantic literature). But although she treats sex as a physical pleasure and even imagines giving herself to anonymous sailors on the docks, she can still indulge in romantic day-dreams about Stephen Dedalus, and criticizes her lover because "he doesn't know poetry from a cabbage". The name of Lord Byron occurs several times in her meditations; in a sense, he obviously stands for her ideal of a lover. All her thoughts are saturated with the romantic and personal attitude to sex.

Conclusion

It might be argued that Don Juanism is too easily understandable to be regarded as "abnormal", even in the least pejorative sense; that it is a mere overflowing of the "normal" sexual impulse, an exuberance. This question can only be answered by a "phenomenological" analysis of the sexual impulse, which I shall undertake in the next chapter.

In the meantime the conclusions of this chapter can be briefly summarized:

Don Juanism – or the urge to promiscuity for its own sake – seems usually to be connected with some mild form of insecurity neurosis. I say "mild form" because while a person is desirable enough to attract large numbers of the opposite sex, the likelihood of more serious perversions developing is not great. The Don Juan of Mozart and Da Ponte is the kind of person who could not exist; at least, Da Ponte was not enough of a psychologist to reveal the neurotic compulsion that would drive a man who could seduce a thousand and three women in Spain alone. Shaw's Don Juan is more credible, for Shaw had the insight to realize that a man whose vitality and intelligence render him irresistible to women would inevitably come to regard seduction as a tiresome frivolity.

The study of Don Juanism makes one thing clear: the sexual impulse cannot be understood within its own terms. The impulse to promiscuity is not explained by saying that a man's sexual desires are stronger than normal, or even by explaining that some inferiority feeling drives him to "over-compensate". This only leads to the further questions: What should be the "normal" desire, and how *ought* the inferiority to be compensated? The sexual part of man's being is not like a small self-governed, self-supporting State; it is closely connected with the economics of the rest of the continent.

CHAPTER III

THE METHOD OF ANALYSIS

The Phenomenological Method. Husserl and Gestalt Psychology.

On the surface, the sexual impulse is as straightforward as the appetite for food, and can therefore be discussed in a limited physical context. On closer examination, this is seen to be untrue. A man may be a gourmet who can only enjoy his meals with a white tablecloth, and who likes to stimulate his appetite with half a bottle of claret. But the fact remains that the whole process has a centre of gravity – the actual act of eating the food. No matter how many mental "frills" are added by the gourmet, they all lead up to the physical act of consuming the food, and digesting it.

Now at first sight the sex act would appear to parallel this closely, the orgasm corresponding to the eating of the food. But is this true? Even the greediest gourmand *needs* food; but no man ever died from the starvation of the sexual impulse. The following extract from Frank Mitchell's *Noonday Sun: An Australian Childhood*, will make this point clearer:

"I had read somewhere that first sexual experiences are always disappointing. . . . I was too shy to even attempt to kiss her – until, that is, she kissed me. After that, she took the lead all the time. . . . A few evenings later, we were lying in the park and kissing, and our bodies were so closely pressed together that she could hardly fail to be aware of my excitement. Suddenly, to my intense delight, she again took the lead, and her cool hand found its way inside my clothes. I felt as if all the sexual day-dreams of my adolescence were coming true. . . . Later, I tried to undress her, but did it so fumblingly that she moved away from me, and quickly unzipped her shorts. I tried to make her lie down but she shook her head, smiling.

She then made me lie on my back and carefully lowered herself on to me. She obviously found it very painful for she kept repeating: 'Don't move, don't move.' A detached part of my mind watched all this with amazement. This was the great experience that had haunted my nights. Surely I should be wracked with ecstasy? Instead, I felt a certain sensation of warmth, but no more. It was far less vivid than many of my erotic day-dreams. This sensation might just as easily have been due to the pressure of her hand, or of my own. . . . Later, I deliberately resisted my feeling that it had been a total failure."

This is reminiscent of "M's" statement that masturbation can be more satisfying than normal intercourse. But most interesting is the statement that "it could just as easily have been due to the pressure of her hand, or of my own". (Mitchell is unusually frank about his practice of masturbation in his teens; in this, he follows the example of his favourite writers, James Joyce and Thomas Wolfe.) A hungry man may titillate his appetite in various ways that have more to do with the imagination than with the gastric juices, but when it comes to eating, there has to be solid food; no matter how good his imagination, he will not feel satisfied until he has actually eaten. Here, Mitchell makes it plain that the "real" act is less satisfying than the imagined version. The nerves of the stomach signal their satisfaction in response to food; the sexual orgasm is a response to an act of will and imagination rather than to a physical reality.

Perception

This brings up an important general question: that of the mechanism of perception in the sexual act. Certain general principles about perception should be stated at this point, if the discussion is to escape from the jargon of the psychiatrist's case book.

If you eat a sausage roll you are participating in an act that has both a mental and a physical component – that is to say, a subjective and an objective component. If you are hungry, you may be able to imagine yourself eating a sausage roll, but it will not satisfy your stomach. There is a certain physical basis, a kind of "reality", to the act of eating it. On the other hand, the process of satisfying your hunger with a sausage roll is not purely mechanical, like putting a coin into a cigarette machine. For although putting the roll into your stomach *may* produce the deduceable effect (i.e. satisfaction and the disappearance of hunger), it might equally well make you sick. If you have a bad cold, you may not be able to taste it at all; it may be as tasteless as sawdust. (If you hold your breath, it is difficult to tell the difference between an onion and an apple.) And if, while you are eating it, someone in the room is sick, you may also be sick, even though you are not close enough to smell the vomit.

It will be convenient to think of eating the sausage roll as the simplest form of perception. You not merely see and smell and touch the sausage roll; you *absorb* it (Whitehead would say you prehend it). In short, you "know" it about as thoroughly as a human being can know an external object. Nevertheless, your digestion of the roll does not depend on the roll alone; it also depends on the state of your senses.

The problem of the rôle of perception was first investigated by Locke and Berkeley; they posed the question of how far we can know "reality" through the senses. They attacked the commonsense position about perception: that there are objects, and that although your perception of the objects may vary slightly (if you are colour blind, cross-eyed, etc.), nevertheless, you see things "as they really are". Berkeley went so far as to question whether objects exist at all when no one is looking at them. Taken to an absurd extreme, this position is known as "solipsism" – the belief that no one exists in the world except yourself.

The next step in the theory of perception was taken by Kant. He also felt that there "are" objects out there, of whose existence our senses inform us. However, he tended to agree with Berkeley that the qualities of objects – shape, colour, taste, etc. – are "added" by the senses, and that we can never hope to know anything about what objects are "really" like. Kant added that we see the world "as it is" because our perceptions impose a certain order on it. We see the external world within the artificial categories of space and time; we cannot see it otherwise. These categories are like a pair of blue spectacles worn on the nose, and they can never be taken off.

The theories of perception propounded by Berkeley and Kant are clumsy in the extreme; in fact, they are no more than a simple recognition of the problem – the problem of how far mental processes enter into eating the sausage roll. Before Locke, perception was accepted as a mechanical process, like putting a coin into a slot machine; Berkeley went to the opposite extreme, and suggested that the coin might be imaginary.

Husserl and Gestalt Psychology

In the twentieth century the theory of perception has at last achieved the rank of a kind of science, and Kant's vague suggestion about the categories has been carefully expanded. There are so far two distinct currents of this theory, that merge only at certain points. One is the science of phenomenology, founded by Edmund Husserl; the other is the so-called "Gestalt" or form-psychology. It is necessary to say a few words about these before passing on to the problem of the rôle of perception and imagination in sex.

Husserl was a mathematician-turned-philosopher, who was dismayed by the chaotic state of philosophy; he felt that it was too much of a vague, speculative art, and not enough of a science. He tried to turn it into a science. Husserl's basic recognition was this: that when we look at the world, we see a series of shapes and colours that might almost be called "symbols" of real objects. And yet we are not confused by this; the mind instantly interprets a certain array of lines and colours as a book, a radio set, a tree. When you read a book, at least half the work of understanding is done by your own mind; the author would be helpless without this co-operation from the reader. But Husserl points out that we "read" the physical world all the time in exactly the same way. If you stare at an object with your mind "a blank", it fails to register or mean anything. Husserl posed the usual Kantian question: How far does the mind affect what we see? But he went further than Kant. He then asked: Is it possible to produce a *method* for deciding how far perception is affected by the perceiver? He invented the procedure of "bracketing". Instead of studying the object, you study only your *perception* of the object; you "bracket out" the object and behave as if it did not exist, concentrating only on the form of the perception.*

What is the final aim of all this "bracketing"? Philosophy is the opposite of taking things for granted. In fact, science could be defined as *not* taking things for granted. The aim of philosophy is to extend knowledge, to understand the universe. But as soon as the philosopher has stated his purpose, he runs into an immediate difficulty. He is rather in the position of the cowboy who shot off his own big toe when he saw it silhouetted against a window in the dark. He is not sure which is "himself" and which is the universe; the dividing line is not very clear. Husserl's point is that the philosopher is always accidentally getting himself into the picture. The psychologist Brentano discovered what he called "intentionality" – that is to say, the way in which the mind *imposes* shapes on the "things perceived".

We tend to think of ourselves as merely "receiving" im-

---

*An obvious example of the "order imposing faculty" is our relation to other human beings. We can never know another person fully in the way we can know an object by walking round it. We observe as many characteristics as possible, and then pass a "judgement" on the person concerned. These judgements obviously depend on one's own personality and needs. Hence our "idea" of another person is a series of observed facets, connected arbitrarily. The equivalent of the phenomenological reduction, on this personal level, would be to attempt to suspend all one's feelings about a person, and to attempt to observe him as detachedly as an entomologist observes the behaviour of a beetle. Correlating this observation with one's observations made in a "personal" frame of mind would throw light not only on the "true nature" of the person observed but upon the biases and feelings that form one's own "observing mechanism". I suggest this only as an approximate parallel of Husserl's method – although, in fact, in the 1930s, Husserl became preoccupied with this type of approach.

pressions and perceptions from "out there"; we think of ourselves, in a sense, as the "victims" of things that happen to us. If a slate falls on your head, it simply "happens" to you, and your mental attitude towards the slate will not make any difference to the pain. So we tend to think of reality as a bully, constantly imposing itself on us. But the Husserl-Brentano picture of the world is the reverse of this; it is our minds that are the bullies. Impressions and sensations present themselves to us timidly; our unconscious minds promptly form them into ranks, and batter them into some kind of order, so that they are presentable for inspection by the conscious mind. The conscious mind imagines that these smart recruits were always orderly and disciplined; it knows nothing of the work that went on before its inspection. Husserl wishes to find out exactly what went on before the inspection, to trap the unconscious mind in the very act of "imposing form" on the perceptions.

All this may seem irrelevant to the discussion of sex; but it will be seen later that such a discussion would be practically meaningless without a background of this sort. For sex is also largely an unconscious matter, which the consciousness takes for granted; the problem is to use Husserl's methods for finding out something about the laws that govern the unconscious in relation to sex.

Gestalt psychology shares many of the aims and methods of Husserl's transcendental phenomenology. It is also concerned with the problem of perception, and its basic statement is that we begin by perceiving things as *wholes*, and only notice later that they are made up of a sum of parts. You see a pair of "identical twins", and yet you know instantly which is which, if pressed, you could not say exactly *how* you know; you could not reply: her hair is a shade darker than that of her sister, and her nose is an eighth of an inch longer. You might discover these facts later, but they are not the original reason for distinguishing between the two. In the same way, you may try to recall a phrase of music; when it finally "comes to you", you whistle it in the wrong key; and yet it is the same phrase, even though all its notes are different. You somehow remembered the phrases as a "whole", as a *shape* of notes, not as a *series* of notes – B flat followed by A natural, etc.

A simple example might help to explain the approach of Gestalt psychology. The police have developed a method of tracing criminals by means of an "identity kit". You have witnessed a crime, and are asked by the police to supply a description of the criminal; but you cannot describe his face in words; it is too much like other faces. But if you are shown a series of photographs and drawings of different men you might be able to say: "He looked rather like that one – except that his face was slightly rounder." The police artist then makes a sketch of a similar face, slightly rounder; you are now able to say: "That is more like it, but the eyes are somehow wrong." And so on. Each new change in the drawing enables you to fill in more *relations*, until finally you have a drawing that seems to you a fair representation of the criminal. Your memory of the face is not a series of facts – the shape of the nose, the eyes, etc.; it is a whole complex of relations.

Another simple analogy might clarify this. Gestalt psychology is an attempt to discover something about the *language* of the unconscious mind, or rather, its symbolism. In the West, we have only twenty-six letters in the alphabet, and all our words are built up from different arragements of these letters. Chinese and Japanese have thousands of symbols, each symbol standing for a different word, so that learning to write Chinese is a great deal more complicated than learning to write English. It is true that the Chinese method is labour-saving, once you have learned all the symbols. Instead of having to place a string of letters end to end to construct a word, you have one small, compact little symbol.

Now Gestalt psychology claims that our subconscious language is more like Chinese than English. When you want to remember a face, you do not "construct" it in your mind by adding together a nose, a mouth, a chin, etc. You sort quickly through a huge box of photos until you find one that more-or-less corresponds to the one you want, and having got the general "form", you then make slight corrections for the nose, chin, etc.

Gestalt psychology, like phenomenology, is an attempt to find out how the form-imposing faculty works, and why.

But most important is the problem of "intentionality". Our minds are less passive than we suppose; in attempting to discover laws it is not unlikely that we shall discover that we are the makers of the laws. If you close your eyes and rub your eyelids hard with your fingers, vague blobs of colour will appear on the inside of the eyelids; by staring at these and "willing", it is possible to make the shapes change continually – they will turn into pink elephants or green giraffes at will. This is the "form-imposing" faculty at work. It is pointless to ask *why* you decide to make them change into pink elephants rather than purple aeroplanes; no doubt caprice and unconscious selection play their part, as in word-association tests; but the *will* is here the most important element.

The Problem of Vision

All this suggests the answer to a problem that is close to the problem of sex: that of vision. Poets have always asked why the moments of affirmation are so brief:

> Whither has fled the visionary gleam?
> Where is it now, the freshness and the dream?

The poet's answer is usually imprecise. Wordsworth talked of a sudden consciousness of "unknown modes of being"; he seems to suggest that the poet can only keep his mind open, and stay "close to nature"; no amount of conscious effort can induce the "mystical" state. The poets and mystics seem to be generally in agreement that language cannot express the mystical vision of "otherness".

But Husserl's psychology provides a new insight into the problem. If the mind imposes its own patterns on all perceptions, it is natural that our experience includes little "otherness". The mind automatically filters off the otherness. The mind's basic mechanism is to perceive similarities between one set of impressions and another. This is the way in which it approaches all problems. A mathematician may be baffled by a problem, until it strikes him that it is similar to a problem he solved the day before. A detective may find a case incomprehensible until certain features remind him of a similar case. Now experiences pour in on us all day long; unless we had some filtering mechanism they would reduce the mind to bewilderment and exhaustion in a few minutes. Admittedly, habit is our ally; but it is no final defence. A home-loving stockbroker may catch the same train every morning, and use exactly the same words of greeting to his secretary; and yet every day is different. For every single circumstance that is "the same" as yesterday, there are another fifty that are different. The weather is different; the people he passes in the street are different; the news in his newspaper is different.

Everyone is familiar with the basic mechanism of the "filter": that its ruthlessness increases as the mind becomes more tired. You are on your way to work in the morning; you are feeling fresh after a good night's sleep, and the attention is wide awake. In the evening, returning from a hard day's work, you no longer notice anything; you prefer to bury yourself in a newspaper, and exclude as much of the outside world as possible. And the filter in the mind obligingly makes you oblivious to the chatter of the two shopgirls in your carriage and the noise of rain on the window.

The tired mind reduces its perceptions to abstractions. In the morning you might have noticed that one of the girls had nice legs and that the other had recently dyed her hair. Now they are merely "two girls"; the filter cuts out all unnecessary detail. If you are *very* tired, you might not even notice that they are girls; you are merely aware that there are two other people in the carriage with you. Later, you cannot remember whether they were men or women. The mind has progressed further in the direction of abstraction. It retains enough sense of time and place to steer you back home, but the "order" it imposes on the world is now of the most arbitrary kind, a few bare lines of latitude and longitude.

Plainly, since life is appallingly complex, the filter is necessary; without it we would all go mad. But it also imposes a certain sameness on our days, a sameness that is the opposite of the "visionary gleam". Children cannot understand the bad memories of adults. They say impatiently: "But don't you remember – it was that day you lost the button off your overcoat on the way to the cinema." They find it hard to believe that you can dimly remember the visit to the cinema, but have totally forgotten losing the button. For the child, every day is thrillingly unlike the one before; with his enormous mental energy, he is more interested in the differences between things than in their similarities. He can remember exactly what you said and did on a day six months before.

But the mind's desire for simplicity and order can become self-destructive. Nietzsche emphasized that it is more important to ask: "Freedom *for* what?" than "Freedom *from* what?"; the same is true of order. The child has no particular purposes; he does not want to make a fortune or support a large family; therefore he has no reason to limit his consciousness. The adult has reasons for limiting his consciousness; he does it to conform to a scheme of values. But he is lazy about his values; he seldom examines or revises them. He does not wake up one morning and think: "I have now made enough money to allow the poet in me a little freedom; I shall now permit myself to 'stand the stare' and notice the reflections of clouds in puddles." He continues, out of force of habit, to limit his awareness of the world to a number of abstractions that serve to keep him sane. But even if he has a sudden illness that forces him to retire, he may continue to live on a kind of psychological bread and water. The values" "that made him choose this diet have disppeared, but he continues out of habit. The result is a gradual dehydration of his springs of enjoyment. The "values" have long ceased to be an active source of pleasure, and he has filtered other sources of pleasure out of his life. No one is really surprised when he dies of a cancer five years after retiring; the undernourished consciousness finally begins to consume itself.

The methods of Husserl and Gestalt are plainly a more practical step in the direction of "vision" than anything suggested by Wordsworth or Blake. If you can examine the mechanisms of the form-imposing faculty, then you can also adjust them to let in "otherness", which is by definition merely that which is normally excluded by the filter.

In short, phenomenology might provide a method for temporarily removing the "blinkers" we all wear on the consciousness. Its fundamental question is: Why is human consciousness so peculiarly limited? This question strikes all of us at some time or other. The factory worker on New Year's Eve feels the sense of "complete confidence" and happiness described by Proust; alcohol and the "holiday spirit" only contribute to it; they do not explain it away. In such a moment he may wonder vaguely why he cannot feel like this all the time. The answer is that it would not increase his efficiency as an instrument of evolution; a constant sense of euphoria would blanket the "challenge and response" mechanism that keeps the will taut.

Once all these basic facts about the nature of consciousness and perception have been grasped, the workings of the sexual impulse become immediately more apparent. These conclusions can be summarized briefly:

(a) Human beings possess an *unconscious* will that filters and selects their perceptions.

(b) Until they understand these "form-imposing" mechanisms, they are in no position to pass judgements on questions about the meaning and purpose of life, human nature, etc. Like the cowboy who shot off his big toe in the dark, they may mistake part of themselves for an alien, an intruder.

(c) The "doors of perception" all have extremely powerful springs. It is occasionally possible to wedge one of them open for a short period and to let in a little light and air – the "otherness" of the world. But they usually slam very quickly, leaving the consciousness imprisoned in its narrow den. This seems to be the method of the "life force" for keeping us from relaxing to much, for getting the maximum of work out of each human will.

Human beings strive all the time to introduce new elements of "otherness" into their lives. Each new achievement produces a sense of power, and opens the "door" momentarily. But although the achievement may be permanent, the sense of triumph is not. The door closes quickly; man has to be driven on to new efforts of will.

Human beings, then, have a common aim; a broadening of consciousness. And the forces of evolution utilize this aim in the same way that we utilize the force of gravity when we harness a power station to a waterfall. They operate on a basis that can only be called a sindle: they keep human beings "poor" in consciousness just as an employer might keep his workers poor by imposing heavy fines and taxes on them, taking back ninety per cent. of the wage packet. This inevitably gives to human life the flavour of futility observed by so many philosophers. The sense of achievement is destroyed almost immediately, so that man is forced to repeat the whole process of striving. Recognizing this, philosophers have pointed out that man needs cunning rather than determination and strength. They play the rôle of agitators, trying to stir men to revolt against this exploitation by the biological forces. If the *sense* of achievement is more important than the achievement, then men had better learn control of their minds and emotions; by doing so, they might be able to hold on to the sense of achievement longer, or even produce it without long and unnecessary striving. Hence Socrates's "Know yourself". They raise an ideal of detachment and of refusing to strive, of cultivating mental serenity. The biological forces seem to depend on rather crude and bullying methods to keep human beings in their rôle of exploited workers. Life is complex and difficult, and merely to keep alive demands most of the available energy and attention. The life forces employ the technique known in America as "the bum's rush"; that is, they crowd and hurry the selected victim to such an extent that he is too confused to grasp the confidence trick that is being played on him. Added to this confusing flow of experience, and the perpetual demands of the body to be fed and tended to, there is the problem of the powerful "spring" on all the "doors of perception", so that even if a man succeeds in stopping to think and take stock of his situation, he finds it hard to think consecutively and purposefully; the doors keep slamming behind him and plunging him back into darkness. He is rather in the position of Alice trying to play croquet using a live flamingo as a mallet, hedgehogs for balls, and doubled-up soldiers for the arches; any of them might move unpredictably.

Once all this is firmly grasped, the mechanism of the sexual impulses becomes easier to understand. Don Juanism, for example, becomes immediately comprehensible. The easiest means of achieving an immediate broadening of consciousness is the sexual orgasm. It will be pointed out that the easiest way of achieving an orgasm is in masturbation. There are no statistics to indicate whether the Don Juan types masturbate more or less than others; but there is certainly no evidence that Don Juanism is inconsistent with masturbation. The ex-officer "M", cited in the last chapter, said that masturbation is in some ways preferable to intercourse; and he conforms in every way to the Don Juan type. Casanova admits to using the hand of Mlle. de la Meure to masturbate himself; it seems unlikely that he masturbated only when he had a compliant sexual partner.

But masturbation can never be as satisfying *to the ego* as the conquest of new sexual partners. Each sexual partner is, in herself, a kind of ultimate, and the actual act of taking her a moment of self-glorification – perhaps even a mystical sense that "everything is for the best", that life is not finally defeat, but splendid adventure.

> What were all the world's alarms
> To mighty Paris when he found
> Sleep upon a golden bed
> That first dawn in Helen's arms?

Immediately afterwards, the consciousness closes up again,

and the whole process must be repeated for another moment of insight. The "inferiority complex" blankets the mind again; man is back in the position of having to "prove" himself in his own eyes. It is to the advantage of the force of evolution that man should be kept in the dark about his own strength.

The principle of the limitation of consciousness is the key to the problem of the human sexual impulse.

CHAPTER IV

THE MEANING OF "PERVERSION"
(1)

The Sexual Criminal. The Black Dahlia murder. Imitative murder. Sexual underprivilege. Sexual fulfilment and the problem of "vision". Blake. Introverted sexuality. Eliot and W. J. Turner. T. E. Hulme. De Sade. Kierkegaard and the Diary of a Seducer.

THE foregoing considerations suggest a new avenue of approach to the whole question of sexual perversion – I mean the philosophical rather than the "pathological" approach. It is easy enough to decide when a machine is functioning normally, and when there is something wrong, for we know about the purpose of the machine. But human beings, it would seem, are machines that have been deliberately sabotaged; a certain frustration would seem to have been "in-built" into us, so that we can never work at maximum efficiency. An even more sinister analogy suggests itself: that human beings are kept in a state of psychological confinement and frustration in the same way that cattle are fattened for the butcher. There is no "mechanical" reason why human beings should be such a poor, degraded, pitiful lot. Degradation and the sense of inferiority are "moods" brought about by a feeling of inadequacy and failure, of defeat by the "present". There is no good reason why any human being should feel this failure. We all possess a vast storehouse of memory, enough material for the deep, broad consciousness of a god. "I knew again, what in my wretchedness I had forgotten . . . the kernel of this life of mine was noble", writes Steppenwolf. Unfortunately, this storehouse is inaccessible; we ourselves might feel that it is a necessity, but the forces of evolution feel that it is a luxury which human beings might well be denied. More: it might even lower their "evolutionary" efficiency, for excess of memory has no survival value, and might promote laziness. So we have to be contented with this thin, un-nourishing soup of consciousness when we know there is no good reason why we should not be allowed a feast.

In the twentieth century our lives have become so complex that we have less time than ever for relaxing and turning away from the repetitious necessities of physical existence. Under the circumstances it is not surprising that there is an ever-increasing emphasis on the simple stimulants of consciousness – alcohol, tobacco, drugs, and sex.

Besides, there is now a difference in the actual quality of our interest in sex. This is because sex is becoming increasingly an object of "contemplation" instead of a simple physical in-dulgence. In primitive societies sex is simply something that a man does to a girl if he is lucky enough to catch her in a dark corner; it is a pleasant physical act, and it is not likely to occupy the mind over-much during the rest of the day. Today, the reminders of sex are continuous. Women dress lightly and elegantly, in a way that is designed to make men aware of what they have to offer in bed. Hoardings are covered with ad-vertisements involving women dressed in their underwear, although the product advertised may only have the vaguest connection with women. (I recall, from my own schooldays, a huge advertisement for a well-known laxative, showing a pretty girl dressed in her bra and panties, standing on a bathroom scale and smiling; crowds of goggling schoolboys used to stare at it as they passed it on the bus.) Certain authors and film producers have discovered the advantages of making their products near-obscene, and the newspaper publicity about such books and films turns them into best-sellers.

All this raises a quite new kind of problem. The Crusader who had spent five years without sleeping with a woman may have felt intense frustration, but it could be satisfied at the first "Christian" brothel on his way home. But as soon as a *mental* component enters into a physical urge, it stretches it beyond its ordinary limits. Boswell records that Dr. Johnson ate his food like an animal, and preferred his meat to be "strong" (i.e. slightly rotten) because he had starved so much in his earlier years. Akutagawa, the "Japanese Maupassant", has a masterly story called *Yam Gruel* about a harmless, half-starved little soldier who develops a passion – an almost insane obsession – about his favourite dish, Yam gruel, and spends his days imagining what it would be like to eat huge quantities of the stuff. (Characteristically, he feels sick and embarrassed when he finally has the opportunity to consume it by the gallon.)

To say that this mental component stretches the physical urge beyond its ordinary limits is not to say that it makes it somehow abnormal. It may cause it to go beyond its "natural" limit; but then, as the last chapter showed, nature keeps us deliberately subnormal in order to keep the will taut, so "beyond its natural limit" does not necessarily imply abnormality.

An interesting illustration of this point can be found in Philip de Bruyn's autobiography, *A Pagan's Hosanna*; de Bruyn writes of seeing a pretty girl walk along the beach in her bathing costume, and speaks of the violence of the desire that he feels. But he goes on:

"The trouble was that I knew it was unsatisfiable. I might get to know her and persuade her to sleep with me. But that would not satisfy what I felt *now*; it would only be a carbon copy of this desire to lay her on the warm sand, remove her bathing trunks, and *take* her with an instantaneous fusion of bodies."

This is important. De Bruyn recognizes that this desire for an unknown girl is of a far more intense order than what he might later feel for a girl personally known to him and willing to become his mistress. It is disquieting to think that, if de Bruyn had been a different type of man, and had the beach been empty, the girl might have been strangled and raped *to meet a need that could not be otherwise satisfied.*

This is not to say, of course, that there are "normal" sexual desires that can only be satisfied by rape. We tend to think and speak as if sexual desire and its means of satisfaction were as

logically connected as hunger and eating a meal. There is no such connection. Sexual desire increases or decreases by no known law; satiety plays its part, but there is also involved a psychophysical complexity that defies analysis. (In the case of the school guard who murdered the three children, for example, the murderer's previous sexual experience had been very wide and somewhat degenerate. Nevertheless, satiety alone cannot be blamed for the crime, for he told Paul de River that he had never before experienced complete fulfilment of his sexual desires, and that he afterwards felt "much easier and sexually satisfied".) There is no more reason why a certain sexual act should produce "ultimate satisfaction" than that a certain poem or piece of music should effect a release of the emotions. Our tendency to associate sexual desire and its means of satisfaction in a rigorously causal process reveals the same kind of loose thinking that causes us to treat our perceptions as somehow "given". It requires only an act of "phenomeno-logical analysis" to show the hidden "intentionality" that selects its own sexual goal.

All the same, the idea of "ultimate sexual satisfaction" leads to an interesting way of restating the question of Chapter I. Instead of asking: Where is the borderline between normality and perversion? we can rephrase the question: What is the permissible limit for human sexual satisfaction? In this form it is possible to carry the analysis a great deal further. For the sentence involves a number of ideas that have been raised in the previous chapter. "Permissible" immediately leads to the question: "Permitted by whom, or according to what standard of values?" And the idea of a limit to sexual satisfaction – some ultimately satisfying experience – raises again the question of the boundaries of human consciousness, and therefore the question of "vision".

Let us state one point with emphasis, for it is the key to every discussion of sex, and constitutes the essence of the viewpoint of this book: in speaking of the values involved in forms of sexual activity, *the "limitation of consciousness" is the villain of the piece*. If the question were being discussed in the

religious language of the Victorians, words like "God" and "sin" could be used, and would greatly simplify the statement. If they are introduced into the present discussion in the form of implications (of terms like "permissible", "nature", "biological force", etc.), it should be understood that this is purely for convenience, in the way that mathematicians use imaginary numbers (the square root of minus quantities). They hide shades and complexities that the discussion has not yet been able to conceptualize.

Nevertheless, the central thesis of this book is in no way falsified when expressed in that form: the limitation of consciousness is the villain of the piece. This is not a justification of sexual "perversion" or sexual crime; but at least it offers us the means of understanding it. A mother who is driven to theft to support her children is still guilty of a crime; but there can be no "justice" that fails to take her motives into account. Human beings are deprived of a consciousness that is arguably "theirs by natural right". Dr. C. D. Broad wrote: "Each person is at each moment capable of remembering all that has ever happened to him and of perceiving everything that is happening everywhere in the universe. The function of the brain and nervous system is to protect us from being overwhelmed and confused by this mass of largely useless and irrelevant knowledge, by *shutting out* most of what we should otherwise perceive. . . ."* [My italics.] This view was first expressed by Bergson. In the last chapter I spoke loosely of the "biological forces" that deliberately blinker the human consciousness to raise it to maximum efficiency. But it should be kept in mind that the "blinkering" may be again *subconsciously intentional:* we may ourselves recognize the necessity of limiting our consciousness (and therefore our "happiness") in order to express our fullest vitality. In that case our ideal self-expression as human beings would involve a certain balance between this unconscious intentionality and the conscious desires.

Bearing all this in mind, we can treat the question of the "permissible limits" of human sexual activity as a problem

*Quoted by Aldous Huxley in *The Doors of Perception.*

about the extension of consciousness. Sexual activity is driven by the same aims and motives as reading poetry or listening to music: to escape the limitations imposed by the need for particularity in the consciousness. Ezra Pound wrote:

> . . . that I
> Am here a Poet that doth drink of life
> As lesser men drink wine.

He has defined the common aim of all humanity: all would like to "drink of life" as others drink wine. Pound's belief is typical of a poet. Hemingway once said that "only a bull-fighter lives his life all the way up", suggesting that physical daring is a better technique for intensification of consciousness. But there is also a joke – of disquieting implications – about a schoolboy who, on being asked what he wanted to be when he grew up, replied "a sex maniac". Nothing is more likely than that many people believe that the "sex maniac" is one of the few members of our society who can "drink of life" in a way denied to the rest of us. To some extent the view is justified. I have already quoted the remarks of Philip de Bruyn concerning the girl walking along the beach, and his feeling that only rape (or at least, instantaneous possession) would be a satisfactory objective correlative for the desire aroused. Henri Barbusse raises a similar point at the beginning of the novel *L'Enfer*; the narrator describes a dinner in a "respectable" boarding house, during which someone speaks of a recent sex crime; the narrator notices that everyone is infected with an excitement that they try to conceal – even the mother of a small girl. All feel a certain secret envy of the sexual criminal.

I have elsewhere suggested that the study of "imitative" sex crimes reveals the same repressed urge. The police dislike the newspaper publication of details of a sex crime because so many of them are followed up by imitative crimes, inspired by the account. (Charles Jackson has written a powerful novel on this subject, *The Outer Edges*.) The Black Dahlia murder that took place in Los Angeles in 1947 is a case in point. Elizabeth Short, an unsuccessful actress, twenty-two years old, was murdered in an exceptionally atrocious manner. Her body was found on a vacant lot; it had been cut in two at the waist. Marks on the body showed that she had been hung upside down and tortured before her death. A man claiming to be the murderer wrote to the police and offered to give himself up, but never did so. The Black Dahlia killer may have been inspired by a murderer named Otto Steve Wilson, who had strangled and mutilated two prostitutes on the same day in 1944 in Los Angeles. (De River also has an account of this case.) But whether or not Wilson inspired Elizabeth Short's murderer, it is certain that the Black Dahlia murder inspired something of a sex-crime wave in Los Angeles in 1947; six more murders of the same type occurred in that year in the same area; in one case, the murderer actually scrawled "B.D." (Black Dahlia?) in lipstick on his victim's breast. Twenty-seven men confessed to the Dahlia killing; all their confessions proved false. The twenty-eighth false confession came nine years after the murder – this time it was a Lesbian. These false confessions might be regarded as a kind of substitute for an imitative crime; they spring from the same envy of the murderer's experience, and a desire to participate in it. Here is a case where one sadistic sex crime triggered off thirty-four parallel reactions – six murders and twenty-eight false confessions – in an area about the size of Greater London. How many other inhabitants of Los Angeles felt the same envy of the murderer's experience, but confined their imitations to the imagination?

Even so, most people – luckily – find such crimes too horrible to feel anything but a certain morbid fascination. Dislike of causing pain is fairly deep in most of us. But sex maniacs are not all murderers – or even mostly murderers. De River again cites a very typical case of a psychopathic rapist. The man was of low intelligence and his photograph shows a loose mouth and weak chin. Before his arrest on charges of rape, he had been in jail several times for indecent exposure and molesting girls on the street. His method was always the same: to show his victim a large knife, and order her to remove some of her undergarments. His brutish appearance seems to have convinced most of his victims that he would not hesitate to use the knife. The victims – they included three women and a nine-year-old child – allowed him to perform various sexual acts on them, including cunnilingus. In all cases he simply allowed the victim to walk away after he had achieved orgasm, making no attempt to molest her further. In at least two cases the girls made the best of their unfortunate situation, and responded with some enthusiasm; one of them asked him to stop exciting her and get on with the job. This is probably closer to what the boy in the joke had in mind when he said he wanted to be a sex maniac.

Sexual Underprivilege

This brings us, the, to one of the greatest problems of modern civilization – the problem of "sexual underprivilege". A century ago the feeling of social underprivilege was to the fore. Many societies – and this was particularly true in England and Russia – were in the process of change; there was neither the old, clear stratification of gentleman and peasant, nor the sense of classlessness, so typical of modern America and (to a lesser extent) of post-war England. The consequence was the state of perpetual social unrest, involving many incidents of violence. In our own time the neurosis of social underprivilege has almost disappeared. It now requires an act of sympathy to understand completely the feelings underlying Dreiser's *American Tragedy* or *John Halifax, Gentleman*, and the snobbery of Disraeli and Oscar Wilde has a curious musty flavour. The last major English writer to be influenced by the sense of social underprivilege was D. H. Lawrence. Occasional throwbacks like Waugh's *Brideshead Revisited* or even Braine's *Room at the Top* now have a sort of novelty appeal that demonstrates how far we have progressed towards a classless society.

But the nineteenth-century social unrest has now been transferred to the sexual sphere. The rate of sex crimes has been rising steadily since before the war; they have actually trebled their pre-war rate in England. This problem will be discussed more fully in the next chapter. For the moment, it is enough to point out that one of its chief causes is the rise in sexual stimulation. Tolstoy complained that there was too much sex in the atmosphere in nineteenth-century Russia; it is not difficult to imagine his reaction to almost any modern capital city, with cinemas showing "X" films involving rape, most advertisements using scantily clad girls, and many bookshops openly selling near-pornography.

The consequence is that the feeling expressed by Philip de Bruyn is now more widespread than ever before. This is partly due to the human tendency to believe that the grass is always greener in the other fellow's yard – an envy of other men's sexual experience. It is undoubtedly encouraged by accounts of sex crimes in newspapers. This envy may also be directed at sections of society where sexual morals are supposed to be unusually free:* the world of artists, criminals, prostitutes, etc. There are times when this "sexual fever" resembles nothing so much as the gold-fever of the Yukon gold rush, a kind of indiscriminate anxiety for any kind of sexual gain.

It is arguable that Nabokov's *Lolita* is about this feeling of underprivilege rather than about sexual relations with a nymphet. Humbert's passion for Lolita is only the passion of modern man for the forbidden. Humbert seems to contain the seed of most of the sexual perversions, with the exception of sadism. He indulges in masturbation on park benches, while peering up the skirts of little girls who raise their knees to adjust roller skates – a form of voyeurism – and later uses the pressure of Lolita's legs to induce an orgasm; his original plan with Lolita is not to seduce her, but to drug her with sleeping pills and use her as a passive sexual object, without actually violating her; this is certainly a close relation to necrophilia.

But whether intentionally or not, Nabokov has certainly

*In 1960 I wrote an article for a Sunday newspaper describing a "Beat" community in Chelsea where the women were more or less communal. I immediately received many letters asking me for the address of the house. These were not, as might have been expected, from art students and other Beats, but from "respectable people", including a schoolteacher and a lawyer, who claimed that they wanted to "study" the community.

created, in *Lolita*, a powerful symbol of the modern sense of sexual underprivilege. I can think of only two possible ways of treating the subject fictionally: to write about a rapist or sexual killer – or to write about some other form of sexual indulgence that can be treated as wholly forbidden.

In the eighteenth century adultery was "wicked" enough to produce an artistic effect of social revolt; by the late nineteenth century adultery had become a commonplace of fiction (particularly in France). The twentieth-century counterpart of *Manon Lescaut* or *The Princess of Cleves* was a novel like Kuprin's *Yama* (about a brothel) or Barbusse's *Hell* (about a voyeur). Proust's *Recherche*, Joyce's *Ulysses*, Radclyffe Hall's *Well of Loneliness*, Faulkner's *Sanctuary*, widened the boundaries to such an extent that a reader who is familiar with them all should be virtually unshockable. Faulkner's novel started a spate of books dealing with gangsters, sadism and rape, the best known of which is Hadley Chase's interesting *No Orchids for Miss Blandish*, whose moral position is so extreme that it challenges comparison with De Sade. Nowadays, a respectable publisher can issue a book that would have brought immediate prosecution thirty years ago; as often as not, reviewers do not even bother to comment on a few rapes or homosexual love scenes.*

All this means that it is almost impossible to write a novel about sexual underprivilege in the mid-twentieth century, since all the symbols have lost their shock value. Nabokov's choice of Lolita as a symbol was perhaps the only one possible – apart, that is, from multiple rape.

*These divide into two categories: books in which the "sex" is a means to an end – as in *Lolita* or the novels of Angus Wilson (which deal openly with homosexuality), and books of altogether less serious intent, like *Peyton Place* or *The Chapman Report*, in which the sex seems to be an end in itself. There are also some interesting "in-betweeners"; Coulter's *Damned Shall be Desire* is an example; as a fictionalized life of Maupassant, its aim is basically serious, but certain episodes – rapes, a detailed description of a girl stripping, a whip-fight between two women – would undoubtedly have been banned as obscene thirty years ago. Today, no one even protests.

This brings the discussion back to the question I stated at the beginning of the chapter: What are the permissible limits of human sexual activity? Nabokov's Humbert is plainly arguing that a society that will not allow him to have intercourse with little girls is treating him unjustly. (The solution of a real-life Humbert would be simply to go to India or North Africa, where he could have any number of nymphets without arousing comment; this is another reason for regarding Humbert's situation as symbolic.) Radclyffe Hall's heroine, Stephen Gordon, is similarly a plea that lesbianism should be treated as permissible.

It is interesting to note the explanation Humbert gives for his fixation on twelve-year-olds. He fell in love at twelve, had some rudimentary sexual experience with the girl, and achieved a sense of freedom, of poetic intensity, that he never again experienced. I have already noted the similarity of Humbert's language describing his feelings in contact with Lolita, and the language of Hesse and Proust describing sudden mystical illuminations. Speaking of his first love, Annabelle, he writes: "But that mimosa grove – the haze of stars, the tingle, the flame, the honey dew, and the ache remained with me, and that little girl with her seaside limbs and ardent tongue haunted me ever since. . . ."

There is an obvious difference here between Humbert's self-defence and that of the heroine of *The Well of Loneliness*. Radclyffe Hall argues that a girl who has been brought up as a boy can only achieve *normal* sexual fulfilment if she is allowed to live and behave as a male. Humbert is not arguing about the kind of sexual fulfilment enjoyed by most people; he argues, in effect, that he is a poet, that he has the poet's *super-normal* capacity to "drink of life as lesser men drink wine", and that he therefore deserves to be allowed the means to this super-normal ecstasy. Radclyffe Hall's plea is reasonable and social; Humbert's is already unreasonable and unsocial, since the essence of poetry is non-rational and non-social.

This introduces an interesting problem into the discussion of what is "permissible". Most of our moral judgements are based on the social *status quo* (in the question of banning books, for example). What happens if the plea for sexual liberalism is based on some other ideal of society? The Oneida Community offers a practical example. Noyes wanted to teach men to enjoy "more freedom" than is possible in a competitive capitalist society; his vision of greater freedom included treating sexual pleasure *as if it were as desirable for man's spiritual expansion as the pleasure of poetry or music, or religious exaltation.* It is difficult to say what Noyes would have thought about Humbert's plea, but it is possible that he might have treated it as reasonable.

In the same way, the early communists of Russia preached free love as an important corollary of the new social freedom. It is significant that the modern leaders of Russia have found this impractical. Noyes succeeded in keeping up the moral tone of his small community; but sexual licence and revolutionary seriousness make uncomfortable partners, and considerable vigilance is needed to prevent one from totally excluding the other. The Russian leaders have been forced to compromise, and maintain the seriousness by taking up a Victorian attitude on sex and the family.*

More to our present point are the views on sex held by William Blake. These are in many ways close to those of Noyes; but Blake was a religious visionary where Noyes was only a religious reformer. Unlike his contemporaries, Blake felt that sex is innocent, desirable and an important part of a man's aesthetic and spiritual experience. Like Whitman and Lawrence, Blake denied the sharp dichotomy between body and soul (and consequently between sin and virtue). His statement that "energy is eternal delight" anticipates the method of phenomenology, and the realization that the "filter"

---

*I should make it clear that my feelings about this are far from unsympathetic. The kind of compromise between freedom and discipline effected in Russia may seem thoroughly undesirable to our Western way of thinking, but Russian art and music – even Russian social life – are by no means as constricted as we sometimes like to pretend. Russian music in particular has an enviable vigour.

becomes more ruthless as the mind grows tired. (See page 71.)

The implications of the Blake-Noyes view of sex should be clearly grasped; they are the key to the problem of sexual abnormality. In *Heartbreak House*, Shaw makes Ellie argue that "the soul" starves without money. "A soul is a very expensive thing to keep, much more so than a motor car. . . . It eats music and pictures and books and mountains and lakes and beautiful things to wear and nice people to be with. In this country you can't have them without lots of money; that is why our souls are so horribly starved."* Blake and Noyes would agree emphatically with this. They would add to Ellie's list of "necessities for the soul" complete sexual expression. Blake can write equally lyrically about political freedom and sexual freedom:

The morning comes, the night decays, the watchmen leave their
    station . . .
Let the slave grinding at the mill run out into the field,
Let him look up into the heavens and laugh in the bright air . . .]
                                        [*America*, plate 6.
. . . Love! happy happy Love! free as the mountain wind . . .

and:

The moment of desire! the moment of desire! The virgin
That pines for man shall awaken her womb to enormous joys
In the secret shadows of her chamber; the youth shut up from
The lustful joy shall forget to generate and create an amorous image
In the shadows of his curtains and in the folds of his silent pillow . . .

This frank recognition of masturbation, and proclaiming of the delights of free love, would have shocked Blake's contemporaries if any of them had troubled to read his prophetic books. That he is speaking of free love is obvious, for in the same poem (*Visions of the Daughters of Albion*), a few lines earlier, Oothoon reproves her husband Theotormon for jealousy, and says:

But silken nets and traps of adamant will Oothoon spread,
And catch for thee girls of mild silver, or of furious gold.
I'll lie beside thee on a bank and view their wanton play

*Collected Plays (Odhams), p. 789.

In lovely copulation, bliss on bliss, with Theotormon:
Red as the rosy morning light, lustful as the first born beam . . .

In *The Book of Los* he makes a similar suggestion for over-coming the ills of society: the vices will be destroyed by allowing them complete satisfaction:

> But Covet was poured full,
> Envy fed with fat of lambs,
> Wrath with lion's gore,
> Wantonness lulled to sleep
> With the virgin's lute
> Or sated with her love. . . .

There is a story that Blake wanted to bring this ideal state of society into his own home, and to begin by sleeping with the maid; his wife felt that this was carrying poetic idealism too far.

Blake's work is full of this glorification of the sexual energies:

The pride of the peacock is the glory of God.
The lust of the goat is the bounty of God.
The wrath of the lion is the wisdom of God.
The nakedness of woman is the work of God.

The road of excess leads to the palace of wisdom.

He who desires but acts not breeds a pestilence.

You never know what is enough unless you know what is more than enough.
Sooner murder an infant in its cradle than nurse unacted desire.

In *Europe*, the present state of society is described as "a female dream". (Blake may have had in mind the matriarchal societies from which modern civilization sprang.) All Blake's favourite hatreds are stigmatized as essentially female modes of thought: the duality of "body and soul" and the accompanying idea of sin and virtue, the limitation of the sexual impulse. The female's central impulse is conservation; consequently, she thinks in terms of boundaries and limitations; her acting principle is caution. According to Blake, this female view reaches an extreme in Newton – that is, in the Newtonian view that man can become god-like through science and reason. This is too much; it brings about a kind of last judgement; the male principle revolts, and the revolution begins, and in the last line of the poem the male creative principle (Los) calls all his sons "to the strife of blood".

Before leaving Blake, it is worth quoting his remarkable anticipation of phenomenology; this occurs at the beginning of *Europe*:

Five windows light the caverned Man: thro' one he breathes the air;
Thro' one hears music of the spheres; thro' one the eternal vine
Flourishes, that he may receive the grapes; thro' one can look
And see small portions of the eternal world that ever groweth;
Thro' one himself pass out what time he please; but he will not,
For stolen joys are sweet, and bread eaten in secret pleasant.

Here the rôle of the five senses is recognized in imprisoning man, in imposing order on the world. But Blake also implies that man can, if he likes, actually see the world *as it is*, without the arbitrary unconscious intentionality. This is certainly a more optimistic view than that of Berkeley or Kant, who regard the *ding an sich* as unknowable. The reason Blake gives for man not "passing out what time he please" is also interesting: self-limitation is preferable to absolute freedom. This is certainly close to Bergson's view of the rôle of the nervous system, and to Husserl's later formulations of phenomenology.*

Blake, then, answers the question: "What are the permissible limits of human sexual experience?" with the statement: Men have a right to all women who attract them; this is a necessary part of man's spiritual development. He who desires but acts not breeds a pestilence.

*For English readers who know only Husserl's *Ideas*, this association with Bergson may sound fanciful. However, Husserl's most penetrating and sympathetic commentator, Herbert Spiegelberg, writing about Husserl's later work, refers to Goethe's "mothers" (*Faust* II), "keepers of the key of being", and speaks of "the unveiling of the hidden achievements of the transcendental ego". (*The Phenomenological Movement*, p. 160.)

To express this in the language of phenomenology: if man is to broaden the limits of his subconscious intentionality, he must broaden his sexual experience. If man is not to allow his intentionality to impose upon himself and upon the world a deadening limitation, then he must retain control of his intentionality; this can be done by keeping in touch with the realm of intentionality – the subconscious – through aesthetic or sexual experience.

We are now discussing – with a new terminology – the question raised in the section on Gurdjieff in Chapter II: whether there is some "ultimately satisfying" sexual experience, some complete expression of the sexual centre. Gurdjieff remained silent on this problem. But many other "mystics" have dealt with the question, and always answered it in personal terms. Blake, like Noyes, believes in free love. Whitman, another sexual mystic, had definite homosexual tendencies; he therefore implies in his work that homosexuality is a permissible expression of the sexual energy. (Presumably this is true for women as well as men.) Lawrence seems to regard sodomy as, in some ways, a more complete sexual experience than normal copulation. The Hindu *Karma Sutra* describes a great many sexual acts that the West regards as abnormal; and yet it could be argued that its doctrines are as closely associated with the visionary mysticism of the *Bhagavad Gita* as Blake's religious views are associated with his sexual theories. It is simply another aspect of the full expression of man's freedom.

All this, plainly, is a restatement of Gide's contention: that the legal definition of "perversion" is by no means the "natural" definition. This is evident enough without bringing Blake and Lawrence into the discussion. Most sexologists are agreed that certain practices between husband and wife cannot be regarded as "perversions" since they are not a total substitute for the normal act of intercourse. And yet there are states in the United States where certain acts between husband and wife are illegal – sodomy and oral stimulation of the genitals – and where, presumably, a husband and wife could be jailed if they were caught indulging in these activities. Dr. Mark Adams declares: "In the country's male population [i.e. in America] authorities . . . estimate that about ninety-five per cent. have at some time violated the criminal codes pertaining to sex conduct."

But all this brings the discussion no closer to a "natural definition" of sexual perversion. Obviously, such a definition is impossible without first answering the question stated at the beginning of this book: what part does the sexual impulse play in man's total being? But the foregoing discussion might have made it apparent that the sexual question and the "philosophical" question help to throw light on one another. Sex cannot be considered *in vacuo*, or solely within the context of the psychiatrist's consulting-room, without the problem turning into a mass of self-contradictions.

Before proceeding to consider the question of particular perversions more closely, it might be helpful to restate some of the points that have emerged in the discussion of "vision".

(a) Man's consciousness is blinkered.

(b) This is desirable from the evolutionary point of view. Man is still too much of a child to conduct himself according to values and principles. Accordingly, the choice must be taken out of his hands. An "open consciousness" would only lead to laziness and stasis; he must be goaded by the inconveniences attendant upon a "closed consciousness".

(c) But this also has its disadvantages. Man is at his best when driven by a sense of purpose, and by a vision of purpose. If consciousness limits this vision, then man's efficiency as an evolutionary agent is also limited.

(d) Blake throws up the interesting remark that man can dispense with the blinkers "what time he please". Can he? Can he? For the moment it is enough simply to state this question.

Introverted Sexuality

De Bruyn's remark about the girl on the beach contains some interesting implications that we have not so far considered. There are, he implies, two types of sexual emotion. The first is the ordinary emotion to be gained by making the girl's acquaintance and seducing her. The second – far more intense – is the sudden fusion of bodies in the unpremeditated animal act. Dogs might reduce their courting to a minimum before coupling, but human society demands a lengthy "personal" preamble. The case of the girl in the cloakroom – cited in Chapter II – is an exception, and would be regarded by most people as "abnormal". It might be argued that the two experiences differ only in intensity, not in quality; this is a decision that can be made later. But the point of the difference can be made more clear by comparing the following two passages, the first from Eliot's *Waste Land,* the second from W. J. Turner's *Hymn to Her Unknown*:

> At the violet hour, the evening hour that strives
> Homeward, and brings the sailor home from sea,
> The typist home at tea time, clears her breakfast, lights
> Her stove, and lays out food in tins . . .
> I too awaited the expected guest.
> He, the young man carbuncular, arrives,
> A small house agent's clerk, with one bold stare,
> One of the low on whom assurance sits
> As a silk hat on a Bradford millionaire.
> The time is now propitious, as he guesses,
> The meal is ended, she is bored and tired,
> Endeavours to engage her in caresses
> Which still are unreproved, if undesired.
> Flushed and decided, he assaults at once;
> Exploring hands encounter no defence;
> His vanity requires no response,
> And makes a welcome of indifference . . .
> Bestows one final patronising kiss,
> And gropes his way, finding the stairs unlit.

The deliberate tone of banality and futility here emphasizes the personal flavour of what is taking place. It is the opposite of pure sexual emotion; it is merely two rather grimy personalities in contact. Compare this with Turner – again writing of "modern love" – a woman he saw on the

24th of August, 1934, in Swan and Edgar's in Piccadilly Circus:

> Could I express the ecstasy of my adoration?
> Mating with her were in itself a separation!
> Only our bodies fusing in a flame of crystal
> Burning in an infinite empyrean
> Until all the blue of the limitless heaven were drunken
> In one globe of united perfection
> Like a bubble that is all the oceans of the world ascending
> To the fire that is the fire of fires, transcending
> The love of God, the love of God, the love of God . . . .

At first it might seem that Turner is simply less of a realist than Mr. Eliot; he sees a married woman in Swan and Edgar's, does not speak to her, but imagines that she would have been the perfect mate. But Turner is capable enough of realism elsewhere; he can write:

> Marriage is but keeping house,
> Sharing food and company,
> What has this to do with love
> Or the body's beauty?

Turner may be idealizing the woman of Swan and Edgar's to some extent, but he is also speaking of the instantaneous, "impersonal" sex that de Bruyn envisaged with the girl on the beach. Eliot is speaking of ordinary, everyday "personalized" sex.

This latter is the sex that was discussed in the chapter on promiscuity: Don Juan sex, the sex of Casanova and Frank Harris and Henry Miller, a coarse but healthy "normality". It might be called extraverted sex. Some amusing examples can be found in A. R. Jones's book on T. E. Hulme.* Hulme seems to have had views on sex and the will to power similar to those of the ex-army officer "M" cited in Chapter II. He liked quick and easy conquests, preferably of shopgirls. Jones tells a story of how Hulme was sitting in the Café Royal when he suddenly looked at his watch and declared: "I've a pressing

*Published by Gollancz, 1960.

engagement in five minutes' time" and strode from the building. Twenty minutes later he came back, perspiring, and commented that the spiral staircase of the emergency exit at the Piccadilly tube station was one of the most uncomfortable places in which he had ever copulated. Hulme seems to have lacked most inhibitions, for another story tells how he was relieving his bladder in the gutter in broad daylight in Soho Square when a policeman remonstrated. Hulme turned on him explosively: "Do you realize you are addressing a member of the English middle classes?" The policeman touched his helmet and walked away. Hulme was famous for his sudden outbursts of physical violence (as when he hung Wyndham Lewis by his turn-ups from some spiked railings in Soho Square), and for his tales of his sexual encounters.

But Hulme's healthy animal copulation on a steel stairway would have been equally repellent to a sexual idealist like Shelley or a "worshipper of the body" like Lawrence. It is completely typical of the extraverted attitude to sex. It is the opposite of Huxley's description of sex in *Antic Hay* or *The Genius and the Goddess*.

At the same time it must be acknowledged that "introverted sex" is always closer to the "abnormal". Hulme's sexuality took the female sex-object for granted; she was the logical focus of the sexual emotions, the rightful recipient of the male semen. The sexual introvert is altogether closer to his emotions; he is aware that the "sex object" is arbitrary. At least he is aware of the fluid boundaries between the "normal" and "abnormal". Even if he is heterosexual, he realizes that the sexual emotion depends upon the invasion of an alien body. It is an act of conquest. Shakespeare makes his Tarquin compare Lucrece to a city that he wants to storm and enter. But if the orgasm is associated with the act of entering the female body, why should her vagina be chosen to the exclusion of the mouth and rectum? For most heterosexual men, the sexual emotion can be exhausted by intercourse in the "normal" way. But if a man has become blasé with "normal" sex, he might well feel the need to make this "natural" extension of his aggressive activities. (In fact, the available statistics indicate that young men practise these "extensions" less often than older men.) And if the desire for the woman is chiefly an aggressive impulse, then the man might well feel that the use of the rectum or mouth rather than the vagina is a more absolute "conquest". There is a notable episode in Henry Miller's *Sexus* that can be taken as typical of the hyper-aggressive male. An aggressive drunk not only forces the girl to perform an act of fellatio on him as he drives a car, but he forces her to hold a lighted cigarette in her vagina, and later rapes and commits sodomy on her. (The episode is related to Miller by his mistress, and forms a kind of inset pornographic novel within the book.) In the same way, the crimes of the "red light bandit" (for which Caryl Chessman was executed) involved forcing two women to perform acts of fellatio on him in a car. Although the "bandit" forced both women to remove their panties (and one of the girls was made to strip to her shoes and stockings), he did not rape either of them. Why, in that case, force them to unclothe themselves? The reason suggests itself: because ordering a woman to undress intensifies the satisfaction of the aggressive impulse.

It is easy to see that if the man is "oversexed", and if he has a more than usually aggressive feeling towards women, a long period of introversion might easily distort the sexual emotions into a sadistic pattern. De Sade, who hated and feared his mother, first came to the attention of the police when various prostitutes complained about his penchant for making shallow incisions with a penknife, and pouring hot wax into them. But the symbolism here is plain enough. All the "natural orifices" are rejected, and De Sade makes his own "entrances" into the female body; he then symbolically possesses her by filling them with wax. At the age of twenty-eight, De Sade was arrested for kidnapping a pastry cook's widow and performing this curious operation on her. (He was forced to pay out a great deal of money in bribes and fines.)

It may seem to be a long way from Blake's innocent talk of

love and copulation to De Sade's need to inflict pain. And yet both are the outcome of a sexual mysticism that strives to transcend the everyday world. Simone de Beauvoir said penetratingly of De Sade's work that "he is trying to communicate an experience whose distinguishing characteristic is, nevertheless, its will to remain incommunicable". De Sade's perversion may have sprung from dislike of his mother or of other women, but its basis is a kind of distorted religious emotion.

This point is of great importance, and should be made very clear. Our basic experience of consciousness is of *passivity*, which is another name for boredom. We look at the world; it is quiet, apparently unchanging. It has a poker face. It gives the impression it can outstare you and outlive you. In comparison to the world, human flesh is constantly changing and seething, longing to be moving on, like an impatient dog on a lead. This is why most people like looking at fires, at waterfalls and rapids; it is pleasant to see the material world being a little less static; it relieves us of our feeling of inferiority in the face of the indifference of a tree.

Because the flesh moves faster than the outside world it dreads boredom and frustration. It wants to *feel* all the time; it hates nothing so much as an internal stagnation confronting the impassivity of nature. It has no memory; all its feelings and boredoms seem doomed to last for eternity. Sex, like alcohol, has the capacity to destroy the stagnation; to turn the consciousness of ourselves into a Niagara. Boredom is a "state of being" from which one finds it difficult to escape into other states, a self-isolating anxiety, like a turtle on its back. But luckily, we have one infallible ladder from one level of being to another. The sexual act is a miniature symbol of conquest. From the male point of view, a woman looks demure, alien, a "city" that cannot be entered; half an hour later she is naked, submissive, she has surrendered; the first impression is proved wrong. But if a woman is not unchangeably distant, unchangeably virginal, then neither is the world. The fear of life-frustration vanishes.

Our social conditioning abets the simple physical impulse. By building up various taboos and fears, it artificially increases the "height" between one state of being and another. Two savages who had known one another from childhood can still take pleasure in breaking down the alien-ness of "the other" in sexual intercourse. If the alien-ness is increased by our civilized habit of wearing clothes, of cultivating various inhibitions about sex, perhaps even by the belief that sex is rather wicked, then the pleasure of breaking down the barriers will be greater still.

Religion, in its simplest form, is the belief that nature is not cold, indifferent, poker-faced, that a tree is not a tree but a god in disguise. And even in its most complex, subjective form, it is still the belief that there is an "otherness" beyond our present boredom and inadequacy, a hidden meaning lying in wait, like a tiger behind a bush. And when a mystic has a sudden insight into this meaning (or thinks he has), he is also performing an act of breakdown of alien-ness, exactly like the sexual breakdown.

De Sade and Baudelaire have in common the need to believe that sex is evil. Then there are more barriers to break through in the sexual act, and the sense of falling from one level of being to another is more exciting, more positive.

Our biological tendency to re-create the alien-ness of "the other" immediately after demolishing it – in other words, to repeat the cycle of desire – often means that the emotions associated with sex remain immature. If a youth is bullied by his father, a day will probably come when he will knock his father down; in that moment he will feel a great sense of emancipation – he will have fallen from one level of being to another, and will feel exhilarated. But it can only happen once; even if he makes a habit of hitting his father every day, he will never again feel the same satisfaction as on the first occasion. But in sex, this is not true; at least, it happens far more slowly. The man who gleefully violates the alien-ness of his newly married wife on their honeymoon will continue to feel the same delight for a considerable length of time; if he is imaginative, he may still feel it half a century later. Some strange conditioning in us re-creates the alien-ness every day.

Even so, men get bored with their wives after a honey-moon. Flaubert says that Charles Bovary soon began treating sex with Emma like a dessert after his supper. The biological conditioning needs to be aided by a sensitive imagination.

Some men, like De Sade, not only insist that the biological alien-ness is re-created, but also like to re-create the "artificial", social taboos that add to the joy of violation. This is why Baudelaire liked to feel that sex is basically evil. Such an attitude is bound to involve a certain immaturity, just as if the youth should spend hours every day working up a resentment of his father so that he gets the maximum pleasure out of knocking him down for the fiftieth time. Emotions are not intended to be cyclic, like the sexual urges.

It will be convenient to refer to this aspect of sexual involvement as "clinging to the emotional cycle". There is an interesting example of it in Sade's *120 Days of Sodom*. Four profligates have assembled in a château, determined to practise every possible kind of sexual activity; they have a large array of young girls and boys brought to the château, most of them kidnapped from respectable parents, and some brothel-madames who will instruct them in the arts of perversion. One of the madames tells a story of how she knew a libertine whose pleasure was to have an orgasm that would deluge the genitals of a young girl with sperm without actually penetrating her. The Duke immediately insists on carrying out the same act on one of the girls present – who is represented as weeping with shame.

This story is a typical example of the infantile sex fantasy. But the full implications of its immaturity can be brought out by comparison with another frustration fantasy, Kierkegaard's *Diary of a Seducer*. Kierkegaard's seducer, Johannes, sees a beautiful but very young girl getting out of a carriage. He then goes to enormous length to possess her, spending months in a complicated pursuit that, at one point, involves getting engaged to her. When, at the end of the story, she gives herself to him, he immediately loses interest.

Now Kierkegaard is more of a realist than De Sade. When he saw a pretty girl in the street, and wanted to sleep with her, his fantasy was far more realistic and circumstantial. De Sade invented an absurd situation in which he could overcome the double alien-ness of a young and inexperienced virgin by force. Kierkegaard, closer to reality, realized that the girl would have to be persuaded to fall in love with him and to finally offer him complete emotional abandonment.

But where Kierkegaard and De Sade both reveal immaturity is in not realizing that the purity of the desire for a pretty virgin would be largely destroyed by the complications of the pursuit. They are a long way from de Bruyn's realization that full satisfaction of the desire could only be achieved by flinging the girl down and raping her. The more circuitous route of a personal relationship would bring the social personality into play. Sooner or later the "seducer" would realize that he is paying a disproportionately high price – in will and energy – for the mere pleasure of penetrating a virgin.

This factor of emotional immaturity, and its cause – the repetition of the emotional cycle – is of considerable importance in analysing the problems of sexual abnormality.

CHAPTER V

THE MEANING OF "PERVERSION"
II

*De Sade and Boredom. Problem of frustration. Fetichism. Under-
wear fetichism. Panty fetichism. Examples of fetichism and sex
crime in literature. Musil's Man* Without Qualities. *Moosbrugger. Joyce's panty fetichism. Heirens. The case of Rodney
Shires.*

THE problem implicit in De Sade's *120 Days* is whether
a number of men could, by concentrating their full attention
on the matter, achieve some *ultimate* sexual pleasure. It is the
romantic striving for the infinite that characterized so many of
the poets of the nineteenth century. At first sight, it may seem
that libertinism is a matter of the body only. But it requires
only a moment's consideration to realize that a dog or a cat
would be incapable of these extremes of pleasure seeking; the
body, unaided by the mind, is quickly satisfied. De Sade might
be compared to a heretical sect of the late Middle Ages known
as the Brethren of the Free Spirit, whose basic doctrine was
the idea "I am God", who believed in the more or less
immediate advent of the Third Kingdom, when flesh would
finally throw off its misery and inadequacy, and who allowed
their worhsip to degenerate into sexual orgies. (They were
ruthlessly suppressed by the Church.) Nine hundred years
later a heretical sect called the Khlysty grew up in Russia;
they worshipped a certain Daniel Philipov, believing that he
was Christ come again, and held Dionysian ceremonies that
often ended in total sexual abandonment, mothers coupling
with sons and brothers with sisters. Rasputin was a member
of the sect.

These visions of an ultimate, of a human kind free of all

inhibitions, and of "original sin", have been the basic drive of all mystics and poets. All men with any psychological penetration are deeply aware of the weakness and inadequacy of "the body of this death", of their inability to learn from experience, their ingratitude for life except when confronting death. Many of the men who feel this inevitably turn to the scriptures, because at least the scriptures are concerned with ultimates that can be taken seriously. But whether they accept the scriptural notion of a City of God, or whether they invent their own City of the Sun, like William Morris and H. G. Wells (whose visions were not the real "ultimate" article), all are possessed by a vision of human perfection, of man lifted somehow above his misery and his weakness. Men very seldom have any deep pleasure that seems to release *all* their emotions and reach to the very bottom of the being. No doubt this is the significance of those lines that Goethe gives to Mephistopheles, when he promises Faust "more pleasure in an hour, than in a year's monotony". Boredom and semi-fulfilment seems to be our common lot; Kierkegaard claims that men built the Tower of Babel out of boredom.

All this has a deep significance, and must be borne in mind in discussing the origins of the sexual impulse. Most of man's ways of dissipating surplus energy are – or can be regarded as – as futile as building the Tower of Babel: his search after political power, after wealth or possessions. An intensely introverted or subjective man regards these activities with amazement, as he might regard a Hindu fakir chewing glass bottles.

But all human beings acknowledge the power of sexual gratification to reach deep into man's emotions and give him a momentary sensation of being a completely fulfilled being. Hence there is not one of us in whom De Sade's quest for total and final fulfilment does not arouse a certain sympathy.

To recognize this is to approach the problem of sex from the only ultimately fruitful direction. The Freudian talk about man's "libido" and his various complexes may help to clear up individual cases, but it takes us no further. Sex cannot be considered *in vacuo*, or in relation to a social entity called Man who probably wanted to kill his father and sleep with his mother. To express this point in an extreme form: the problems of sex and the problems of teleology (man's ultimate purpose) are bound up together, and neither can be understood in isolation. (In a later chapter I shall discuss briefly the modern school of "existential psycho-therapy", developed on this basis by Binswanger, Minkowski, Straus, etc., and making use of concepts borrowed from Heidegger and Husserl.)

The problem of sex, then, and the problem of "abnormality", is bound up with some vague notion of "fulfilment" and with the limits of "human nature". The notion itself may be vague, *as a notion*, but it is clear enough when it presents itself in the form of an intuition of some deeper, more "godlike" state of satisfaction for the individual.

The problem can be expressed most simply in this form: let us suppose a man of unusual intelligence and vitality, fundamentally "un-neurotic", well disposed towards his fellow human beings, and with the power and influence of an Eastern despot. (An anarchist would deny that a despot could be uncorrupt and un-neurotic, but we will by-pass his objection.) Such a man now asks himself the question: Is it possible for me to progress a little further than most human beings in the direction of godhead by making full use of my power? Not only is he able to point at any girl in the street and say: "Take her to my bedroom at once", but he is also intelligent enough to profit by his experience – in so far as the experience has any content.

If we now assembled a committee, made up of Blake, Whitman, Lawrence, De Sade, Noyes, and Casanova, to discuss the problem of how the despot should best employ his powers, we might gain from them their notion of the limits and capacities of man's power and energy. Their opinions would conflict in some curious ways. Blake, for example, would declare that a man cannot hope to move in the direction of godhead except by developing his "inner eye", the "fourfold vision", striving to contemplate the human race as a unity, recognizing the imagination as its highest and most powerful faculty, developing to the full the intellect and emotions, and striving to see "a world in a grain of sand '. But he would undoubtedly go on to add that the ideal conditions for this exercise would be a South Sea island, full of healthy men and beautiful, uninhibited girls, who would unashamedly offer themselves to the visionary at any hour of the day, singly or in larger numbers. Noyes would no doubt basically agree with this picture – adding that all the inhabitants of the island should be moved by moral earnestness, and should spend a great deal of time in discussing together how best to build the City of God.

Whitman would substantially agree with this picture, except that, in his expansive way, he might feel that an island was rather a small place, and that this paradise of healthy men and women should extend over the whole world. He would probably also add that he reserved his right to sleep with the men as well as the women.

D. H. Larence would probably reject the whole idea with disgust, asserting his basic principle of the untouchability of the great man, *noli me tangere*. His own paradise would include only one woman, boundlessly healthy and wilful, and their sexual activities would involve mutual stimulation of "the fount of darkness" by sodomy and the manual process. Blake and Noyes would undoubtedly find Lawrence's paradise half-hearted and unsatisfactory, particularly as Lawrence would fail to satisfy them on the subject of an ultimate; Blake would find the idea of eternal warfare with the woman neurotic and unnecessary.

Casanova would no doubt reject the idea of an island entirely. His own idea would be to use the wealth and power to dazzle society, and to have endless love affairs with demure young convent girls, newly married women, beautiful courtesans, and intelligent young bluestockings. He would meanwhile produce a ten-volume work summarizing the history of the human race in a manner that would combine devastating cynicism with sparkling wit. This, in his opinion, would be the closest that man can ever come to the "god-like existence".

De Sade alone would horrify everybody by some vision of a monstrous, universal orgy. (All, that is, except Blake, who would whisper: "Let him get on with it. He'll get it out of his system by the time he's disembowelled a dozen virgins then you'll see what a nice fellow he'll turn out to be.") De Sade would declare that man can only become god-like by dismissing the idea of God, and (paradoxically) doing his best to plumb the depth of evil in himself. He would then explain that he had already given his attention to the problem of godhead, and had written a treatise on the subject. The *120 Days* would then be produced as a textbook on how to plumb the depths of evil – beginning with such harmless activities as sodomous incest and debauching six-year-old girls and, ending with orgies of torture, conducted with the help of demons. De Sade would explain that all these efforts would finally establish man in God's place, and make him all-powerful.

And yet De Sade might be powerfully assailed for confusing the issue with neuroses and immaturity. One of the earliest perversions described in *120 Days* is the drinking of a child's urine; later, it progresses to the eating of her excrement, and even the eating of menstrual blood and miscarriages. Finally, one of the libertines declares his taste for sucking dirty feet, and even his hardened companions are sickened; one of them observes that these infamies are inspired by satiety and boredom; they are frenzied attempts to stimulate a jaded appetite. It can be argued that De Sade produced *120 Days* after many years of imprisonment, when frustration and bitterness had driven him to dreams of revenge. But it is posited of the Eastern despot whose problem is the subject of this debate that he should be un-neurotic, well disposed to his fellow men, and able fully to satisfy his appetites long before frustration builds them up to this terrifying extreme.

This hypothetical debate makes one thing clear: frustration is the basis of much "abnormality", and a satisfactory (and un-self-contradictory) notion of some "ultimate sexual satisfaction" *must* be bound up with some larger mystical vision about the purpose of human existence. Lawrence's purely sexual mysticism is a halfway house, an incomplete vision that extends only as far as a curious state of unresolved conflict between a man and woman.

This notion of the rôle played by frustration in sexual perversion deserves to be closely examined. For it immediately involves a question of the relationship bewteen frustration and various stages of fluidity in the developing sexual bias. These relationships in turn suggest a total picture, a kind of map, of man's psychological being, on which an area labelled "sexuality" can be clearly marked out.

Frustration

Before considering the frustration problem more closely, the "frustration" factor in human consciousness should be given its full importance. *Forgetfulness is in-built in us.* We are inefficient machines. This inefficiency is to be 'blamed' for aberrant sexuality if there is to be an apportionment of blame. The life force has fitted human consciousness with a powerful door-spring that automatically closes the door after a few moments. This doorspring must be kept in mind in considering the following instances of "perversion".

First of all, let us make it clear that we are discussing the sexual impulse, the animal desire, as distinguished from various forms of emotional attachment. Many writers on sex confuse the issue by pointing out that a lover may steal his mistress's handkerchief or a lock of her hair, they then use this as the "missing link" between "normal love" and aberrated sexuality. Hirschfeld notes that Goethe, at fifty-four, asked Christine Vulpius for a pair of her slippers, so that he might "press them to his heart", and asks if Goethe was perhaps a shoe fetichist. The answer is obviously no, and only an initial confusion of thought could have led to the question being put. On the other hand, Marghanita Laski mentions that when she became a television personality, one of her many corres-

pondents asked her to send him a pair of her soiled knickers.*
This, equally obviously, *is* genuine fetishism. Miss Laski was
apparently so shocked by this request that she speaks of
writing it down "to exorcise the beastliness". But the interest
of the request lies in its being simply a sexual response to the
same illusion – springing out of the limitation of consciousness – that led other admirers to write asking for her autograph
or offering her their lifelong devotion; it is intrinsically neither
more nor less shocking than the request for an autograph.
But it is an excellent illustration of the working of the principle
of limitation of consciousness. It is important to the "life
force" that the sex urge re-forms soon after it has been
satisfied; it would be most inconvenient for the human race
if we learned from the sexual experience as quickly and finally
as we learn from certain other experiences. The craving for
yam gruel of Akutagawa's little soldier presumably never
returned after he made himself sick on it. The sexual urge
alone can re-form with undiminished power a few hours
after it has been satisfied. In the case of Miss Laski, the sexual
instinct was abetted in its work of illusion by the social instinct of admiration-for-the-leader. She was involved in a
double-alienation from the point of view of her admirer: the
simple alien-ness of the strange female, and the alien-ness of
the leader, the person who has been selected to appear before
the eyes of millions of other people, and who is therefore, by
the strange arithmetic of these illusions, a million times as
important as each individual watching her.

At this point it is interesting to try to formulate a kind of
table of aberrations, beginning with the minor deviations from
"normality"; in this way it might be possible to gain some insight into the mechanism of the deviation. For the moment, I
shall speak only of deviations in the male, since the work of
Krafft-Ebing, Ellis, and Hirschfeld indicates that men are
more prone to aberration than women.

For practical purposes, normality can be taken as a simple
animal sexuality that plays a relatively small part in the con-

*The Twentieth Century, November 1959.

sciousness of the male. Men who lead a strenuous physical life – as labourers, soldiers, professional athletes, etc. – probably have little time for thinking about sex, and the energies are otherwise occupied. This is Tolstoy's idea of normality – the peasant who makes love to his wife once a week, and fathers a baby every year.

The simplest deviation from this "ideal" is the man whose attention strays to other women, and who may take any opportunity for infidelity to his wife. This Tolstoy would regard as the beginning of perversion. (Herein, of course, he is less extreme than St Paul, who seemed to regard all sex as a movement away from man's rightful – and therefore normal – preoccupation with God.)

The number of men's magazines specializing in sophisticated stories of adultery, and in pictures of girls in their underwear, indicate that most men regard the "roving eye" as more or less normal. All the same, it will be observed that very few men *stare* at a picture of a half-naked girl if there are other people present; the examination will be briefer and more cursory than if the man is alone. This is undoubtedly due to fear that other people may suspect him of committing mental rape on the girl. A quick, masculine appraisal of a half-naked girl is felt to be natural. A longer examination may indicate that the man is thinking of sex in a masochistic way, since he cannot satisfy his desires on a picture; the shame springs from the admission of being a thinker rather than an actor; it may even point to the self-enclosed circuit of masturbation.

What is in question now, and in all other deviations, is the illusion of alien-ness. Once a man has slept with his first woman he now has a basic knowledge of what a woman is like. He is like a traveller who has always longed to see India, and who then goes there. The basic, and greatest need, is now satisfied. Lawrence has spoken of this with considerable power in the poem "Manifesto" he writes of:

... another hunger
very deep, and ravening ...
redder than death, more clamorous.

The hunger for the woman . . .
which we must learn to satisfy with pure, real satisfaction;
or perish, there is no alternative. . . .
A woman fed that hunger in me at last.
What many women cannot give, one woman can . . .
She stood before me like riches that were mine.
Even then, in the dark, I was tortured, ravening, unfree,
Ashamed, and shameful, and vicious.
A man is so terrified of a strong hunger;
And this terror is the root of all cruelty.
She loved me and stood before me, looking at me.
How could I look, when I was mad? I looked sideways furtively,
being mad with voracious desire. . . .

Following this extraordinary description of the violence of
sexual desire, unequalled except by certain pages in Wedekind,
comes the climax of the poem:

> I could put my face at last between her breasts
> And know that they were given forever
> That I should never starve
> never perish;
> I had eaten of the bread that satisfies
> And my body's body was appeased,
> there was peace and richness,
> fulfilment.

But Lawrence is remarkable largely because, in this particular way, he was so free of the modern neurosis of sexual
underprivilege. He declared – whether it was wholly true or
not – that his major sexual experience (not his first) *had* taught
him something permanently.

This is not true for most men. Shaw remarked in one of the
later prefaces that in the twentieth century most men have
their first sexual experience too late. In the Elizabethan age
many girls were mothers at thirteen; many boys lost their
virginity at twelve – the age when the hunger for sex begins to
trouble men. Lawrence had his first sexual experience in his
late teens. How much of his later sexual mysticism is the outcome of this long frustration? Whatever the cause, men do not
feel that they have been given something permanently when

they have had their first satisfying sexual experience. At least Lawrence had penetrated the sexual illusion to the extent of realizing that "what many women cannot give, one woman can". But if the sense that his wife's breasts "were given forever" had been really deep, he would have lost sexual interest in her fairly quickly. The Don Juan urge may have disappeared, but the ordinary illusion of alien-ness remained – otherwise the marriage would have been very brief. Sexual desire is not like the need for food; it does not re-form according to a simple mechanism of nourishment, but by means of a mental habit, which I have compared to a spring on a door.

The magazines that specialize in pictures of girls in their underwear are catering for a mild form of voyeurism. Some psychological text-books distinguish between the voyeur and the Peeping Tom. Most men are Peeping Toms, since most men would turn their heads if a naked girl walked along the street, or if a girl's dress blew up in the wind. But not many men will place themselves on the wrong side of the law to gratify the desire to see unclothed women, so for police purposes the Peeping Tom is the man who makes a nuisance of himself by trying to watch women undressing or couples making love. The voyeur is the man who actually likes to watch an act of sexual intercourse taking place. (Faulkner's Popeye, in *Sanctuary*, is incapable of taking Temple's virginity himself, but lies on the bed – wearing his hat – and watches while she has intercourse with Red.) I shall use the term "voyeur" to cover all men who are sexually stimulated through the sense of sight, whether the excitement reaches orgasm or not. The hero of Barbusse's *Hell* is a curious case of voyeurism. At the beginning of the book he watches a woman undressing in the next room (although Barbusse is careful not to mention any sexual excitement), but for the most part, the scenes he watches have no sexual interest; his voyeurism springs from a desire to overcome the fundamental loneliness of human beings, to penetrate other lives and live them vicariously.

It should be noted that voyeurism cannot be called a per-version in the sense that it is a complete substitute for the

normal sexual act. Many men like to watch a woman undressing before they possess her. Most Peeping Toms would
happily possess the woman they are watching if it could be
done without danger, or without causing pain. Charles Floyd,
who was sentenced to life imprisonment in Texas in 1949, was
a Peeping Tom as well as a rapist. One of his victims was in the
habit of undressing without drawing her curtains. After
watching her for several nights, Floyd climbed into the apartment one night, bludgeoned her into unconsciousness, and
raped her. He actually spent the night in bed with the corpse,
leaving after daylight. This indicates that the long anticipation
had intensified the appetite so that one act of violation was
insufficient to satisfy it. Over a period of seven years, Floyd
committed at least five murders with rape, and several attempted rapes; after his arrest he was found to be only partly
responsible for his actions, and was imprisoned in a mental
institution. Floyd is a typical example of simple frustration
(his photographs show an unattractive little man) intensified
by the stimulation of careless women; his low intelligence
combined with these factors to remove the normal restraints.
But the desire to rape is not confined to the mentally unstable
and the morons. Hesse's Steppenwolf admits that he would
like to seize a "roe":

> And feast myself deep on her tender thigh,
> I would drink of her red blood full measure,
> Then howl till the night went by.

This is an intelligent man admitting the element of the
rapist in himself, the desire to take by violence.

This raises the question: Why should a man feel the need to
commit violence on the "alien" flesh? Why is its alien-ness
more satisfactorily destroyed by inflicting pain? Here is a
simple case of the misdirection of an impulse. The need to
watch a woman undressing springs from the feeling that she is
alien. A man is bound to feel a certain simple resentment at the
way in which "ultimate sexual satisfaction" always eludes him,
at the way in which the sexual impulse, like a conjurer, presents

him with satisfaction and then snatches it away. The sexual urge clamours for an object; five minutes after being presented with its object, it is clamouring as noisily as ever. It is like scratching an itch, only to have the itch transfer itself to another part of the body. But there is no point in getting angry with the sexual impulse; consequently, some of the resentment is irrationally transferred to the sexual object, the girl.

Again, the annals of sexual murder provide many illuminating examples. Patrick Byrne, the Birmingham YWCA murderer, declared that he wanted to terrorize all women "to get my own back on them for causing my nervous tension through sex". He made a habit of peering through windows in the Edgbaston YWCA to watch girls undressing. On December 23, 1959, Byrne was exceptionally drunk – and therefore free from restraints – as well as feeling resentful about being ordered off a building site by the foreman for his drunkenness, and it was in this state that he murdered and raped Stephanie Baird, cutting off her head with a carving knife. He also apparently made some attempt to eat one of the breasts with sugar. (This eating of the breasts – or the nipples – is a frequent motif in sex crimes; there are two such cases cited in Paul de River.) On the same evening he attempted to kill another girl by hitting her with a stone; he declared he felt a desire to kill several "beautiful women". (He decided not to attack one girl because she was plain.) Byrne admitted that he indulged in sexual fantasies in which he cut a girl in half with a circular saw.*

This murder is plainly the outcome of years of sexual frustration, an overwhelming feeling of the sexual underprivilege in our society, and *the idea that the women themselves are*

*This kind of irrationality is not, of course, peculiar to sexual criminals; it is a common criminal trait. Stephen Nash, who murdered a boy on a beach at Santa Monica in 1955, is quoted as saying: "I was proud of him. I was sorry it had to be a boy, but I had to get even." He had committed several murders – and intended to go on committing them – to get even with a Los Angeles judge who gave him the maximum sentence for some minor crime.

to blame for this. No doubt Charles Floyd had something of the same feeling. This was certainly the case with Heinrich Pommerenke, the twenty-three-year-old German sex murderer, who committed ten murders. Pommerenke, who was sentenced to life imprisonment in 1960, claimed that he was inspired to commit his first murder after seeing the Hollywood epic *The Ten Commandments*; the sight of women dancing round the Golden Calf convinced him that women are the source of all the world's evil, and he murdered his first victim immediately afterwards in a park. However, it is notable that he claimed the killing was incidental; he only wanted to render the women unconscious while he raped them. Women might be evil, but they could be sufficiently punished by having intercourse with them. This is an aggressive attitude towards sex that is curiously typical of the male viewpoint. (I have observed this particularly among working men. On one occasion a builder's labourer had a difference of opinion with a woman in a canteen – a middle-aged and not particularly attractive woman – and commented angrily: "She needs f – ing." He obviously conceived this as a form of punishment to "take the starch out of her" and assert his masculine rôle.)

Pommerenke, like Byrne, was described as "sexually immature". Although he claimed that he had seduced his first girl when he was ten, he admitted that girls ignored him or made fun of him.

This resentment motif may take even more curious forms. Werner Boost, the German sexual murderer, declared that courting couples enraged him, and that "these sex horrors are the curse of Germany". In this virtuous frame of mind he would hold up couples in cars and force them to take a drug that stupefied them; he would then rape the women, as well as robbing the men. It is difficult to see how he rationalized the act of rape. The point to note here is that there is almost no attempt to find a rational outlet for the resentment and frustration; it is allowed to express itself in the simplest way, through the act of violation. Later, Boost murdered two couples; in one case he pushed the car into a pond, and in the other burned it in a haystack. It can be seen that the resentment motive is profound.*

There has been, as far as I know, only one competent literary treatment of a "sex maniac" (if one discounts the episode of rape on a child in the banned chapter of Dostoevsky's *Possessed*) – the character of Moosbrugger in Musil's novel *The Man Without Qualities*. Moosbrugger is actually arrested for stabbing a girl who solicited him; but in all other respects he fits into the type of the frustrated murderer dealt with above. Musil's analysis of Moosbrugger is worth quoting:

"As a boy, Moosbrugger had been a poverty-stricken wretch, a shepherd-lad in a hamlet so small that it did not even have a village street; and he was so poor that he never spoke to a girl. Girls were something that he could always only look at, even later when he was an apprentice, and even on his wanderings as a journeyman. Now, one must just imagine what that means. Something that one craves for, just as naturally as one craves for bread or water, is only there to be looked at. After a time, one's desire for it becomes unnatural. It walks past, the skirts swaying round its ankles. It climbs over a stile, becoming visible right up to the knees. One looks into its eyes, and they become opaque. . . .

"So it was understandable that even after the murder of the first girl, Moosbrugger had vindicated himself by saying that

*A disquieting feature of this case – and of the situation generally – is that many of the assaulted couples made no complaint or report to the police. In the case of Gerald Thompson in Peoria (see p. 157), the police suspected that the killer might have raped other women who were ashamed to come forward because of publicity. The press therefore agreed that no names of victims would be printed. The result was staggering; more than fifty women came forward; all had been knocked unconscious and raped by Thompson, who photographed them in compromising positions and pointed out that his capture would lead to publicity and the discovery of the photographs. None of these women complained. An important step in combating sex crime would be to pass laws forbidding publication of any information about the victims of sex crimes.

he was continually haunted by spirits, which called him day and night. . . ."

There is a powerful description of the brutalizing effect of sleeping out in winter, never washing, being insulted and arrested as a vagrant. Moosbrugger insists that he felt only disgust for the women he raped and strangled, or the objective cruelty of the cat for the mouse. He also day-dreams of becoming a "destroying angel, slaughtering thousands, an incendiary, setting theatres on fire, or a great anarchist".*

Musil has here caught the basic sexual hunger of the male, in the same way as Lawrence in "Manifesto". Given a hunger as great as this, it is not surprising if a man develops certain "abnormalities".

Closely related to the simple forms of voyeurism, and equally widespread, is the deviation called fetishism. A fetich is an object that assumes sexual significance because of some association with sex. Since it is a part of the life-mechanism that men should learn very little from sexual experience, and are therefore driven to repeat it *ad infinitum*, it also follows that the basic mechanism of selection of the sexual object should be faulty and inefficient. Any "deviations" that get accidentally included in the original "hypnotism" of the sexual desires, are likely to be perpetuated by the repeating mechanism. Stekel cites a case in which a man was able to have an orgasm only when the woman wore an apron. Analysis revealed that the patient associated the apron with his nurse who used to play with his genitals when bathing him. Stekel's *Sexual Aberrations* (which deals entirely with fetishism) contains accounts of hair fetishists, crutch fetishists, beard fetishists, etc. But I am inclined to doubt whether these aberrations are of any great general significance, except as illustrating that the sexual impulse can be "hypnotized" by the most unlikely objects. Strangely enough, most of the writers on fetishism devote very little attention to what is most certainly its most widespread form in the twentieth century – garment fetishism, and in particular, panty fetishism. This may very well be because

*See Chapter VII, on the character of Peter Kürten.

the emphasis on female underwear has been a development of the past twenty-five years (that is, since the mid-1930s). The magazines and advertisements of the early part of the century – the age of Freud, Stekel, Ellis, and Hirschfeld – did not carry seductive pictures of girls in almost non-existent underwear. (Undoubtedly there are fashions in fetichism, and I doubt whether, for example, corset fetichism is now as widespread as it appears to have been around 1900.)

To a certain extent, underwear fetichism may be regarded as being as "natural", in its simplest forms, as voyeurism. The following passage, from Nelson Algren's novel *A Walk on the Wild Side*, illustrates my point. The boy Dove is fascinated by a plump Mexican widow who keeps a general store.

"A scent of the Orient came to him. He left the book and followed his nose, sniffing like a rabbit, right up to the bureau drawer.

"A chiffon blouse, a white slip frayed at the hem and a black brassière like the vestments of some holy order. Dove felt of them with that special reverence of men who have lived wholly apart from women. Under these clothes, it came to him like a mystery, the señora walked naked. The realization weakened him so much that he sat on the bed's edge with the slip lying limp across his knees and stroked it as if it were her flesh. In the nippled cup of the black brassière he smelt her special smell, like that of *Russian Leather*. . . .

"A yearning deep as need can go stretched him on to his stomach, clasping her slip to his chest. Pressing the pillow where her head had lain, his limbs convulsed, and a dizzying surge left him limp as the slip. Sweating and passionless, guilty and spent, the boy lay a long moment with shuttered eyes. This had never happened to him before while waking."

The last sentence indicates that Mr. Algren is less of a realist than he appears. There are probably very few boys of sixteen who have never experienced a sexual orgasm except through a wet dream. But his description of a simple act of fetichism is wholly convincing.

In fact, the earliest example of underwear fetishism in literature occurs in Joyce's *Ulysses*; the action of the book takes place in 1904 (in the days when panties were known as bloomers or drawers, and were vast tents of coloured rayon). Bloom is a panty fetichist. Mrs. Bloom observes: "Of course hes mad on the subject of drawers thats plain to be seen always skeezing at those brazenfaced things on the bicycles with their skirts blowing up to their navels. . . ." And later: "Anything for an excuse to put his hand anear me drawers drawers the whole blessed time till I promised to give him the pair off my doll to carry around in his waistcoat pocket." In the beach scene, where Bloom masturbates after seeing a girl lean backwards with her hands around her knees, his exitement is caused by the sight of the girl's underwear:

'And Jacky Caffrey shouted to look, there was another and she leaned back and the garters were blue to match on account of the transparent . . . and she had to lean back more and more to look up after it, high, high almost out of sight, and her face was suffused with a divine, an entrancing blush from straining back and could see her other things too, nainsook knickers, the fabric that caresses the skin, better than those other pettiwidth, the green, four and eleven, on account of being white . . . and she was trembling in every limb from being bent so far back he had a full view high up above her knee. . . ."

Professor Wilson Knight has suggested, in the essay already quoted, that Bloom's excitement was due to the sight of Gertie Macdowell's buttocks. This seems to me unlikely, in view of the evidence in the rest of the book. In the Night Town scene Lynch raises the slip of a prostitute, using the poker. Bloom's father, Virag (who is present only in Bloom's imagination), comments: "Inadvertently her backview revealed the fact that she is not wearing those rather intimate garments of which you are a particular devotee." (Joyce was also apparently a devotee of these "intimate garments"; a story about him tells how he once performed a drunken dance in the middle of a bridge, waving a pair of panties that he usually carried in his pocket.*)

Ulysses, of course, is a compendium of sexual perversions (mostly attributed to Bloom). Bloom carries on extra-marital love affairs, has attempted at least one sexual assault on a housemaid, is an underwear fetishist, writes indecent letters to attractive socialites (if the evidence of the mock trial in the Night Town scene is to be taken literally), and even asks one of his correspondents to "soil the letter in an unspeakable way" (use it as toilet paper). He has not had normal sexual intercourse with his wife for ten years, but likes to lie at the other end of the bed and kiss her buttocks and the "smellow yellow furrow" between them. (It has also been suggested that he inserts his tongue into her anus in one of the final scenes of the book. Joyce's language is often so obscure that this may be correct, but I have not been able to find the passage in question.) At a very early stage in the book Bloom recalls making love to his wife in the days before they were married, and how she forced chewed seedcake from her mouth into his. Finally, at one point in the book, Mrs. Bloom mentions that her husband liked to wash and iron her knickers. So Bloom's sexual peculiarities range from minor deviations to definite abnormalities.†

I do not know whether Joyce ever made any suggestions to explain Bloom's sexual orientation; but the portrait has an intuitive accuracy and "roundness" that makes it possible to consider Bloom as if he is a case out of Stekel, and certain conclusions seem to stand out. Bloom has a strong inferiority complex – this becomes most obvious in the episode that follows the Night Town scene (Eumaeus), where the chapter is related in a flat, cliché-ridden language that is actually the language in which Bloom would write it. Bloom suffers from

*I Frank Budgen mentions that Joyce was a panty fetishist, and that, like Bloom, he carried a pair of "doll's drawers" in his pocket.

†In *Finnegans Wake*, Joyce's interest in perversion is further developed (see Clive Hart's *Structure and Motif in Finnegans Wake*, pp. 205–8). His hero persuades his wife to excrete in his mouth.

the "fallacy of insignificance", an inferiority feeling about his race, his lack of education (in comparison with the students with whom he mixes) and his physical appearance. He has a strong masochistic tendency, which appears in the Night Town scene when he turns into a woman, and allows the brothel madame to beat him. He is shown throughout as a good-natured man, incapable of inflicting pain. The sense of sexual underprivilege, the frustration, expresses itself in minor perversions, chief among them being his fetichism.

What exactly is the significance of fetichism as an outlet for frustration? To begin with, it is a kind of symbolic rape of the alien female. The kind of sexual desire felt by Moosbrugger is essentially impersonal. The hero of Barbusse's *Hell* remarks: "It is not a woman I want – it is *all* women." Personal contact might even spoil the experience. But impersonal sex is rare; both partners are drawn into a vortex of each other's personality. Rape performed on an unconscious woman might be described as impersonal; but the Blooms of the world are luckily incapable of rape. An outlet is therefore found in onanistic fantasies, intensified by the possession of a garment that would normally be accessible only to a lover.

This idea of the passivity of the sexual object – touched upon in the discussion of "instantaneous and impersonal" sex – is of great importance to the understanding of the nature of sexual abnormality. Leonid Andreyev brings it out very well in a short story called *Abyss*. A male and female student take a country walk together; they are in love, and have a long and idealistic discussion about life. They pass some tramps who are attracted by the girl; the tramps follow them and attack them. Having knocked out the male student, they strip the girl and all of them rape her. When the male student recovers, he finds his companion unconscious. He starts to cover her up, then, excited by her unconsciousness and nakedness, rapes her himself. This is the "abyss" of the title.

Andreyev never elaborated the idea of the story, but it seems probable that the student is excited as much by her unconsciousness, and by the fact that she has just been violated, as by her nakedness. Consequently, he *is* able to satisfy that instantaneous violence of lust that Philip de Bruyn describes.

Similarly, I have heard of a case of a homosexual who was unsatisfactory to his sexual partners because he most enjoyed making love to them while they were *asleep*, and was not excited by them when awake. This, of course, is the pure sexual impulse attempting to evade the sense of personal contact that dilutes it.

The point I wish to make – and it is no doubt the central point of this study – is that all these "perversions" can be regarded as *attempts by individuals to escape the repetition mechanism*. Plato has a parable about how humankind came to be divided into male and female. Men were once globular objects in which male and female was united. But they showed such extraordinary energy and astuteness that the gods became worried that these creatures would become gods themselves. They therefore divided each human being into two halves, slicing him down the middle, and the two halves became male and female. This had the desired effect. The self-divided beings spent all their time and energy trying to unite again male with female. They stopped being a challenge to the gods.*

Only a parable – but in the light of existential psychology, it contains more truth than many "scientific" theories. It is true that the basic sexual striving is a striving for godhead, for the "god-like" sensation of affirmation in the orgasm, and that this is true of *all human effort*, from writing symphonies to committing murders. It also seems that the unconscious biological forces that move us have hit on the device of the repetition mechanism to keep us moving and reproducing. This is rather like tying a carrot on a stick attached to a donkey's collar in order to keep the donkey moving forward. Or the mechanism might be compared to one of those swing

---

*Symposium, Aristophanes' speech. Plato mentions three "primal sexes"; the other two became "male" males (homosexuals) and "female" females (lesbians).

boats at a fair, that swings completely over a bar and back to its original position. Sex carries us to a desired climax of momentary godhead, then immediately deposits us back where we started.

I want to emphasize again that this is not true of all human activity. The life force allows us to learn something from most experiences; we grow and mature to some extent. The intellect learns easily. Even the emotions learn in time, so we can no longer be wrecked by absurdities like jealousy and envy. Even the body learns a little. If you eat a certain type of food until you are thoroughly sick, your stomach will shrink from that food *of its own accord* for a long time afterwards.

The sexual experience is the only one from which we are permitted to learn *almost nothing*. Learning means, of course, that some residue of the experience is left in "the system" permanently. Some learning is intellectual; you can actually express the "lesson of an experience" in so many words, and mean it when you say "It taught me a lesson". Even getting drunk, or taking drugs, leaves a certain residue, although it is a well-known experience that you may seem to "know" all kinds of things when drunk that have completely vanished the next day. But no experience is as baffling and frustrating as that of sex. No matter how much it brings visions, unites the "divided self" into a momentary sense of what it would mean to be an efficient machine, its "lessons" are almost totally ungraspable to our present clumsy way of expressing ourselves.

The history of human evolution has been the history of an attempt to escape the terrific limitations that "the gods" have planted into animals for their self-preservation. Man catches a glimpse of some vision outside in the garden; he rushes out of the room, down the stairs, along a corridor; finally, he flings open the door that leads out to the garden – and finds himself back in the room in which he started. This is sex. To the very simplest living organisms, this is *all experience*. Men painfully devised a language to overcome this limitation; they learned to use words to preserve the essence of certain experiences –

how to make a fire and build a house, for example. Later still, they invented writing – symbolism – to enable them to catch even more complex experiences. They invented mathematics to help them keep a check on the material world. They invented the scientific method – the greatest evolutionary leap since the ape learned to walk upright. And yet for all that, ninety-nine per cent. of their experience remained ungraspable, unusable, like land that stubbornly refuses to be drained and ploughed. This is the position today. Our few tiny steps in the direction of godhead have been taken over millions of years; in many ways, we *are* god-like creatures, and have every reason to be proud of ourselves; compared with any four-legged animal, our lowest and most degenerate criminal is a Zeus. And yet we do not live like gods; we live like some nervous king perpetually in fear of the assassin's knife. We live a beaten, defeated existence; life beats us at every turn, and leaves us exhausted – broken dray horses, glad to lie down and die, not understanding what it has all been about or why we have been made to pull a cart for so many years. And the Einsteins and Bernard Shaws die as bewildered as the most exploited workman.

It is not therefore too far-fetched to say that the gods have hit on the device of the repeating mechanism to prevent men from advancing too far towards the godhead that lures them on. *But plainly, if the "new existentialism" has a starting point, it is in sex: to devise ways of blocking the repeating mechanism – which at present is as useless to man as a bad stutter – and producing a concept-language for grasping some of the meaning of the sexual experience.*

A sexual "deviation", like Leopold Bloom's fetishism, is the attempt of the healthy organism to tear off the blinkers that frustrate its self-knowledge, the widening of its self-consciousness. There is a well-known psychiatric joke, in which a psychiatrist says to his patient: "I have at last discovered the cause of your inferiority complex. You *are* inferior." Objectively speaking, no one is inferior. Looked at from one point of view, man is the culmination of an evolutionary process; if every man saw himself in this light, the "inferiority complex" would be unknown; every human being would wear a broad smirk of self-satisfaction. (In consequence, our civilization would be far more decadent than it actually is.) The repeating mechanism is designed to prevent us from feeling too much superiority (and ceasing to be intensely responsive to challenges of environment). Casanova's promiscuity is a repetitious attempt to "prove himself". Casanova stayed jammed in his seduction-neurosis because the repeating mechanism sneaked in and robbed him of his proof after every successful seduction. If it were not for this wholesale thieving of the fruits of our experience, human life would not be such a pitiful and agonizing struggle for such small rewards. Casanova, his social and sexual superiority proved by conquest, would pour his immense energies into literary work and leave behind him the achievement of another Voltaire instead of the memoirs of a clever fool. The great writers and artists, for the most part, are not men who are "born with genius", but men who with either effort or good luck have escaped the burden of the repeating mechanism that dooms most men to futility. To say that Voltaire or Shaw or Tolstoy "had genius" is only to say that they were less weighed down by the inferiority neurosis than most people. It is a fallacy that neurosis is another form of genius. It *can* sometimes be an asset, a negative stimulation of the will when no positive stimulus is available. But in most major artists who were also neurotics – Dostoevsky, Schiller, Lawrence – the neurosis can be seen as the factor that gradually destroys the work.

The sexual deviation, then, is man's attempt to outwit his inferiority neurosis by supplying himself with an intenser quality of experience than would be possible within the "normal" limitations. It is his attempt to breathe more deeply, to uncramp himself from his stance of unfulfilment. "I am nothing and I deserve nothing", says the hero of *L'Enfer*. It is not a woman he wants, but *all* women; but he knows he does not deserve them. The attitude of a Pommerenke is a little less abject, even if it is more anti-social; he at least makes a misdirected attempt to have all women. What is pathetic about Pommerenke – and about most sexual criminals and deviates – is that they learn nothing from the experience; the repetition mechanism is as ruthless to them as to Casanova. And this is what makes a case like that of Chessman so tragic: that it seems that he *was* stimulated by his danger (when on trial for his life) into reversing the usual downhill roll of the criminal, and developing in stature as a human being.

The minor sexual deviates, then – the voyeur and the fetichist – are men who wish to broaden their sexual experience, without using the most obvious and simple method to this end: knocking women unconscious and raping them. (I am also, of course, leaving out of account the fetichists who are simply "hypnotized" by some object – like a rubber apron or a nightcap – that *must* be associated with any woman they possess.)

A typical case of minor fetichism will clarify this point. It is quoted in Israel Beckhardt's book *The Violaters*. Beckhardt calls his fetichist "Rodney Shires", and he came to Beckhardt's attention as a juvenile offender needing the help of a probation officer. Shires was the son of a famous actor, who had been married several times; not all his wives were sympathetic to the boy, who was girlish in appearance, had a morbid craving for affection and stuttered badly. As a small boy, Shires was left alone a great deal; he used to drape some of his mother's clothes on the bed and imagine she was there. Later, this turned into the onanism described by Nelson Algren. Whenever he could, Shires obtained women's undergarments – stockings and nightdresses interested him as much as panties – and used them to masturbate. In his mid-teens he obtained a casual job as a messenger boy with a theatrical agency – of which his father was the most important client – and met there an elderly stage magician who taught him how to open simple locks with a strip of cellophane, and with skeleton keys. For various reasons, Shires was in a state of sexual tension that summer. The sight of so many young actresses at the agency increased his excitement. Finally, he got the idea of burgling their apartments to secure underwear.

One day he learned by chance that a certain girl would leave her apartment empty that evening. He rang the apartment to make sure no one was in, then went into the building. He was able to let himself into the apartment and steal panties, stockings and a nightdress. Back at home he spread these out on his bed and masturbated. After this, he felt ashamed and frightened, and threw them into an incinerator. At this point the release of the sexual tension, the symbolic act of copulation with the pretty actress, the symbolic overcoming of her "alien-ness", might have decided him to take no more risks for such a small result. But a few days later another opportunity presented itself, and he repeated the procedure. Beckhardt writes: "He approached each theft with trembling, his body bathed in cold sweat. Yet despite his fear . . . he was fascinated by the idea of entering bedrooms surreptitiously and received pleasurable sensations which he was unable to describe." This is again a familiar part of the fetichist pattern; the mindless repetition mechanism associates all the feelings in a messy lump. The underwear is associated with the thought of undressing a girl. (There is no question of the underwear itself becoming the focus of the sexual emotion; no doubt it would be even more satisfying if it could be taken off an unconscious girl.) The entering of her bedroom is associated with the underwear. The idea of theft is associated with entering the bedroom. And all the various emotions of fear and shame, culminating in orgasm, are a kind of catharsis.

Shires made the mistake of choosing all his victims from the same agency, and often from the same immense apartment building. The police followed him one night and caught him with several undergarments under his jersey. Instead of being treated as a neurotic who needed treatment, he was tried in a juvenile court, which agreed not to send him to prison if he went into the army. A few weeks after entering the army he died in hospital from a sudden illness.

The case of Shires makes certain points clear. This kind of fetichism springs out of frustration; it is symbolic Casanovism. In some respects it is also like drug-taking. It *can* be used to obtain an intensity of experience that would other-wise not be available; i.e. in a kind of scientific spirit, to obtain new data. But like drug-taking, it is also capable of getting the upper hand of the "experimenter" and under-mining his will-power.

A Jungian psychologist once made a jocular suggestion to explain panty fetichism, and its apparent independence of the ordinary hypnosis mechanisms that produce crutch fetichists, hair fetichists, etc.; he suggested that it might be some deep racial memory, from the days when a woman handed her panties to a man as a symbolic act of surrender. The idea was not offered seriously, of course. (Knickers are a fairly recent invention, dating back less than two hundred years; our Elizabethan ancestors wore nothing under their skirts.) It was probably meant as a parody of the Freudian notion that shoe fetichism springs from the feeling of the shoe as a symbolic vagina. And yet it catches something important about the problem. Certain fetiches are associated *arbitrarily* with the sexual act, through some early hypnosis of the sexual impulse. Others have the character of *inevitable* substitutes for the sexual act, separated from it only by some thin barrier of frustration, in the way that a sexually excited dog will choose to rub itself against a child's arm or leg.

In 1933 Havelock Ellis could write: "[Sexual anomalies] are especially liable to occur in a civilization like our own, where the stimulations to sexual activity and the restrictions on that activity – both external and internal – are alike so powerful." Since that time, the "stimulations to sexual activity" have in-creased, and sex crime in England has trebled. Even to com-pare the popular "true crime" magazines of the 'thirties and the 'sixties is to recognize the same point: the number of crimes associated with sex and sexual abnormality has increased. It would be interesting to discover the exact statistics by comparing fifty issues of the "True Police Cases" type of magazine of the early 'thirties with fifty issues of the same magazine today. In the magazines of the 'thirties, wives were buried in back gardens, baby farmers murdered their charges, and husbands were poisoned – probably in much the same numbers as in 1962. But the reader was far less likely to come upon a story entitled "Panty Fiend" or "Crazy About Girls" in the 'thirties. There were multi-murderers and sex killers, but none who, like Peter Manuel (who was executed in 1956), apparently killed two girls solely in order to steal their panties.*

The problems involved in the origins of fetishism are probably exaggerated by such writers on the subject as Binet, Freud and Hirschfeld, Krafft-Ebing, for example, suggests that shoe fetishism contains a component of masochism, since the foot is a symbol of conquest – being "trodden under foot". A philosopher would counter this hypothesis by invoking Ockham's Razor – that is, the idea that it is never useful to propound more theories than are *absolutely necessary* to explain a problem. It is easy enough to understand how the shoe can become a "sexual object" if it happens to get associated with the idea of sex in some casual relation. A case cited by Hirschfeld provides an illustration. A fourteen-year-old boy was staying with friends, whose only daughter was an attractive girl of twenty. He used to enjoy lying on the hearthrug in front of the fire. One evening the girl wanted to reach something on the mantelpiece, and jokingly stepped on him, saying that she would show him "how the hay and straw feels". She raised her skirt and held out one foot to the fire. The boy was in a feverish state of sexual desire by this time, took hold of her foot, and drew it down to his penis. She stepped on him with her full weight, and he experienced an orgasm. This soon became a regular "game" between them. The girl would stand on him and move her feet around against his ribs and

*Unfortunately, no psychologist's report on Manuel has yet been published, and books like John Gray Wilson's study of the case confine themselves to presenting the "facts" of the crimes – Manuel committed ten murders – and offer no speculations about his mentality. However, hints were dropped at the trial of a "peculiar sexual perversion", and the evidence makes it fairly clear that this was panty fetishism. Although eight of his victims were women, there was no rape; in the two cases of girls who were murdered out of doors, the panties were missing.

stomach; he would finally seize her foot and she would step on his penis. The patient never mentioned whether the girl also experienced an orgasm, but he describes her with "bright eyes, flushed cheeks, and trembling lips" as the palpitations of his orgasm communicated themselves to her foot.

Now to speak of symbolic sadism and masochism here is surely unnecessary. At fourteen a boy's sexual emotions may be overwhelmingly strong. Even if he is in every way normal, he is likely to be excited by the sight of a girl's legs in silk stockings above him, and if she also raises her skirt, the effect will be intensified. At this point, the penis is like a gun with a hair-trigger; at the slightest pressure it will explode. That the two continued to do this until it grew into a habit is no proof of sexual perversion, but only of sexual frustration, an intense pressure of sexual emotion. (Nevertheless, the youth was sufficiently inconvenienced by the habit to later become a patient of Havelock Ellis.)

The point to be observed, though, is that any number of "deviations" might have resulted from the continued repetition of this experience. The boy might have associated the pleasure with her shoe, with her silk stockings, or with her panties (if he could see them) – or he might simply have developed a taste for being trodden on (which, in fact, he did). The sexual energies have all the power of a fast river, and they are likely to cut their channel in almost any direction in which they habitually overflow. The "repetition mechanism" then magnifies the inclination into a "perversion". No special hypotheses about the character of the patient are necessary; the power of the sexual emotion and the repetition mechanism are capable of causing sexual deviations in *any* type of personality.

The point that stands out clearly from these considerations is that "fetichism" is a definite name for an indefinite state. Once, fetichism meant only the sexual craving for inanimate objects; later, it had to be extended to include parts of the body – the hair, feet, etc. But is there any logical reason why a sexually normal man should not be called a "girl fetichist", and a homosexual a "man fetichist"? If, as all these analyses indicate, sex is "mental" (i.e. made up of a raw sexual energy – the bullets in the gun – and a mental component that determines choice of the finger that pulls the trigger), then even convenient words like "fetich" must be mistrusted. To many readers it may seem a dubious advantage to blur the lines of our terminology, a step in the direction of total muddle-headedness. In fact, this blurring of the lines helps to destroy the "object" view of sex (i.e. the view that sex is a straight-forward appetite, like hunger, that requires a straightforward satisfaction – food) and throws the emphasis upon the element of mental choice – upon *freedom*. The old Freudian analyses of sex proceeded from a basis of materialism. The conclusions of existential analysis are in the opposite direction. They can be stated in this way: *Treat sex without preconceptions, and apply to it the methods of phenomenological analysis, and it will be seen that the study of the sexual impulses leads the discussion into the area of human freedom.* The study of sex, by phenomenological methods, is perhaps the most powerful method yet discovered for pursuing the existential problem.

In discussing the sexual impulse, the word "selectivity" is in some cases preferable to "intentionality". In the case of Ellis's patient, a number of subjective factors "selected" their object, or rather, the shape of his future sexual experience.

The case of Rodney Shires shows how this intentionality of selection may go even further afield in the process of association; he admitted that entering the women's bedrooms also caused him sexual excitement. (Disciples of Freud would explain that a bedroom is a hole, and therefore a female sex symbol.) The sexual emotion was also apparently intensified by the fear and excitement of risking capture. It is not a long step from the mentality of a Rodney Shires to the mentality of the kleptomaniac who is driven by sexual excitement to steal from big stores.

The process of association is interestingly exemplified in the case of the Chicago killer, William Heirens. Heirens, who was eighteen when he was sentenced for three murders, had a record of juvenile delinquency dating back to the age of thirteen. He had spent two periods in "correctional institutions" for burglary. But apparently it was not realized that Heirens broke in to apartments to steal panties. He began to obtain sexual excitement from stealing underwear before he was twelve. When he was thirteen he began to commit burglaries. *Soon, the sight of an open window would induce an erection.* It was after he was released from the second reformatory that he committed his first attack on a woman, knocking her unconscious with an iron bar and tying her to a chair. (Later, he claimed that he attacked women only when they interrupted him in process of stealing.) There followed two murders of women. Now a sadistic motive began to assert itself. The first woman he stabbed in the throat, and then bound a nightgown round her neck. The second was more badly mutilated. On the wall above her bed Heirens scrawled in lipstick: "For God's sake catch me before I kill more. I cannot control myself." Finally Heirens murdered and dismembered a six-year-old girl when she woke up and spoke to him as he passed through her room. He dropped parts of the body into sewers and manholes. He was caught when the police were alerted about sounds coming from an "empty" apartment. In the attic of his home the police found more than thirty pairs of panties.

Heirens's testimony to psychiatrists reveals the typical pattern of the sexually obsessed criminal. The urge to commit burglaries would overwhelm him. If he resisted it, he would suffer from headaches. While committing the burglaries he was in such a state of tension that he killed unhesitatingly when interrupted or startled. To justify these crimes to himself he invented an "alter-ego" called George, and declared that it was George who committed the burglaries and murders.* On one occasion he locked his clothes in the washroom and threw the key inside to prevent himself from going out. Halfway

*After his sentence, Heirens admitted that George was pure invention to help a schizophrenia defence.

through the night the urge overpowered him, and he crawled along the house gutter to get his clothes, then went out. Finally, the act of entering the window was able to induce an orgasm.

Heirens was found sane and sentenced to life imprisonment.

The interesting point about this case is the way in which sex became associated with the idea of *evil* (or with anti-social activity). At first it was unnecessary to commit any crime in order to obtain satisfaction from his fetichistic urges. But as soon as he began to steal to obtain the panties – from clothes lines – the sexual excitement became associated with the excitement of danger – as with Rodney Shires. Finally, he develops a typically criminal attitude to himself and to society. The criminal attitude is the exact opposite of the attitude of the social and religious reformer. The reformer feels that he is right and society wrong, and that he must use his powers of persuasion to make society accept his own values. The criminal sees society as his unsuspecting victim; but society is potentially his judge, and will judge him in the wrong. He develops the subjective attitude of a rat cowering in its hole, the attitude of the "underground man". He is surrounded by potential enemies, by hostility. But his 'idealistic powers" have no chance to develop; he will never indulge in constructive thinking because all constructive thinking is basically for *one's own sake*. The criminal can never be confidently subjective, because his basic picture of life is of a struggle against society, and his criterion of "useful thought" is of thought that will help him in his battle against society. Consequently, he lacks a true centre of gravity, for he never ceases to think of himself in relation to other people. Instead of developing the healthily egotistic position: truth is what moves me deeply; evil is what hurts me or destroys my relation to myself, he thinks in terms of a simplified good and evil. He enjoys sex; but sex is evil. (This is the exact opposite of the Blakeian position.) But he must have sex, so he is willing to accept himself as evil.

Once he has fallen into the habit of thinking of himself as evil, as a kind of dangerous wild animal that must exercise cunning to avoid being destroyed by society, then he is in the right frame of mind for slipping into sadistic crime. When he has committed a murder he feels no twinge of conscience, because it only confirms his gloomy view that he is incurably wicked. His wickedness is a burden, so he writes a plea for society to catch him. He also invents a "Mr. Hyde" called George, so that at least he can feel that he is still partly good. (Heirens's Roman Catholic upbringing may have increased this tendency to a split in his personality; although the practice of confession undoubtedly has a great deal to be said in its favour, it hardly increases the individual's tendency to be morally self-reliant.) Blake or Noyes would find Heirens a sad example of the destructive effects of a commercial civilization. The sexual vitality – which according to Blake is "the bounty of God" – is misdirected at every point. Shaw's Peter Keegan spoke of a man as a "poor lost soul, cunningly fenced in with invisible bars". This would be the verdict on Heirens by anyone who feels an intelligent interest in education and the problems of our society. The problems raised by Heirens's crimes are too complex to be solved by broad generalities about education. They are problems of communication; problems whose solution demands a profounder psychology than any that exists at present.

CHAPTER VI

THE MEANING OF "PERVERSION"
III

Shepherd who divided his penis. Sex murder. The Christie case. Heath. Necrophilia. The case of "D.W.". Sergeant Bertrand. Homosexuality and the homosexual community.

THE analysis of sexual abnormality and sex-crime reveals a difficulty that, as far as I know, has never been clearly stated. Two distinct elements can be made out in all "perversion", two factors that have usually been treated as one. There is an element of vitality striving to cut its own channel, and the element of degeneration, of exhaustion making a last feeble effort to achieve "alien-ness" through a new sensation. It is important to make a clear distinction between these two elements. De Sade touched on the second when he made Durcet remark that the most extreme perversions are the outcome of boredom, satiety and worthlessness. Hirschfeld cites a case that is almost a symbol for destructive degeneration. This concerned a shepherd whose loneliness caused him to masturbate excessively until normal manual stimulation ceased to have much effect. He began to inflict wounds on his penis, dividing it. He died in his thirties after an operation on his bladder.

The first thing that strikes us on considering this case is the *emptiness* of the patient's life, when he could find nothing better to do than masturbate fifteen times a day. Either from shyness or feelings of guilt, he never had sexual intercourse with a woman. (This is not as unusual as it might seem; the most famous example of a totally celibate man, whose guilt about masturbation tortured him, is Nicolai Gogol, whose stories are full of strange images of his guilt.) Presumably he was unable to read or write, and probably had little general education. Life would have been a long, dull burden of unwanted consciousness without his single pleasure. But the sexual instinct was never intended to bear the whole burden of man's need to discharge his energy. Excessive emphasis on sex leads inevitably to degeneration; the divided penis might be regarded as a symbol of the destruction of the psyche

This immediately raises the problem of "more suitable" routes for the evolutionary energy, and emphasizes again the distinction between the degenerative and the creative elements in sexual activity. Blake wrote:

> When thought is closed in caves
> Then love shall show its root in deepest hell.

That is to say, the frustrated vital energies will express themselves in destruction.

But this should not lead us to lose sight of the nature of these energies. Of all philosophers, Nietzsche understood them most profoundly, and laid full emphasis on their rôle. The whole human organism is obsessed by a will to power. Nietzsche regarded this will to power as the highest will of which human beings are capable. The outward striving for social or political domination is its least important and stupidest manifestation. It is the drive for "complete consciousness" that was discussed in the last chapter. The man who turns it outward to personal domination is guilty of self-delusion and self-betrayal, since the misdirected energies now enter a circuit of frustration, and the evolutionary drive is completely wasted. Power is another name for Whitehead's notion of an "absoluteness of self-enjoyment".

Before Nietzsche's concept of power can be understood, this idea of "outward power" – the domination of other people – must be dismissed. Only then can a passage like the following be understood correctly:

"What is good? Everything that heightens the feeling o power in man, the will to power, power itself.

"What is bad? Everything that is born of weakness.

"What is happiness? The feeling that power is growing, that resistance is overcome.

"Not contentedness, but more power; not peace but war; not virtue but fitness. . . ." (*Antichrist*, Section 2.)

In Gurdjieff's "well-balanced man", the striving for sexual power is only one line of struggle towards "higher evolution". The despair of philosophers and mystics springs from perception of the power of the "repeating mechanism", which prevents maturity on an intellectual and emotional, as well as on a sexual level. One only has to read the work of H. G. Wells to become aware of a monstrous appetite for ideas, a vital enthusiasm, that is as insatiable as De Sade's sexual enthusiasm. When this kind of enthusiasm has a strong emotional component it tends towards religion, or a kind of poetic idealism, as in Shelley, Wordsworth, Blake. But one only has to read about the lives of these men to realize that their "idealistic" experience was as heavily taxed by the life force as De Sade's sexual experience; that is to say, it was as inadequate as sexual experience to serve as a ladder towards "godhead". Its "widening" effect on consciousness is almost as short-lived as that of the sexual orgasm, and the evolutionary enthusiasm of *Men Like Gods* and *Prometheus Unbound* turns into the gloomy sense of the futility of all human effort. And yet the residue of great intellectual or emotional experience is undoubtedly more considerable than the residue of the sexual orgasm.

The battle against the "repeating mechanism" is conducted on many levels. The healthy and well-adjusted man (assuming for the moment that he could exist) would conduct his war against the "partial nature of consciousness" on many fronts. (It is interesting that both Wells and Shelley believed in a multiplicity of sexual experience, and Wells at least practised it vigorously.) The Nietzschean "Will to Power", the craving for complete consciousness, expresses itself on several levels. But it is always a striving to overcome the repeating mechanism. Somewhere in the human machine there is hidden a kind of thermostat. Just as an ordinary thermostat turns off a heater when a certain temperature has been reached, so this conscious thermostat turns off the consciousness when a certain level of power and intensity has been reached. We hope continually for a steadily rising flood of consciousness, a flood that begins from some insight of intuition, and invades the brain with a sense of "otherness", other places, other people, other experiences, and new relations between half-forgotten pieces of experience. But the thermostat switches off. It is like a miserly matron who holds the keys to the pantry, and who will only dole out minute quantities of food, enough to keep us from starving. We dream hungrily of tying her up, stealing her keys, and eating as often and as much as we like. Or, to use another metaphor (and the language of images is indispensable in a discussion of this kind), we dream about finding the hidden lever that operates the flood-gates of vitality, so that we can turn the feeble, muddy dribble into a clear, strong flow of consciousness. The quality of our everyday consciousness is incredibly poor; we only realize *how* poor when some new stimulation or excitement intensifies it for a moment. (Mr. Huxley claims that mescalin has this effect.) Half our living is a dull ritual that *ought* to be fascinating. For a child, a trip to the seaside brings floods of "otherness" that gives him an intuition of some magnificent and powerful consciousness when he reaches adulthood. In fact, adult consciousness is all watery soup and half-rotten bread that keeps him psychically thin and "oppressed". It is this poor quality food that keeps men un-godlike. Consciousness is synonymous with vision, and vision means godhead. While man is so heavily blinkered, while consciousness flows in such a thin, reluctant dribble, it is inevitable that man should walk with a stoop, and cringe away from experience in case it snatches away his miserable crust of subjectivity and "self-enjoyment".

Instead of thinking of humankind as divided up into the "normal" and "abnormal", the socially well adjusted and the criminals, we should see all men as engaged in more or less the same kind of fight against this automatic robber of their intensity, this robot-thief planted in the mechanism of the brain. The badly defeated may become neurotics or actually insane – some defence mechanism of illusion preventing total collapse – or may make some clumsy attempt to redeem the defeat by force, and become criminals. It is significant that most criminals have the same misdirected feeling of hostility. It is "The world owes me a living" or "Society has driven me to crime", etc. The psychologist who points out to them that "the world" and "society" are abstractions that cannot owe anybody anything or drive him anywhere is throwing out the dirty water without offering to replace it with clean. The criminal is right in his vague intuition of having an enemy who is treating him unjustly. He will be closer to the truth if he says that "Luck is against him" or "Life has a down on him". He *is* being robbed and beaten; his mistake lies in supposing that, because other men look happier they must be in league with the oppressor.

This is the reason that the socially unfit become so often sexual criminals. We would find excuses for a starving worker who threw a brick through the window of a big store because its owners were charging prices that condemned him to starvation. But the sexual criminal is frequently a man in the same position. The repeating mechanisms rob him so that he is induced to attach great importance to sexual conquest, but the price he is asked to pay for these infinitely desirable sexual goods is prohibitively high. It is not surprising if some of the oppressed minority try to smash the window and take the goods without paying the price in energy and will-power.

I should repeat that this image of underprivileged and exploited human creatures is intended to be understood relatively. All "law" is simultaneously a safeguard and an oppression. Until human beings have reached a degree of power and self-determination that would make a backward slide down the evolutionary scale impossible, the artificial stimulus of hardship remains necessary. *The man who wishes to escape the heavy tax in consciousness that is the safeguard of our continuous effort must prove himself capable of self-determination and resistance to the reflexes that cause boredom and collapse of purpose.*

But although the "law" may be necessary, its universality inevitably involves a certain oppression. Many human beings may be as happy as their weakness allows them to be under the constant pressure of unfulfilment. Others – the more sensitive and intelligent – may even be glad of "body and its stupidity" (Yeats's phrase) that acts as a buffer against their weakness. But there are also men who are born with certain handicaps, and who are doomed to a kind of perpetual starvation of the vital instincts – men who, by the time they have paid the heavy "tax on consciousness", are left totally incapable of any affirmation. Sometimes such men as these revolt and become sexual criminals to obtain a few moments of the Nietzschean sense of power, of mastery of existence. An interesting example is the sexual murderer DeWitt Clinton Cook, who is cited by de River. Cook, who was twenty when he was executed in 1941, attacked girls with a piece of wood and raped them when unconscious. His sexual member was so tiny that he and his wife were forced to satisfy one another orally. Cook was a weak-chinned young man with a marked inferiority complex, and de River suspected that the piece of wood with which he stunned his victims may have been a symbol of the erect male organ. His attacks occurred usually at the time of the full moon, and Cook claimed that the sight of the moon made him unable to resist the urge to rape. He was plainly a man whose only moments of freedom from his inferiority neurosis occurred in the act of rape on an unconscious girl.

Even more to the point in this connection is the case of John Reginald Halliday Christie. Christie murdered at least six women in the house at 10 Rillington Place, Notting Hill Gate – five of them for purposes of rape. Like Cook, Christie was a man who suffered from an inferiority neurosis. He was born in Yorkshire, in a poor, working-class family, son of a father who treated his children with Victorian harshness. He was coddled by his mother and bullied and dominated by his sisters, three of whom were older than he. At school he showed himself to be below average in intelligence, and was poor at games. Being his mother's favourite, he used his weakness as a means of gaining sympathy, and was frequently ill. At the age of fifteen Christie made his first attempt at sexual intercourse with a girl in Lovers' Lane, and failed completely. When this story got around he was nicknamed "Reggy No Dick" and "Can't-do-it Christie". Two years later – in 1915 – Christie was gassed and blown up in France. As a result of fright he lost his power of speech for several weeks, and was able to speak only in a whisper for many years. (Christie also claimed that he was blinded by the mustard gas shell, but this seems to be a lie.) In 1920 he met his wife, Ethel, and married her; but they had no sexual relations for two years – a result of the inadequacy that had led to his nickname in Halifax.

Christie was a habitual petty criminal, who had been in trouble with the police since childhood. He seemed to be unlucky in being discovered in minor offences that most healthy boys commit. In his early teens he lost two jobs for petty theft; later, after his marriage, he spent seven months in prison for stealing postal orders when he worked for the Post Office, and for various other offences, including striking a woman on the head with a cricket bat. At the beginning of the war, in 1939, he became a War Reserve policeman, and became known in Notting Hill for his harshness to petty offenders; he enjoyed bullying as far as he dared. For four years he gained some kind of self-confidence by his ability to dominate his neighbours. Apparently he even started to have some kind of sexual relation with a married woman whose husband was a soldier. One day the soldier returned, found them together, and gave Christie a beating.

Ludovic Kennedy, who has written about the case, believes that this beating triggered Christie into sexual murder. He invited a young prostitute named Ruth Fuerst to the house when his wife was away in Sheffield (her home town). He strangled her and had intercourse, then later buried the body in the back garden. This was soon after Christie had been beaten by the soldier. And a year later, in 1944, Christie again killed a woman and buried her in the garden. This time he used a ruse that he later found valuable for stupefying victims; he told her that he could treat her catarrh with various inhalants in a jar, and introduced a tube that was connected to the gas tap. When the woman became unconscious, he undressed her and raped her, strangling her as he did so.

Five years passed before he committed another murder. Perhaps his wife was constantly at home, or perhaps he felt that it would be tempting providence too far to kill again. Or, more likely, *the two rapes may have performed a catharsis*, removed a psychological burden, and left Christie a healthier man – for the moment. But in 1949 the temptation became too great. A young married couple had moved into the flat above the Christies. The husband, Timothy Evans, was a poor specimen, physically and mentally; only five feet high, with a lame foot, he was so mentally backward that he had never learned to read and write. His wife Beryl was a pretty eighteen-year-old girl. They had a baby daughter, and when Beryl discovered that she was pregnant again, Evans became worried and consulted Christie. Christie's mind worked quickly; the sexual hunger revived; he saw an opportunity of access to the body of the desirable wife. He talked mysteriously to Evans about his qualifications as an abortionist. The result was that, one afternoon in November 1949, Christie went up to Beryl's flat to perform an abortion, and ended by strangling and raping her. It is doubtful whether he intended to do this; with her husband still alive, detection would be inevitable. Probably he intended only to satisfy some voyeur's urge, or render her temporarily unconscious with his gas device and satisfy himself before she woke up. Ludovic Kennedy suggests that Beryl struggled before she succumbed to the gas; Christie was too sexually excited to hold back, and battered her unconscious, then strangled her.

What happened next is uncertain. It seems likely that Christie told Evans that his wife had died during an abortion, and that they would both be tried for murder if they were not careful. He offered to take the baby to Acton to be looked after by friends. Two days later the baby was also murdered by strangulation, almost certainly by Christie. (All that is known of Evans's character indicates that he would be incapable of such a crime; although he was an inveterate and imaginative liar, he had a strong trait of family affection and loyalty.) Evans probably believed that the baby was at Acton. A week later Evans went to Wales to stay with an aunt, and on November 30 gave himself up to the police at Merthyr Vale, saying that he had murdered his wife. This part of the case remains mysterious. Although Evans at one point accused Christie of the murder, he withdrew the accusation when told that his daughter's body had also been found. And he allowed himself to be tried and executed, with Christie as one of the witnesses against him.

Three years later, Christie began his final "murder rampage" that ended in his arrest. At the end of 1952 he strangled his wife and hid her under the floorboards – probably to have the house to himself. Then, in the next two months, he killed and raped three more women – all girls in their twenties – probably using the "inhalant" device to render them unconscious. He hid the bodies in a cupboard, which he covered with wallpaper, and then left the house. Four days later the bodies were discovered by a Jamaican tenant. The body of Mrs. Christie, and the skeletons in the back garden, were quickly uncovered. Christie was arrested, tried, and executed. A great deal has been written on the question of the innocence of Timothy Evans, and the case undoubtedly contributed to the suspension of the death penalty in England in 1957. (Even under the new Homicide Act, however, Evans would still have been sentenced to death, since he was accused of committing two murders on "two different occasions".)

But for the present purpose the interest of the case lies in the murders themselves. Christie's murder of the baby Geraldine, as well as his past criminal record, reveals that this is not a simple case of "frustration murder"; there is present a strong element of criminal degeneracy. But the frustration element is very strong indeed, and entitles Christie to be considered as another "Moosbrugger-type" killer, breaking the shop window for the food he is too poor to buy. Christie's case represents a struggle between the elements of sickness and health. He was always inclined to hypochondria, and to the inferiority neuroses that accompany it. His revolt against inferiority was a healthy response of the organism; but like all revolts by the weak, it was too violent. It led to the bullying and officiousness of his period as a policeman. It was undoubtedly a form of schizophrenia. Rollo May has pointed out* that schizophrenia is a loss of contact with "the real world" caused by fear, disinclination to face it honestly; this is covered over by a constructed personality, by rationalizations, in the way that a dangerous hole might be temporarily covered with a board instead of being determinedly filled in. But the strain is great – like maintaining an elaborate swindle – and can lead to breakdown or to various forms of violence. May also points out that cases of schizophrenia are increasing steadily in number. The "typical" case for the Freudian analyst of fifty years ago was "hysteria"; today it is schizophrenia.

Christie was condemned to schizophrenia by his weakness; his response to life had to be either a turning away or an attempt to impose himself by deception. (There are many examples of his attempts to pass himself off as a man of fashion, etc. Duncan Webb claimed that he married Ethel by pretending to be a rich man.) Although his sexual appetite was strong – it had been awakened at the age of ten by his sisters, according to his own account – his fear of women was equally strong. He developed the usual furtive sexuality of the subjective type. He may have been a fetichist; the knickers were missing from all the corpses, and he kept female pubic hairs in a tobacco tin. The ideal sexual object for Christie was an unconscious woman. In several of the cases he admitted to feeling a strange sense of peace and happiness after he had committed the murder and rape. He may even have felt proud of himself. With the balance so heavily weighted against him,

*Existence, edited by Rollo May (Basic Books, New York), p. 56.

doomed by "life" to frustration, he had met the challenge; he had shown the enterprise and cunning of a wild animal, and satisfied an apparently unsatisfiable appetite. Life had played him an unpleasant trick in making him a mild, defenceless, cringing little man, afraid to make love to a healthy, demanding woman; he had refused to lie down under the burden. Society was opposed to his appetite; he set himself up as judge, and decided that the appetite would be satisfied in any case. In that moment he may have felt as Steppenwolf describes his alter-ego – like a powerful wild animal. Life had beaten him, victimized him, defeated him; but at least he had won one battle. Man is not a worm after all; with enough fight in him, he could be a god. The sexual fulfilment could re-unite the divided ego for a moment, bring back a sense of contact with reality and power.

In Christie the two elements of sex crime can be clearly seen: the degenerative element, and the urge towards health. The sadism (the need to strangle as he had intercourse), the murder of the baby, reveal the man who has stopped willing, who has allowed his instincts to slip towards disease. But the acts of violation were an attempt to right the balance, to supply himself with an experience that he felt to be his by "right", to escape a spiritual stagnation. This is not to say, of course, that the sex crimes were somehow "right". It is only to point out that there are two forces at work in opposite directions, one making for increased sickness, the other for health. If human nature was as simple as it seems to be – that is, if nature did not "tax" our experience so heavily – a sex crime *could* be a step in the direction of conquest, of godhead. A neurosis is temporaily dissipated; life is attacked and defeated. If the criminal could then take a Sartrian attitude towards his crime – a refusal to disown the act, and a determination to develop beyond it – it might conceivably result in "health". The Sartrian attitude to crime is perfectly expressed by Thomas Middleton's De Flores in *The Changeling*, who commits a murder solely in order to blackmail a woman to sleep with him; when he is caught he comments:

> . . . her honour's prize
> Was my reward; I thank life for nothing
> But that pleasure; it was so sweet to me,
> That I have drunk up all, left none behind
> For any man to pledge me. . . .

This is the ideal existentialist attitude to all experience; to lose nothing, to refuse to pay the tax on experience, and consequently not to feel "cheated", having obtained a pleasure that once seemed infinitely desirable. But only characters in literature evade the tax to that extent. A Christie may feel like De Flores for a moment, as he feels drained of a sexual energy that has become mixed with a poison of frustration; five minutes later his own daring crushes him; he panics, schemes how to dipose of the body, and again lets in the enemy he has just ejected so vigorously.

If Christie is compared with a sadistic killer like Neville Heath, the point of this analysis becomes immediately apparent. Heath is the typical criminal-Casánova type; weak-willed, good-looking, a born liar and *poseur*, who found sexual conquest very easy. Like Casanova, he feels himself to be a failure in all things but seduction; consequently he channels all his vital energies into seduction – with the usual result: degeneration. Satiety and worthlessness lead to the development of perversions. At first the perversions – inflicting pain on the sexual partner – are a kind of curry-powder to flavour the sex; eventually they become the main component. A careful examination of the case of Heath – who murdered and mutilated two girls in 1946 – fails to reveal any of the element of urge towards health. The crimes were not a despairing attempt to escape his own sickness, but a deliberate wallowing in it by a man who is too weak to feel any sense of purpose.

This distinction between the completely degenerate and the health-motivated crime is becoming widely recognized in a rather vague way. The judges who refused to condemn *Lolita* and *Ulysses* were recognizing that, although these books may express an unpleasant aspect of sexuality, they are at least expressions of a creative and not a degenerative urge. The attempt to "cure" criminals whose crimes are the expression of an anti-social rage is also a recognition that the vital energy might be turned from its destructive channels. No doubt the widespread agitation about Chessman sprang from the same feeling.

This point is no doubt already clear to the reader; yet it is worth enlarging to bring out all its implications. Nowadays, most parents would not beat a small boy who tried to undress his female cousin to examine her; they would feel that it was a natural expression of curiosity that should be satisfied. And what of the sexual experience of the ex-officer "M" with the nymphomaniac? Opinions may be divided; but there will inevitably be a body of opinion that feels that such an experience is, on the whole, healthy. It should be noted that the sense of triumph expressed by "M" as he looked over the room of "prostrate bodies" is not at all dissimilar to the "peace and happiness" of Christie looking at his victims. Both express the satisfaction of an urge to self-fulfilment. Again, although it is hard to imagine that the works of De Sade could ever be openly published in English-speaking countries – their effect would undoubtedly be harmful – yet De Sade himself is widely regarded with a kind of sympathetic interest that shows an awareness of the strange mixture of creative and degenerative forces in his work.

Again, consider the case of "Felix and Eddie", cited by Beckhardt. Both men were in their seventies; they spent a great deal of time playing draughts together, and used to sit out in the alleyway in the sunshine and talk. Three girls made a habit of playing near them, aged ten, eleven and fourteen. The fourteen-year-old was mentally retarded, but sexually awake. It was she who used to beg sweets from the men, and who one day allowed one of them to take her on his knee and fondle her before he gave her sweets. The relationships developed; soon, all three girls were allowing themselves to be fondled in exchange for candy, and partly undressed. A neighbour suspected what was going on; the men were arrested, and both sentenced. (For some reason, one was sentenced to twenty years, the other to three.) And yet, as Beckhardt says, the seriousness of their crimes depends very much on the point of view. Evidence showed that the fourteen-year-old was at least as responsible as the men for the development of the relation. It was she who persuaded the other two to offer themselves. The rôles of the two men could be compared to that of a receiver of stolen property who is offered a bargain that is too good to miss. Any seventy-year-old widower might accept the offer of intercourse with attractive "nymphets". If the scene had been India or Morocco instead of New York no one would have raised an eyebrow. And yet in helping to corrupt young girls the men had undoubtedly committed a crime, and their activities might be labelled "perversion". Here, one might feel, is the borderline between normality and perversion, crime and legality.

If the distinction between "perversion" and "normality" is to mean anything, it should surely correspond fairly closely to the distinction between the creative and degenerate elements in sex. Tolstoy was right to condemn the listless adulteries of bored aristocrats; boredom and degeneracy are almost synonymous. But the question of degeneration or evolution cannot be considered solely within the sexual context; *it is a teleological question*. This means that the whole question of sexual perversion must be considered in a new way. Questions that would have been irrelevant to Freud – and that would most certainly have been irrelevant to "atomistic" psychologists like Mill and Spencer – are now seen to be essential to the development of the subject. In short, an "existential psychology" is needed – one that is, perhaps, even broader and deeper than that of Binswanger and his colleagues. This will be discussed at length in the final chapter.

There is a certain sense in which Christie can be said to be less "abnormal" than the fetichist Rodney Shires. Christie was averse to "normal" sexual intercourse, but at least he continued to need the female body.* Rodney Shires gained complete satisfaction from the underwear – a stage further away from "normality".

Both perversions derive from the need to escape the *personal* contact with the sexual object. Consequently they cannot be regarded merely as results of the weakening of the "normal" impulse; they are an attempt at a sexual experience that is different *in kind*, not merely in degree.

This urge reaches a certain natural extreme in necrophily, the preference for sexual intercourse with dead bodies. It has been suspected that Christie was a necrophile because he admitted that his morbid interest in death began when, as a child, he saw his grandfather's body laid out for burial. The truth of this is doubtful; but it is not improbable that Christie kept some of the bodies around the house for some time before concealing them.

Again, although necrophily can undoubtedly be called a *perverse act*, it need not necessarily spring from a specific necrophiliac impulse. Sexual desire and sexual curiosity can be very intense in a young man; given the opportunity, he may accept sexual intercourse with a corpse in rather the spirit that Alfred Packer, America's famous cannibal, ate his companions in the wilderness. De River writes: "The necrophiliac is a psychopath. He is of decidedly perverse and abnormal sensuality." Such a judgement is too detached. Lawrence's poem "Manifesto" reveals" abnormal sensuality". Joyce and Wolfe admit to abnormal sensuality in autobiographical

*Dr. Francis Camps, the pathologist on the Christie case, has made some interesting speculations about Christie. He discovered sperm in the seams of Christie's shoes, and guessed that Christie was in the habit of masturbating standing up. (He may have been standing over the corpses.) This led him to suppose that Christie had no plan of killing the women when he rendered them unconscious; he only wanted them to be unable to resist his advances or to render him impotent by active demands. The murders were then committed out of fear of the consequences when the victim awoke and accused him of rape. There is probably some truth in this theory.

novels. The probability is that almost every healthy young man is abnormally sensual. The other objection to be made to de River's statement is that a necrophiliac is not necessarily a man who performs a necrophiliac act; he may only be doing so *faute de mieux*.

Nevertheless, a "perversion" called "necrophilia" does exist, and its study helps to clarify certain points about the nature of the sexual impulse.

First of all the distinction between the genuine necrophiliac and the person who happens to have indulged in necrophilia should be clearly made. One of the cases cited by de River seems to me to belong to the latter group. The accused was a twenty-one-year-old student, a college graduate who now worked in a morgue. The youth, whom de River calls D.W., was shy in the presence of girls, and had a negative sexual history before he commenced his acts of perversion. He had been in love with a girl of seventeen who had died of tuberculosis; he had only one act of sexual intercourse with her. The sight of her body in the coffin excited him sexually. He wanted to become a medical student but, because the course was too expensive, was forced to take a course in undertaking and embalming as the next best thing. Inevitably he drifted into acts of necrophily with the corpses. D.W. was arrested, found guilty and committed to an insane asylum.

And yet there is nothing in the evidence to show that "D.W." was either insane or a genuine necrophile. The idea of having sexual relations with a corpse may revolt most men; but then most men feel no revulsion about the "alien-ness" of a living woman, while a sensitive child may feel that the whole idea of sexual intercourse is as nasty and "alien" as eating excreta. Clearly it is a matter of degree, and of accepting intercourse with alien flesh. Any excitable teenager would, if given the opportunity, have sexual intercourse with every pretty girl he met. (In one case in Chicago a nineteen-year-old boy, Samuel Hryciuk, committed nearly seventy rapes before he was caught; there are few teenagers who would not feel a certain envy of his experience, even if they find it basically distasteful.) Committing sexual acts upon helpless naked women – even if they happen to be dead – may be less a sign of perversion than of overpowering sexual hunger. And this case makes even clearer than usual the arbitrary definition of the word "perversion". Sexual perversion is taken to mean "against nature"; but how can "D.W." be accused of behaving against nature? Is the action of a female ape clutching her dead baby "against nature"? Obviously not. It is only anti-social because it will sooner or later inconvenience the neighbours. But in that case perversion should be defined in terms of social convenience. Far from being "against nature", most sexual perversions are the fault of nature. Nature should be blamed as a bad engineer who spoils the ship for a ha'porth of tar. If nature were more efficient, sexuality would not depend upon a single all-purpose instinct that can easily go wrong: the sexual instincts would be delicate, selective, and precise. And if nature's aim is evolution through civilization, and the historians are right in believing that the decline of ancient civilizations is hastened by sexual perversion, then nature can be accused of a kind of bungling that actually defeats its own purpose.

The interest of the case of "D.W." – particularly the assault that led to his arrest – has very little to do with its necrophiliac aspect. Plainly he found dead women so satisfactory for the reason mentioned by Philip de Bruyn at the beginning of Chapter IV (p. 80): The sexual impulse is an *instantaneous* thing; in its most violent form it wants to overleap the obstacles set up by personality. A poet like Turner may speak idealistically of "bodies fusing into a flame", but such purity of sexual emotion is almost an impossibility for two human personalities. "D.W." was able to obtain practically what Turner can only speak of in theory. The episode that led to his arrest underlines this. The desire to drink a girl's urine and to eat her flesh reveals an intensity of sexual emotion, a vanishing of the *meum-tuum* sense – in short, an absence of "alien-ness" – that are very rarely achieved by "normal" human beings in sexual intercourse. The fact that he then chose to perform an act of sodomy – rather than normal copulation – makes this even plainer. Lawrence, with his talk of the "fount of darkness" would have understood this. "D.W." might argue that, through his "perversion", he had come closer to the "absolutely satisfying sexual experience" than most people in a lifetime.

This is a point of very considerable interest in pursuing the problem of the nature of the sexual impulse. It should be clearly understood that these considerations do not prove that such perversions as necrophily and fetishism (to which it is closely related) are somehow "preferable" – or even equivalent – to the normal act of intercourse (as Gide might argue). They only indicate the truth of the main argument of the preceding chapters: that the act of sexual intercourse is so involved with the peculiar limitations of human consciousness that a partial or perverted act may achieve an intensity – as an expression of the "sexual centre" – that is rarely achieved in the more complex world of "normality".

This becomes even more evident in considering the "classic" case of necrophilia, that of Sergeant Bertrand, cited by Hirschfeld (who quotes Epaulard). There is, admittedly, an element of sadism in Bertrand that may confuse the issue; nevertheless, the case records give an unusually clear picture of the perversion. Bertrand is beyond doubt a "genuine necrophile", as distinguished from a youth like "D.W.". (The difference between them is as clear as the difference between a genuine fetishist – like Heirens – and the example given in Nelson Algren's *Walk on the Wild Side* – p. 108.)

As given by Epaulard, Bertrand's case history is regrettably incomplete; since he was arrested in 1849 – long before psychoanalysis – this is only to be expected. He was born in 1822, and began to develop an abnormally strong sexuality at the age of eight, when he masturbated while imagining that he was torturing and violating naked girls. His sadism may have been tied up with his irritability and explosions of impatience. The usual child's urge to smash things was exaggerated in him; when he grew older he was unable to keep a pipe or a penknife for more than a day; the urge to break it was too great. When drunk, he was inclined to smash everything within reach. Nevertheless, he was a good soldier, obsessed with smartness; he was also a good Catholic, and disliked obscene talk. His attitude towards women was extremely gallant. He was successful in love, and had many mistresses – village girls – who often wanted to marry him.

At the age of twenty-four he began to treat animals in a sadistic manner. Nevertheless, the examples Epaulard cites – killing dogs and tearing out their intestines – do not indicate genuine sadism; the fact that he killed them first reveals that the infliction of pain was not the object – only satisfaction of the urge to smash.

Bertrand described his first act of necrophily in a confession; he was twenty-five at the time:

"At midday I went for a walk with a friend. It so happened that we came to the garrison cemetery, and seeing a half-filled grave I made an excuse to my friend and left him, to return to the grave later. Under the stress of a terrific excitement I began to dig up the grave with a spade, forgetting that it was clear daylight and that I might be seen. When the corpse – a woman's – was exposed, I was seized with an insane frenzy and, in the absence of any other instrument, I began to beat the corpse with the spade. While doing so I made such a noise that a workman engaged near the cemetery came to the gate. When I caught sight of him I lay down beside the corpse and kept quiet for a while. Then, while the workman was away in search of the police, I threw some earth on the corpse and left the cemetery by climbing over the wall. Then, trembling and bathed in cold perspiration and completely dazed, I sat for hours in a small spinney. When I recovered from this paralysis I felt as though my whole body had been pounded to a pulp, and I felt weak in the head."

Later he dug up the grave with his hands and tore open the abdomen of the corpse.

Bertrand committed a number of acts of this nature while continuing to have affairs with village girls, and to satisfy them completely. An interesting feature of the case is the power of the urge to make him immune to discomforts and difficulties. In one case he was forced to dig up fifteen corpses before he found a suitable female. In another he was shot as he was climbing over a wall; but the experience did not deter him. He also went out on icy winter nights seeking for pleasure, and even swam through a pond and lay motionless for a long time in wet clothes when he heard voices.

Bertrand was finally caught through a booby-trap; he tripped over a string connected to the trigger of a rifle, and was shot. He was eventually sentenced to a year in prison, and after his release apparently "disappeared".

Plainly Bertrand's case is very different from that of "D.W.". In a certain sense, Bertrand was not a true necrophile, since the basic instinct in him was purely destructive. And this raises certain problems. How is this destructive impulse to be explained? Many children are destructive – but this is natural, since the child spends a great deal of time repressing various animal impulses to fit into civilized society. The act of destruction is symbolic of the release of Dionysian energy. For this reason, children derive more pleasure than most adults from watching fires or rivers in flood; they enjoy breaking bottles or windows. The adult, with his greater knowledge of the material world, sees life as the problem of maintaining order in spite of nature's tendency to chaos. The child, aware only of an orderly world, wants to introduce chaos. But this urge to destroy is usually weakened as the child grows older. Life demands from him an ability to organize and create, and so increases his respect for organization. The destructive or anarchic urge is usually confined to the mentally retarded, or to those who are brought artificially into contact with overpowering authority. Epaulard does not offer enough details to provide a reliable basis for theorizing about Bertrand's destructiveness. No doubt a Freudian psychologist could have produced certain "traumatic incidents" from Bertrand's childhood to explain it.

Whatever the reasons, Bertrand never outgrew his childish

destructiveness. But he was apparently a good-natured man, who would have been incapable of cruelty to a conscious human being; his male and female acquaintances were unanimous on this point. If Epaulard is accurate in saying that Bertrand began to masturbate at the age of eight (which is at least five years earlier than most male children) then it may be that his sexual development and the natural destructiveness of a child happened to overlap, so that they eventually became associated in his mind. As a good-natured man, he would feel frightened and revolted by the idea of murdering and torturing living women. Therefore, the ideal object for his erotic-destructive impulses was a female corpse. It will be noted that Bertrand was unlike "D.W." in that his prime interest was in mutilating and disfiguring, not in satisfying the normal sexual urge. Bertrand's attitude to his "victims" was one of hatred; "D.W.'s" was almost certainly one of love, as his final offence seems to demonstrate.

The most interesting part of Bertrand's testimony is his description of his feelings after his first attempt at necrophily, "trembling, bathed in cold perspiration, and completely dazed". The repressions, the discipline of the destructive urge, broke like a dam as the opportunity of satisfying them offered itself so suddenly. The repressed urges burst to the surface with a force that shatters him and robs him of all normal caution, so that he beats the corpse with a spade, and attracts attention. All the evidence shows that Bertrand was astounded by his own impulses, but delighted at the same time to realize that there was a possibility of a deeper personal fulfilment than he had so far suspected. This again is evidenced in his statement: "All my enjoyment with living women is as nothing compared to it". The partial consciousness is momentarily completed; the divided personality unites.

There can be no possible room to doubt that Bertrand was a "sadist *manque*" – if such a term is conceivable. But also of interest is his claim that the sadistic impulses had begun to disappear after his last orgy of destruction, during which he went further in mutilation than ever before. This may, of course, have been only temporary. On the other hand, it is possible that, since Bertrand was a strong-minded and religious man, he made an effort of will to arrest the degenerative process, and was only following Blake's formula of exorcizing the "dark energies" by allowing them full scope.

The revolting nature of these cases make it difficult to discuss them with analytic detachment. When Blake writes that it is untrue that "good is of the soul and evil of the body", that "energy is eternal delight", and that repression and frustration are the source of all evil, we can accept the theoretical content of the words without seeing to their practical consequences. But Blake's ideas have a practical application to the Bertrands and "D.W.s" – even to a Christie. Man cannot evolve while he struggles with a split personality. All evil is the result of frustration and of the lop-sided working of the "centres". (Blake symbolizes the centres in his various mythological personages – Urizen, Luvah, Tharmas, etc.) If energy is allowed to flow outwards naturally, without repression, "evil" is an impossibility. Repressions result in psychological "ulcers", curious pockets of poison, that must be drained. The first results of the draining may be disgusting and horrifying – like draining a physical ulcer or boil – but this is necessary. The end will be the health of the organism.

All this, of course, is if the man has the "courage of his own sins", and does not allow the degenerative process to set in by a relaxation of the will. It seems likely that Blake was unaware of the strength of the "repeating mechanism", and therefore of the likelihood that acting-out repressions would lead to degeneration.

And yet Blake's psychology is in many ways more penetrating than the psychology we apply to the "criminally insane". He recognized, for example, that unless a man can cure himself, then he cannot be cured. Psychology can help; but the very idea of psychology contains a fundamental contradiction, for there cannot be a science of the living psyche that sets out to treat it as a mechanic repairs radio sets. In a section of *Thus Spake Zarathustra* called The Pale Criminal, Nietzsche writes of a criminal who is self-condemned by his own contempt. "What is this man? A ball of wild snakes that rarely enjoy rest from each other. . . ." Zarathustra advises the judges to execute the man, because he has already pronounced sentence on himself. This is the judgement that Nietzsche might have passed if he could have seen Christie standing in the dock. But the converse is also true: the criminal who has not condemned himself – Chessman is an obvious example – is always "curable", for his will is actively working towards self-unification.

These considerations lead the argument into curious complexities. The various neurotic types who have been dealt with in this chapter have attempted to act-out their neuroses, to explode their repressions. These neuroses were produced by unusual conditions. When Bertrand became a necrophile his response to the pressure of his neurosis brought him an intensity of experience that surpassed anything that had happened to him. But we are again thinking and judging as if there was a sexual "norm". No doubt Bertrand's responses were abnormal, conditioned as they were by some peculiar destructive neurosis. But is it possible to assert that a certain conditioning is "normal"? It seems likely that "D.W.'s" conditioning was normal, and that only the intensity of adolescent sexual desire and a certain breakdown of inhibitions about death (that came from seeing a girl with whom he had been intimate in her coffin) led to the act of necrophily. De River's assumption that "D.W." was, to some extent, insane, and that his insanity was the result of his conditioning to the death of his sweetheart, ignores the possibility that "D.W." may have exercised an unconscious intentionality – but nevertheless an act of choice – at every stage of his "disease". In a limited situation, with certain desires, he made an act of choice. We may criticize his interpretation of the possibilities of his situation, which led to the act of choice; but it is meaningless to criticize the act of choice from the standpoint of some ideal "norm".

And yet if the act of choice results in sadistic murder, as in

the case of Kürten, there is no alternative to criticizing it from
an "absolute" standpoint. It is possible to make a simple
distinction here, and say that a "moral judgement" becomes
valid if the sexual act involves an invasion of the rights of
another person, as in rape and murder; this would parallel the
case of the Englishman who replied to an anarchist who claimed the right to punch his nose: "Your rights end where my
nose begins". But this would be an evasion of the issue; for
while our laws may declare that consenting adult homosexuals
have a right to sleep together, we can hardly declare that
necrophily should be legalized because it does harm to no one.
In short, we are called upon for a definition of "normality"
within a framework of intentionality. Is it possible to dispense
with moral judgements and the talk of social norms, of talk
of sanity and insanity, and still to arrive at a sensible and
consistent theory of sex that can criticize the intentionality that
results in sadism, necrophily, etc.? If it were possible, the new
theory of intentionality would bear much the same relation to
Freudian psychology that Einstein's relativity bears to Newtonian physics; it is not a denial, but a necessary extension to
meet new cases and problems. This possibility will have to be
left for discussion in the final chapter.

Homosexuality

There is one class of "aberration" with which I do not pro-
pose to deal at length in this book: homosexuality (under
which heading I include also transvestitism, the preference of
certain men for dressing up as women). This is because the
study of homosexuality can contribute nothing distinctive to
the existential theory of perversion that I am attempting to
outline. Of all sexual aberrations, with the exception of
Casanovism, it is the easiest to understand.

To begin with, the borderline between male and female is
blurred. The general public has been made more aware of this
in recent years by the publicity given to cases of "change of
sex"; if men and women can change sex, then it is reasonable
to expect that there should be a whole class of men who are

partly women, and women who are partly men. This is a matter of glands and hormones, not of "perversion". Donald Webster Cory in his book *The Homosexual in America* (1953) states that he was unaware of the fact of homosexuality for at least two years after his first experience of attraction to another man. He speaks of his bewilderment at the feeling, and writes: "I had never been taught that there are men who are attracted to other men. No one had ever attempted to seduce or tempt me". Hence, for a person such as Cory, homosexuality *is* normal, and any other way of life is unthinkable.

De River, however, expresses the belief that only a small proportion of homosexuals can be placed in this category – that is, of men or women whose homosexuality can be explained in terms of endocrine changes. But even agreeing that this may be true, it does not follow that all other types of homosexual are in some way wilfully responsible for their tastes.

At the bottom of homosexuality, as of all other perversions, lies the problem of the "tax on experience". The efficiency of our "feeling mechanism" seems to have been deliberately impaired. This is one of the few generalizations that one can make about human nature with confidence; there appears to be an automatic cut-out, a sort of thermostat, attached to consciousness. So that when the poets complain that man is incapable of gratitude, has an absurdly short memory, is devoured by ambition, is incapable of "counting his blessings" and being happy, they are observing only the mechanism that has led to the achievement of civilization. They are also observing the mechanism that leads to all sexual abnormality. The major component of the sexual urge is the sense of sin – or, to express this more moderately, the sense of invading another's privacy, of escaping one's own separateness. When this contact with another being has been established the sexual cycle is temporarily completed. But the sense of achievement fades, and the continued success of the relation depends upon how far the two beings can maintain their sense of mutual "strangeness". With the Casanova type of man, the strangeness fades inevitably, and can only be renewed with another

sexual partner. For others, minor sexual perversions – cunnilingus, sodomy, or the introduction of other refinements –
serve to overcome the loss of intensity. The "damper" mechanism is to blame.* The "perversion" is an attempt to circum-
vent the damper.

Homosexuality is easily understood as soon as it is grasped
that the effect of the "damper" is to enfeeble the sexual urge
and make it unsure of its objective. The body of a person of
the same sex is, after all, as "private" as the body of a person
of the opposite sex, and its privacy can be violated just as
effectively by the introduction of the sexual member. If
cunnilingus, fellatio, and sodomy can be regarded as attempts
to restore the strangeness and intensity to sexual contact, then
it can be seen that homosexuality might be accepted as the next
logical step.

Homosexuality is easily established as a "norm", particularly if early sexual sensations are associated with a member of
one's own sex. Frank Harris describes how, at his public
school, prefects selected younger boys as pathics, and allowed
their pathics certain privileges. Harris describes how the head
boy in his own dormitory used butter as a lubricant on his
favourites. It can be seen that, under these conditions, intercourse with a younger boy might duplicate fairly closely the
physical and psychological sensations of intercourse with a
girl, with the same elements of dominance, violation, etc., and
that, once this has become established, the pattern might
easily persist into later life. The pathic might later seek out
men who would be willing to violate him – and the tendency
could easily be exaggerated into masochism – while the active
partner would presumably continue to be attracted to feminine
men.

Inevitably the homosexual may drift into other perversions

---

*The analogy is borrowed from atomic physics. Atomic piles contain
"dampers", an absorbent metal that can slow down the reactions, or even
halt it completely in the event of an emergency. These could be compared
to the automatic fire-fighting devices in warehouses used to store in-
flammable goods.

more readily than the heterosexual. To begin with, homosexual relations tend to be more casual than those between heterosexuals. Cory remarks that, although he often thought of proclaiming his temperament and "Live a full and complete life in unison with another male", he found that permanent love attachments in the homosexual world are difficult to achieve. Permanent homosexual "marriages" are known, but they are not frequent. Where a long series of erotic courtships follow one another, the need for diversity may soon lead to "experiment". A fairly typical case is cited in *The Sexual Criminal in Prison* by Mark E. Adams.* "D.G." declared that he had his first sexual experience at the age of ten, when a man with whom he had been swimming committed an act of sodomy on him. After this, he was seduced by a barber, who made him wait behind after the other customers had gone, and performed the act with "D.G." bending over a chair. The subject developed suicidal tendencies, and was treated in a clinic for his homosexuality, but without effect. In New York he lived with a man who taught him to commit fellatio, and then used artificial penises on him, as well as carrots and cucumbers. He soon developed a preference for intercourse with more than one man at a time. He was arrested for the murder of a homosexual who liked to insert vegetables, broom handles and even a Pepsi Cola bottle, into his rectum. The final indignity was the insertion of a sash weight; "D.G." used the weight to murder his companion. The accuracy of De Sade's observation can be recognized here; promiscuity leading to satiety and boredom, which in turn leads to more extreme methods of stimulation.

To summarize: homosexuality, like all other "perversions", is the attempt to compensate for the maddening inefficiency of human consciousness. Insofar as it is a "disease", it is the squirming of a creature with too little freedom; but whether it should be regarded as a disease is an open question; for, like religion, it is man's attempt to improve the poor quality of the consciousness he has been granted.

*Chapter 25 of de River's *The Sexual Criminal*.

There is one important distinction between homosexuality and most of the other "aberrations"; it seldom springs from a distortion of the sexual impulse by the "will to power". Sadism, fetichism, necrophily, all spring from a form of "rape complex"; they are based on the need of the individual to *impose* himself on the sex partner (or the substitute). In homosexuality this is, on the whole, untrue (although Lesbianism is often accompanied by the domination urge). It is also untrue of transvestitism – which is the reason that I classify it with homosexuality rather than with fetichism (although it obviously contains elements of both). A psychologist who accepted Plato's myth of sexuality as symbolically true might say that the transvestite is attempting to unite in himself the male and the female elements that have been artificially sundered by the purposes of procreation, and that the act is an attempt to unite the "divided psyche" and escape the consequences of "original sin". However, these speculations are unnecessarily remote from the centre of the discussion. (It has frequently been remarked that transvestitism is partly a "social disease", since women are not accused of transvestitism if they dress as men.)

The Homosexual Community

Some interesting light is thrown on a neglected aspect of homosexuality in a paper called *The Homosexual Community* by Evelyn Hooker (University of California).* Doctor Hooker is concerned with the "normal homosexual", the homosexual who lives an ordinary social life and regards himself as a member of the homosexual community. Doctor Hooker's researches were conducted in Los Angeles, and they may be taken as typical for any large city in the world.

Homosexuals might be divided into three classes. There is the lone-wolf homosexual, who may feel that his deviation is a "disease" that must be kept carefully concealed, and who feels himself to be an "outsider". But the majority of homosexuals are to be found in the other two classes; the "married" class (that

*Vol. 2, *Personality Research,* Munksgaard, 1962.

is to say, a more or less stable household of two homosexuals) and the "casual class". This third group is probably the largest. In Los Angeles there are apparently about sixty "gay" bars. When a homosexual was asked to define "gay", he replied: "To be gay is to go to the bar, to make the scene, to look and look and look, to have a one-night stand, *to never really love or be loved*, and to really know this, to do it night after night and year after year". (My italics.)

Doctor Hooker describes the "scene" in the gay bars. The bar is a sexual market. Homosexuals stand around and talk – and look. The "look" is important. Two pairs of eyes meet, and observe one another for a moment. A few minutes later the two men may leave the bar casually, sometimes without speaking together. Minutes or hours later the sexual act is performed; they may separate again and go to other bars, or they may stay together for the night. Doctor Hooker writes: "The promiscuity of the homosexual has been attributed to his psycho-dynamic structure; among other things to his primary narcissism which prevents him from forming enduring emotional relationships". The homosexuals who "marry" usually tend to withdraw from this communal activity, in order to safeguard their relationship. They may live in the "homosexual suburbia" – whole streets or blocks that have been taken over by homosexuals (although this may not be known to the neighbours).

The behaviour of the casual "gay" homosexual may be regarded as an example of the Casanovism treated in Chapter II. But the interesting question now arises: How far can this behaviour be regarded as "abnormal"? Doctor Hooker suggests that homosexual relations are more casual than heterosexual relations because sex means more to a woman than to a man, and because she stands to lose so much more by promiscuity. It can also be argued that women have a stronger instinct for security that is a part of their child-bearing capacity. But in that case, the male–female relation is not "normal", in that it is a matter of taboos that may strike the male as arbitrary. The female imposes these taboos in order to channel the "casual" sexual instincts of all men into narrow currents of social acceptability.

There are also many arguments to be urged against this point of view. Societies in which the women have drifted into the casual attitude to sex are usually decadent. Moreover, casual sex and mental instability often seem to be related. The reason for this is plain enough. Casual sex leaves nothing behind; when it is over there is a sense of being back at the beginning again. The more often it is repeated, the more meaningless it becomes. For anyone with any instinct for "meaning" in life, too much casual sex would produce a suicidal despair because it always brings a sense of having been successfully "conned", of having tried hard to grasp something that has melted away. This problem has been touched on in Chapter II.

If homosexuality has so far been given prominence in books dealing with sexual deviations, this is mainly because it has previously been associated with social ostracism, and has consequently been the cause of neuroses. It is difficult for the homosexual of today to realize the torments of guilt felt by a Tchaikovsky or Schubert, and their agonies of concealment. Since Gide, many well-known writers have openly proclaimed their homosexuality without unpleasant consequences. Although it is now generally recognized that certain social evils associated with homosexuality (corruption of minors, etc.) must continue to be legally condemned, sexual inversion is no longer counted as proof of moral obliquity.

CHAPTER VII

SADISM AND THE CRIMINAL MENTALITY

Existentialism and its categories. Inauthentic existence, bad faith, etc. The Pieydagnelle case. Case of sadistic rape. The Stacey case. Freud. John Cowper Powys and sadism. The Kürten case. Freud's death wish and theory of aggression. The sexual impulse in animals. Gestalt theory. A case of bestiality. The Existential alternative to Freud. A note on the prevention of sex crime.

SADISM presents far the most complex of problems to existential analysis.

We should begin by making a distinction between true sadism and sado-masochism. The true sadist experiences no more identification with his victim than a diner experiences for the steak he devours. The sado-masochist "identifies", to some extent; he is also hurting himself, but enjoys the pain. Sado-masochism is not difficult to understand. The least masochistic person knows that pain can, to some extent, be "enjoyed". Seven-year-old children enjoy tugging at loose teeth, although this is slightly painful. Pain is a stimulant, in small doses.

Happiness – or pleasure – might be defined as the intensification of consciousness, dissipation of the dullness of our senses. Physical pleasure can be divided into two types: stimulating and soothing. The pleasure of a good meal to an empty stomach is soothing. The pleasure of stretching the muscles when you get out of bed is stimulating – a kind of discharge of a static electricity stored in the muscles. Masochism is associated with this second type of pleasure. The discharge of this "static electricity" seems to clear the head and the senses. And small degrees of pain – like being pinched or gently slapped – can affect this discharge. When a person becomes accustomed to being slapped or pinched, he (or she) becomes capable of taking larger "doses". And since sexual pleasure is also a kind of discharge of static electricity it is easy to see how the pain stimulus can become associated with sex. In some cases, of course, the inflictor of pain has a sexual motive that is not necessarily sadistic. Hirschfeld mentions a case in which a governess caught two boys masturbating, and beat them on the buttocks. "It burned my behind like fire, but the same time it prickled so pleasantly, so delightfully. It was the blows that did it; it had never been so nice when we masturbated. . . . And later I noticed that the governess's hands, during the now regular chastisement, frequently strayed between my legs and stayed there. So we were glad of the blows, and when the happy days were over we longed for them". All that has happened here is that the governess has found an excuse for participating in the sexual play of the boys while providing herself with an excuse.* Another case describes how a schoolmistress "always arranged her clothes in such a manner that when we were being thrashed we could push our hands in and feel her breasts, the heaving of which frequently gave us a pleasant sensation. Many of the boys earned a flogging merely in order to experience this sensation".† In *Crime and the Sexual Psychopath*, de River prints a photograph distributed by prostitutes for flagellants, showing a schoolmistress chastising a boy; she wears a short skirt, and has one leg on a chair; the photograph is taken in such a way as to suggest that the boy's genitals are in close contact with those of the schoolmistress.‡ In all these cases it is clear that the "sadism" is only the initial excuse for sex-play. Another case cited by Hirschfeld makes this even clearer.§ A young widow with two daughters, aged twelve and fourteen, asked a male friend to chastise them for misbehaviour. At first the girls had only to pull down their knickers, but later, were made to strip naked to be

*Sexual Anomalies and Perversions, London Encyclopedic Press, p. 359.
†ibid., p. 367.
‡Crime and the Sexual Psychopath, Charles C. Thomas, p. 63.
§Hirschfeld: p. 361.

beaten. "When the elder girl refused to appear naked in front of the 'family adviser' she was permitted to wear a tiny pair of red bathing shorts which hardly covered her genital organs. The mother held the child, and the chastisement was carried out in such a manner that the girl lay on her back on the sofa, and her legs were bent back towards her head. The mother frequently let the bathing shorts slip off so that the chastising man could see the girl's vagina." Finally, the mother, after having all three children chastised together (there was also a boy) asked the "adviser" to beat her, which he did. Hirschfeld does not add whether the two adults finally threw off the pretences and became lovers. But again, it can be seen that the element of sadism may or may not have been present; the beatings were an excuse for establishing a kind of sexual relation between the children and the adults. But it is obvious that the sexual stimulation and the pain could easily become associated in the mind of the children and the adults, causing the children to develop masochistic, and the adults sadistic, tendencies.

In all these cases the sadism is a matter of *faute de mieux*. But it must also be remembered that the secretive element is important, and intensifies the pleasure to a point that would be impossible in a more open relationship. The idea of the forbidden is essential in sex; without the sense of the violation of an alien being, sexual excitement would be weakened, or perhaps completely dissipated. (Both Maupassant and Stendhal have amusing accounts of "fiascos" that occur when the desired object is suddenly made *too* available.)

But the above considerations explain only minor degrees of sadism and masochism. They do not explain sadistic murder, or the true sadism that has no element of masochism. This is an altogether more difficult matter. The difficulty here is in understanding how the sadist can so completely fail to "identify" with his victim. Bertrand, as has already been noted, was too good-natured to be a sadist, in spite of his curious craving to break things. He "identified" too easily. This identification is a natural outcome of man's place on the evolutionary ladder;

man is the most "social" of all animals. We note that the least
social animals are the cruellest. There is a definite connection
between cruelty and loneliness. The remote ancestors of the
dog probably hunted in packs, like wolves; it is hard to imagine cats associating in packs. It follows naturally that the dog
is an affectionate animal, with almost no cruelty in his com-
position, while the cat is strangely selfish, and enjoys torment-
ing its living prey. Man, as the most social of all animals,
should therefore be the least cruel. This is what makes true
sadism so difficult to comprehend.

But there are many other factors to take into account. First
of all, the least energetic animals are the least cruel; we cannot
imagine cows or deer – or even crocodiles and hippopotami –
being cruel. They are too lazy. But we can associate cruelty
with the tiger and the cat (even with the spider, another "lone
wolf", noted for his tireless industry and patience). Cruelty is
often the outcome of surplus energy seeking an escape. (The
word "energetic" occurs frequently in the advertisements of
sadists and masochists: "Energetic lady offers her services to
men requiring discipline. . . .") When energy is associated
with stupidity, the result is frequently sadism, since the stupidity finds it hard to devise outlets for the energy.

Equally important is the element of fear or inferiority feeling. Either of these prevent identification. To say that a man is
afraid of another is almost synonymous with saying that he is
capable of cruelty to him. Children can be crueller than most
adults because they feel inferior to adults, and altogether
less sure of themselves in the face of the world and other
children.

The study of statistics of sex crime reveals that sexual
criminals fall into three main groups: (a) idiots and morons,
who inevitably feel inferior to the rest of society, and whose
conditions condemn them, to some extent, to being "lone
wolves", (b) men with a criminal record for other offences,
and who therefore feel a certain guilt and resentment towards
society, (c) abnormally sensitive and neurotic men who lack
a sense of "contact" with society. Typical of the first group is

the school guard cited by De River, who murdered the three children; Straffen, the English child murderer, is another example; obviously an idiot, he was confined in a mental institution.* The second type of criminal may be extremely intelligent, like Chessman or Kürten. But early clashes with the law develop a feeling of resentment against society, and this becomes an excuse for indulging an over-developed sexual instinct. He may also feel that he has been treated unjustly by society, and is entitled to get his own back. It is the third type of criminal who gives most cause for alarm, for it is inevitable that the number of such men should increase in a highly mechanized civilization. He feels that he has nothing in common with the people who pass him in the street; they are all strangers, as alien as Martians. Since he is immature, emotionally undeveloped, he may be as serenely selfish as a child. The Peoria murderer, Gerald Thompson (executed in 1935) is typical of this type of criminal. Thompson knocked out his female victims, raped them in the back of his car, and took photographs of the girls in the act of violating them. He then told the girls that the photographs would be sent to their friends if they laid any complaints. He also wrote about these rapes in detail in a diary – more than fifty of them. His murder of Mildred Hallmark led to a manhunt and his arrest. Here is the true sadistic attitude – total lack of identification with the victim, who remains an "object" even when he is involved in conversation with her. It would be interesting to know details of Thompson's earlier life – whether a lack of affection in childhood led to this "independent" attitude to other human beings.

Although Thompson killed only one of his victims – and this was probably by accident – he is undoubtedly a "true sadist"; he played with his victims like a cat with a mouse. One girl told how he kept her in his car for nearly two hours before

*From which, unfortunately, he succeeded in escaping a few years after his confinement. Before he was caught, he murdered another female child. The case led to an investigation into the precautions taken against escape from the Broadmoor Institution.

completing the assault. Most sexual criminals prefer the victim to be unconscious, and get the assault over as quickly as possible; many testify to feelings of remorse afterwards; they may even, like Heirens, feel themselves to be double personalities, Jekyll and Hyde. Thompson was apparently quite single-minded in his delight in rape, gloating over the details later with no element of remorse. Such total lack of "identification" is unusual. Far more typical is the case of Morris Leland, the rapist of Portland, Oregon, who stated, in his confession to the murder of a fifteen-year-old girl: "She was such a nice, sweet kid, I didn't want to kill her at all. . . . I slugged her over the head. When she was out, I didn't mind stabbing her". And yet Leland, like Thompson, made a habit of holding women prisoner and threatening them with a knife until he had completed the assault. (He was executed, four years after the murder, in 1953.)

It might almost be said that men like Thompson and Leland are "outsider" types; they feel no connection with the rest of society. I have pointed out elsewhere that a society like ours inevitably creates "outsiders", men who live in society and yet do not feel as if they "belong". This is not to say that the "outsider" is the potential sex criminal, for sex crime usually seems to be associated with arrested emotional development, the child's tendency to grab what he wants without thinking of the consequences. But if the increasing impersonality of society causes outsiders to multiply, it is logical that the number of "outsider" sexual criminals should multiply in a certain mathematical proportion.

It should be recognized that the tendency to discount other people is not necessarily a sign of social unfitness. In his *Stories of Mr. Keuner*, Bert Brecht has an anecdote that underlines this point.

"What do you do", Mr. Keuner was asked, "when you love a person?" "I make a sketch", said Mr. Keuner, "and then make sure that I get a good likeness." "To the person?" "No," said Mr. Keuner, "to the sketch."

That is to say, the condition of Mr. Keuner's love is that its object should fit herself to his idea of her. But here the attitude is that of an intolerant man of genius who wants to raise people to the level of his ideals. Brecht, the "intellectual outsider", treats the other person as an object to satisfy an intellectual ideal. The sadist treats the other as an object in order to satisfy a physical appetite.

Existentialism and the Psychology of Sadism

Sadism is plainly connected with the need for self-assertion. At the same time it cannot be separated from the idea of *defeat*. A sadist is a man who, in some sense, has his back to the wall. Nothing is farther from sadism, for example, than the cheerful, optimistic mentality of a Shaw or Wells.

This sense of defeat requires closer analysis. It was Heidegger who first introduced into existentialism the concepts of "authentic" and "inauthentic" existence. For Heidegger, authentic existence is existence in the race of death – the sudden knowledge of the value of life, the intensity and determination.

Clearly this "authentic existence" of Heidegger has something in common with Gurdjieff's idea of a man with all seven centres working in harmony. In fact, Gurdjieff makes one of his characters (in *All and Everything*) say that what man needs most is an organ whereby he can always perceive the hour of his own death. Our laziness, our lack of sense of urgency, our boredom, leads us to live in this curiously half-hearted and inefficient way. This "normal living" Heidegger calls inauthentic existence.

Sartre extended Heidegger's psychology by adding another term to it: the idea of "bad faith". Sartre pointed out (in *Being and Nothingness*) that inauthentic existence means that man is seldom aware of his own existence. His attention is turned outwards to natural events. He knows himself as a kind of "hole in Nature" rather than as a solid reality. It is only in certain moments of intensity – in the sexual orgasm, for example – that man becomes aware of himself as an active existence, not merely as an object that is always acted upon.

But man dislikes this feeling of nonentity, this perpetual self-doubt. So he is inclined to enter into a compact with other human beings to turn away from it, a compact of mutual praise and self-respect. He asks to be treated as an *identity* – as a "man of substance", for example – because the respect of other people reassures him when he faces the emptiness inside himself. It is rather as if a man who had a stiff neck, and could not therefore look down to reassure himself that his body existed, built himself a hall of mirrors so that he would find himself reflected in all directions.

Sartre calls this compact of mutual reassurance *mauvais-foi*, or self-delusion. His work is mainly of value in analysing the various species of self delusion. For example, two of his finest works deal with anti-semitism – his story *Childhood of a Leader*, and the essay *Portrait of the Anti-Semite*. Both these treat anti-semitism as man's attempt to escape his own futility.

Sartre also points out that even the brittle self-belief given us by our sense of identity can be taken away very easily. If you are caught doing something discreditable, you "see yourself" through the eyes of the person who has caught you; identity vanishes completely; you become wholly an object observed by the other person, a mere hole in the universe. There is no small internal spark that declares "I exist". The intuitions fall into the subconscious as if down a lift-shaft; man is left stranded in his mere reason and in feelings that spring from outside – humiliation, pain – instead of the feelings that come from inside.

Being caught doing something discreditable is an extreme example. (A man about to be executed would be an even more extreme example; he would feel that whatever "reality" he possesses is in the hands of his executioners, and is about to be thrown away as useless.) But almost every moment of the day brings some minor emergency that snatches away a tiny part of our identity. Mr. Eliot points out that merely missing a step as we are walking downstairs gives us a sense of being a mere object, a victim of fate. (I should point out that "existential psychology" is by no means the invention of Sartre and

Heidegger; it pervades modern literature from Dostoevsky onwards.)

Whitehead invented a term that is invaluable for the existential psychologist: the idea of "prehension". Prehension is the act of digesting our experience. Sartre once made the dubious assertion that our most fundamental experience is one of nausea – that a kind of sickness lies at the bottom of our consciousness. Whitehead's prehension is a less extreme version of this notion. When you feel sick, you frequently make an effort *not* to be sick; if it is successful, whatever is troubling the stomach is persuaded to allow itself to be digested. But nothing is ever digested *automatically*; all the workings of the body spring from an unconscious act of will. So the conscious effort not to be sick might be regarded as an extreme form of the effort the stomach makes after every meal. And prehension is also a non-stop process, since the meal of experience never ceases. It may be a very difficult experience to digest – like some personal tragedy or humiliation. It may only be the experience of slipping as you walk downstairs. But the living being makes a non-stop effort of prehension.

This prehension is obviously closely connected with intentionality. As you read a newspaper attentively, you *prehend* its content. If your attention wanders, you will read without "taking it in" (prehending). But this is only another way of saying that "intentionality" has ceased to function – the act of filtering, selecting, arranging the meanings of each sentence. Intentionality is the ante-room of prehension, as necessary to it as the mouth to the stomach.

Before passing from these general considerations to the problem of sadism, a further approach should be indicated. We might pose the general question: How much attention "ought" we to accord to each individual in order to feel ourselves "correctly" involved – that is to say, not involved in a way that could lead (in the case of a potential lover) to an abnormal sexual relationship, like that of the sadist to his victim? The Christian would answer unhesitatingly that we should be completely and deeply involved with each individual, aiming at total understanding and love. This may be so, but an immediate objection presents itself. When we speak to a single individual, we may suddenly experience him intensely and uniquely as an alien world. The Christian would declare that this relation is preferable to treating the other as a mere object, as a kind of equation or symbol rather than as a unique world. But human life being what it is, how is it possible to behave to everyone in this "Christian" manner? The problem is analogous to that of Oscar Wilde's happy prince, who suffered acutely because of other people's misery, but had to realize that he could not carry all the misery of the world on his own shoulders. A good Christian (or a good humanist) may feel that there is something immoral in treating anyone as less than a complete human being; but we could not live in any other way. The indifference of the sadist to his victim's "true being" is only an extreme form of the indifference that even the most "Christian" of us is forced to practise on ninety per cent of his acquaintance.

Heidegger's notion of inauthentic existence supplies the basic concept for grasping the mentality of the sadist. A man caught spying through a keyhole – and thus reduced to a sense of being a mere object, pinned like a butterfly on the end of another's regard – has lost all vestige of "inner direction", of subjectivity, and therefore of the ability to treat another person as a complete human being. Shaw remarked that our interest in the world is the overflow of our interest in ourselves. A man who has been completely robbed of his subjectivity cannot be expected to take very much sympathetic interest in the world, or to make the Bergsonian effort to penetrate the being of another by an act of loving intuition.

The first thing one realizes about the sadist – as about the criminal in general – is that he is a man who has lost his battle with the world, lost his subjectivity. There is essentially an element of prolonged adolescence, of immaturity, about sadism. The sadist, like the habitual criminal, is usually a compulsive liar. His lying reveals his immaturity, for most men know that lying is usually a bad bargain, a social miscal-

culation that wastes far more energy than it saves. The case of
Neville Heath, mentioned in the previous chapter, is typical.
When finally arrested for the murders of Margery Gardner
and Doreen Marshall, Heath had a long record of petty crime.
One of the writers on the case has said that most of Heath's
crimes were connected with vanity and the need to impress.
(Crime writers often take a regrettable "high moral tone", as
if to answer in advance the accusation that they are exploiting
crime for cash.) But vanity and the need to impress are not in
themselves signs of a criminal; they might also be the main-
springs of the most selfless social reformer. We are all vain;
we all want to impress; as Shaw points out, we all bid for
admiration with no intention of earning it. This is nothing.
What is pathetic in reading about men like Heath or Christie
is that their notion of how to gain admiration is so unimagina-
tive. For Heath, a typical Don Juan type, it meant endless
sexual conquests. Since he lacked Casanova's resourcefulness
in finding money, he swindled in an unenterprising way, passing dud cheques and borrowing money on false security. The
poverty of his imagination made his world a far duller place
than that of Casanova. As De Sade predicted, this lack of
imagination and the satiety that was its natural consequence
led to an overstraining of the pleasure nerve.

According to a book written by an acquaintance of Heath's,
he was known at school as a bully, and one day beat an eight-
year-old girl so badly that she had to be admitted to hospital.
But it is interesting to note that his first victim (his first known
victim, that is) was a masochist who accompanied him to a
hotel with the full knowledge that he wanted to ill-treat her.
Heath mutilated and killed her. And yet only a few days before, Heath had picked up a respectable girl who spent the
night with him (on a promise of marriage); she asserted that
she had no suspicion of Heath's sadistic tendencies. Heath's
wife also declared that he treated her gently. This tendency to
inflict pain on the helpless is distinctly a characteristic of early
childhood; its persistence is a sign of Heath's retarded development.

This, however, is no help in the understanding of the sadistic impulse as it revealed itself in Heath. It is important at this point to distinguish between the genuine sadistic impulse, and the desire simply to punish by inflicting pain. We say loosely that the Grand Inquisitor Torquemada was a sadist. There is no evidence whatever for this view. Shaw's Inquisitor in *Saint Joan* is a perfect example of the kind of man Torquemada may have been – completely sincere, preoccupied only with the "eternal damnation" of those whom he punished.

But it is possible to be far more involved in the pain inflicted on a "culprit" without being a sadist. Torquemada might have felt a certain grim pleasure in watching heretics die – and those who were condemned were only those who had defied him by refusing to become Christians – without being a "sadist" in the precise sense of the word. A man who relieves his anger, or outraged righteousness, by inflicting pain is not necessarily a sadist, although he may be disguising a sexual component from himself. The sadist is the man who is *sexually excited* by pain.

Hirschfeld describes an interesting case of genuine sadism that will make this distinction clear. He was speaking of the French murderer Eusebius Pieydagnelle, upon whom Zola based Jacques Lantier in *La Bête Humaine*. Pieydagnelle was tried in 1871 for four murders. When Pieydagnelle was a child he became fascinated by the butcher's shop opposite his parents' house in Vinuville; it was owned by a M. Cristobal. "The smell of fresh blood, the appetizing meat, the bloody lumps – all this fascinated me, and I began to envy the butcher's assistant because he could work at the block with rolled up sleeves and bloody hands." Unfortunately we are not told whether Pieydagnelle masturbated in childhood, or why he came to associate the smell of blood with sex. He persuaded his parents to apprentice him to M. Cristobal, and he began to drink blood in secret and wound the cattle. (Blood is an emetic; Pieydagnelle does not mention how he managed to drink it without being sick.) He was also allowed to slaughter cattle himself, which gave him the greatest pleasure of all. However, his parents decided that he should be apprenticed to a lawyer. He became depressed, and began killing people. He felt some guilt about his murders – six of them – and tried living alone in a cave in a wood; the urge was too strong for him, and he returned to kill. His last victim was his employer, M. Cristobal. It is apparent, from the brief account given by Hirschfeld, that Pieydagnelle derived pleasure solely from the sight of blood, not from committing any sexual act on his victims (most of whom were women). Pieydagnelle finally gave himself up voluntarily; his acts horrified him so much that he begged the jury to sentence him to death.

Here, the split personality noted in an earlier chapter becomes apparent. The sadist has a sense of himself as two persons; his sexual urges actually frighten him. De River cites a case in which this is interestingly apparent. A twenty-one-year-old youth spoke to a girl at a bus stop late at night, and offered to walk her home. She accepted, and even turned into a lonely park with him. When he tried to kiss her she pulled away (probably out of coquetry, since she had agreed to walk with him and allowed him to put his arms around her). He put his hands around her throat, and after a struggle, throttled her into unconsciousness. He raped her, and when she recovered, knocked her unconscious again, and tied some clothing round her neck; he then carried her some distance, into a building, and raped her again; he also bit off one of her nipples and swallowed it. Then he went to the nearest house, telephoned the police, and gave himself up. (He stated: "I knew I had done wrong.") De River believes that the girl's resistance excited the sadistic urge; if she had allowed him to kiss her she would probably not have been killed. The youth had no criminal record, was not addicted to alcohol or drugs, and lived with a girl who had borne him a child and with whom he was happy. His immediate response to his crime was to give himself up; it is evident that he was shocked by the urges that suddenly overwhelmed him. (He was sentenced to life imprisonment.)

In certain respects this case is similar to any other case of violent rape; it might be argued that, like Pommerenke, this youth only wanted to render his victims "incapable of resisting". But there is an obvious difference between this act of violation and the cases cited in the previous chapter. Most young men would find their sexual excitement diminishing as they had to struggle with the girl; here, it was increased. The brutality required to silence the girl would cause a certain remorse to most men after the act of violation; here, the excitement of knocking her unconscious (by beating her head against the concrete road) so inflamed him that he carried her to a place where they would not be interrupted, and violated her again, as well as indulging in various sadistic practices.

Again, not enough details are supplied by de River to explain how, in this case, the sexual impulse had become associated, on a certain level, with the infliction of pain. Admittedly it may never be possible to explain this satisfactorily. The sheer power of the sexual impulse defies close analysis. In air raids during the war, rescuers noted the anomalies of bomb-blasts; a whole house would be reduced to ruins, and yet a feather duster lying on a table would be unmoved. Obviously there is no hope of one day creating an infallible science of bomb-blasts that will be able to explain exactly why these things happen. A man who observed that, in a storm, heaps of leaves were being driven before the wind, but that one single leaf was travelling in the opposite direction, might well feel that his sanity depends upon a simple and scientific explanation. But wind is one thing; bomb-blast is another. So the vagaries of the sexual urge may ultimately defy analysis. Usually the explosion is well controlled; the man making love to his wife is not likely to be suddenly overwhelmed by a desire that makes him aware of his split personality. But if the circumstances are unusual and sudden, the uncontrolled blast may throw up all kinds of strange and forgotten urges from the bottom of the subconscious. Bertrand's feverish excitement on seeing the woman in the open grave is an example. A recent Chicago murder case illustrated the same point. A sixteen-year-old housewife was found battered to death; she was wearing only an open dressing-gown and panties. A baby lying in its cot was unhurt. Eventually it was discovered that a young photographer named Stacey had called that day. He turned out to be a religious young man with a strong sense of "sin". Finally he confessed that he had called to photograph the baby; the mother had received him in her dressing-gown (at mid-morning). As she bent over the cot the gown fell open, revealing that she was almost nude. Stacey was immediately overwhelmed by sexual desire; he seized a baseball bat that he carried in his bag and battered her to death. Then, horrified by his crime, he fled without assaulting her. It is not difficult to understand the psychology of this particular murder. The girl may have intended the open gown as an invitation; for the somewhat repressed young man, the need to possess her suddenly became the only important thing in the world. Too uncertain – and perhaps too excited – to try an ordinary sexual advance, he knocked her unconscious. It is possible that Stacey became a murderer by pure bad luck; in his position a great many other young men might have ended as murderers – or at least as rapists; others might have known how to take advantage of the situation, and ended only as satisfied lovers.

Cases like this – and the case cited by de River – might give the impression that sadism is easily comprehensible as a kind of bastard derivative of the sexual impulse. Even the least cruel of men might take a certain pleasure in feeling that he dominates a woman; sadism is only this domination pushed to abnormality. And most healthy men would be capable of rape under extreme circumstances; is this not also a type of sadism? But these conclusions are less reliable than they might seem at first sight. Although Pieydagnelle murdered women with a sexual motive (he described his desire to kiss a sleeping woman, and then how the impulse to stab her overcame him), the original impulse of sadism was connected with the smell of blood and the butcher's shop. In his *Life of Conan Doyle*, John Dickson Carr cites a curious case in which Doyle played detective; at Great Wyrely, in the Potteries, a maniac made a habit of creeping up to cattle asleep in the fields at night, and disembowelling them. In letters to the police he gleefully re-counted details of his mutilations, and added that he would start on small girls in the near future. A man named George Edalji – son of a Persian clergyman – was arrested and tried; he was sentenced to seven years' penal servitude, although the case against him was very thin indeed. Doyle, convinced of his innocence, played "Sherlock Holmes", and finally traced the real culprit, a youth whom Carr calls "Peter Hudson". This youth had been to the same school as Edalji, and had always borne him a grudge; even at school he had showed a predilec-tion for using a knife; he used to rip open leather cushions on the railway, and his father had to pay several fines for leather straps that his son had destroyed. Although Edalji was freed after three years, and admitted to be innocent, "Peter Hud-son" was never prosecuted. Hudson probably used a large horse lancet to mutilate the animals; the incisions were long, but not deep. Apparently he ceased to mutilate cattle after the case; Doyle's investigations had probably frightened him.

"Peter Hudson" is closer to the type of the genuine sadist than de River's sex killer. The need to slit leather cushions and straps is a pure destructive impulse that may be totally unconnected with sex. Many children find knives irresistible; a surface of tight leather seems almost to ask to be cut with a razor edge. This is the same kind of urge that leads to building elaborate reservoirs of sand, filling them with water, and then poking a small hole in one of the walls for the pleasure of watching the water sweeping them away.

Carefully observed cases of sadism are remarkably in-frequent in psychological literature. This may be because the theory of sadism is so incomplete that psychologists see no point in multiplying their data. Freud, for example, writes in *Three Contributions to the Theory of Sex*: "That cruelty and the sexual instinct are most intimately connected is beyond doubt taught by the history of civilization, but in the explanation of this connection, no one has gone beyond the accentuation of the aggressive factors of the libido." He adds that it is possible that in sadism and masochism "many psychic strivings unite herein into one effect", and says that sadism and masochism originate from a special source in the impulses that differentiates them from the other perversions. But Freud himself made little advance beyond this position, and in the book already quoted, devotes only two pages to sadism and masochism. The peculiar limitations of the Freudian approach can be seen in the following comment:

"I have no doubt that the concept of 'beauty' is rooted in the soil of sexual stimulation, *and signified originally that which is sexually exciting*. [My italics.] The more remarkable, therefore, is the fact that the genitals, the sight of which provokes the greatest sexual excitement, can really never be considered 'beautiful'." (*Op. cit.*, footnote to Chapter I.)

It follows from such a comment that objects of beauty – landscapes, for example – must be somehow regarded as sexual symbols: the hills are breasts, a lake is the vagina, etc. This approach reveals a naïve kind of "fundamentalism". The sexual urge is undeniable, even to the most old-fashioned nineteenth-century materialist. The "love energies" (libido) may also be taken as "given". The idea of a sense of beauty rooted in an intuitive hunger for freedom must be dismissed as too metaphysical. So instead of treating all manifestations of beauty – including music, visual appreciation, religious strivings and the sexual impulse – as expressions of the same evolutionary freedom-hunger, all must somehow be reduced to the one certain factor, the libido. Freud then finds himself faced with a paradox: all beauty is somehow a reflection of the lust aroused by the sight of the genitals, and yet the genitals are less beautiful than a lake or a Beethoven symphony. Because he could not think of sex as an evolutionary urge – in fact, could not admit the existence of a non-mechanical evolutionary striving – he is left with a barren reduction of all such impulses to the level of libido. He might have made a start on deflating his own hypothesis by reflecting that Venus sitting with open thighs exposing her genitals would somehow be less beautiful than the form Praxiteles gave her. Not only are the genitals not particularly beautiful, but it is also untrue that the "core" of the perception of beauty is directed towards the genitals. Most men would agree that a woman lying naked with her legs open is usually less sexually desirable than a fully or partly clothed woman.

Freud's error here arises from an employment of an "analytic" instead of a Gestalt psychology. It is somehow the total "Gestalt" of the woman that is sexually attractive. Freud implies that the vagina is a kind of light-source, and that if a lover finds the neck and hair beautiful, it is because they reflect this light. Gestalt psychology declares that the light-source is somehow behind the whole body, in some more ultimate evolutionary urge; and that, what is more, it is exactly the same light-source that lends beauty to a landscape, a symphony, a social-reformer's urge to improve society. It is true that the genitals are a kind of whirlpool in the midst of the sexual rapids, and that appreciation of a girl's face and figure can suck a man towards the vortex of desire; this is because the evolutionary "light-source" is reflected most intensely at this point. But it is also true that the power of the whirlpool depends upon detachment from it; the greater the detachment, the greater its power. A woman's attraction diminishes in proportion as she is seen as an isolated object, as a "mere woman", a "mere body" or even as a "mere vagina"; it increases as she is seen as a portion of a whole, a social or a biological context. The ladies of King Arthur's knights derived attraction from their social context, the conventions that made them modest, withdrawn embodiments of a kind of angelic "eternal feminine". Aldous Huxley's Katy (in *The Genius and the Goddess*) derives her attractions from making men aware of her as a part of a biological context, as a sort of symbol of womanhood. It can be seen that the Gestalt treatment of the sexual problem is somehow more adequate than the Freudian analytical approach.

These considerations explain why Freud and his followers never succeeded in producing a "unifying theory" of sadism. With the libido as the only "ultimate", to which all "aberrated impulses" must be somehow reduced, it is hardly surprising that the problem of sadism should remain impenetrable to Freudian analysis.

An interesting – if somewhat vague – suggestion to explain sadism as an "evolutionary perversion" is made by John Cowper Powys in his novel *A Glastonbury Romance*. Powys himself admits freely in his autobiography that "from earliest childhood up to the present hour, my dominant vice has been the most dangerous of all vices. I refer to Sadism." Powys confined his abnormality to sadistic fantasies up to his fiftieth year, after which he "cured himself" – at least of the tendency to indulge voluntarily. Professor Wilson Knight writes of Powys:

". . . in *A Glastonbury Romance* we meet one of the strangest and most terrifying studies in fiction – the sadistic Mr. Evans. Mr. Evans is a lovable, academically minded man with a fondness for old Welsh manuscripts but tormented by a recurring sadistic obsession utterly at variance with his better nature. The problem is not handled as a 'perversion' attributable to some fault in upbringing or charcter; rather is Mr. Evans' sexual mechanism shown as directly reflecting and responding to that side of the creative process, or great 'First Cause' which is responsible for the manifest cruelties of the cosmic scheme."

Powys writes about Mr. Evans:

". . . [he] was able to get rid of every embodiment of his dark temptation, except one single passage in 'The Unpardonable Sin' which some supernaturally crafty devil might have composed especially to devastate and overwhelm him. Certain images called up by this particular passage were so seductive that his knees grew weak as he thought of them. The worst of these images had to do with a killing blow delivered by an iron bar. . . . Such abominable wickedness came straight out of the evil in the heart of the First Cause, travelled through interlunar spaces, and entered the particular nerve in the erotic organ of Mr. Evans which was predestined to respond to it."

Such language may seem unnecessarily literary or symbolic. And yet it deserves careful consideration. Powys admitted to feeling himself all the torments he describes in Mr. Evans: "He saw his soul in the form of an unspeakable worm, writhing in pursuit of new, and ever new mental victims, drinking new and ever new innocent blood." In a powerful passage in his auto-biography, Powys describes how he one day walked over the hills obsessed by this urge to destroy and torture, struggling with a desire to smash things and kill animals and birds. A man who has wrestled with these problems (in such a personal form, and who has applied his very considerable analytical intellect to understanding them, might be expected to produce profounder conclusions than a psychologist whose interest is solely academic or professional. Powys's idea of "evil in the first cause" (which can be found in many Christian mystics including Boehme) may be as symbolic as Plato's myth of the gods cutting men into two; it may also contain as much psychological truth.

At least Powys's vision is basically that of Gestalt and existential psychology. Sex *can* be analysed down to its components – with an emphasis on the genital organs – and the result is self-contradictory. Sri Ramakrishna once told his disciples that if they felt lured by a woman, they should reflect that women were made up of disagreeable things like blood, gristle, and bones. This is good Freudian reasoning; sex is not explained by reducing it to its elements, any more than life is explained by anatomizing the body. But to do Ramakrishna justice, he would not have considered that sex was adequately explained in terms of blood and gristle, nor would he have felt in the least surprised that the genital organs themselves are not beautiful. He would have declared that all beauty is a reflection of the Divine Mother, the eternal creative power of Brahman, and that each woman is a tiny mirror reflecting a small part of that power. The mirror is made of silvered tin; but this does not mean that the power is an illusion. And like Powys, Ramakrishna would have had no difficulty in understanding sadism, since Kali is simultaneously creator and destroyer, portrayed as a black-faced woman who holds a sword and a severed head in two of her hands, and who offers blessings to her children with the other two; she wears a necklace of human skulls, and stands on the body of her husband Shiva, for he symbolizes only conscious life. She is the complete irrational power of the life force, a glimpse of which made Nietzsche write that "war is a deeper and nobler impulse than the urge to peace".

Incomparably the best study in sadism that has so far been produced is Professor Berg's *Der Sadist,* a study of the mass murderer Peter Kürten. Berg does not theorize; he offers only facts. But no previous study of a sadist offered so many facts that illuminate the deeper motivations.

Kürten, who was executed in July 1931, admitted to committing nine murders and fourteen attacks that involved serious wounding. Professor Karl Berg, who acted as psychologist for the Düsseldorf police, saw a great deal of Kürten in jail, and soon won his complete confidence. At first Kürten declared that his crimes had been committed to revenge himself on society. (He had spent twenty-seven of his forty-eight years in prison.) Later he admitted that the motive was wholly sexual. He proved to be a man of exceptional intelligence and of unusual honesty. Unlike Nietzsche's "pale criminal", he accepted his perversions as a part of his nature, and experienced no pangs of conscience. His case history, as related to Berg over a period of many months, is as follows:

Kürten was born in 1883 in Köln-Mulheim, the son of a brutal and violent moulder. The family of thirteen lived for a time in a single room in conditions of extreme degradation.

From a very early age the element of sex became important in Kürten's life. When his father came home drunk he frequently beat Frau Kürten, and just as frequently forced her to have sexual intercourse. To the young Kürten, who could often see and hear this quite plainly, it seemed that his mother was being violated. His father also attempted incest with one of Kürten's sisters, as a result of which spent fifteen months in jail. Kürten claimed that all his sisters were oversexed, and that one of them attempted to seduce him. He also attempted

– unsuccessfully – to have intercourse with the sister whom his father had tried to rape.*

In this atmosphere of misery and degradation the sole outlet for evolutionary energy was the sexual urge. When he was about eight years old he became a friend of a sadistic dog-catcher who lived in the basement. This man taught Kürten to masturbate the dogs; Kürten also watched him torturing them. The relation between sex and pain was being underscored in his mind. Kürten claims that at the age of nine he pushed a boy off a raft on the Rhine, and when another boy tried to save him, pushed him under the raft so that both were drowned. At this age the crime need not necessarily have been connected with any sexual impulse. A child lives in an adult's world in which he feels helpless; he is always being tempted to assert his presence by breaking the glass of fire alarms, pulling communication cords, slashing railway seats, etc. Most children are afraid to give in to the impulse; besides, the pressure is not strong enough if their lives are reasonably sheltered and pleasant. Kürten had very little to lose, and his unhappiness led him to regard the world with a cold hostility, as a ruthless enemy. At the age of eight he had been unhappy enough to run away from home and live in furniture vans for a while. A child who possesses this much independence of purpose might well assert his power against the "adult world" by committing a double murder.

Before he was in his teens Kürten masturbated excessively, and had attempted rape on his sister and on schoolgirls. At the age of thirteen he made a habit of wandering along the Rhine meadows looking for animals with whom he could attempt

*Sociologists have pointed out that incest is extremely frequent in slum areas and in large families, where brothers and sisters are frequently forced to share the same bed. But it should not be assumed that slum conditions are entirely responsible. Madame de Brinvilliers, the poisoner who was executed in 1676, came of a wealthy and aristocratic family. In her confession, she admitted to having had intercourse with all her brothers before she entered her teens, and to have indulged in various perversions that forced the seventeenth-century publisher to print her confession in Latin.

sexual intercourse. He claims that he succeeded with goats, pigs, and sheep. He discovered that he would increase the pleasure of bestiality by stabbing a sheep at the same time that he had intercourse. This was undoubtedly the major step in turning Kürten into the most horrible of mass murderers.

At sixteen he was apprenticed to a moulder, greatly against his will, since he had a loathing of his father's profession. He was ill-treated, and finally stole money and ran away to Coblenz, where he lived with a masochistic prostitute. Shortly after this he was arrested for theft, and received the first of his seventeen sentences. Among hardened criminals and "old lags", Kürten felt bound to turn himself into something more like a professional criminal, and had himself tattooed. When he was released in 1899 he took a girl out into the Grafenberger Woods and strangled her during sexual intercourse. He declared that this taught him for the first time the pleasure of hurting while he had sexual intercourse. Although he thought he had killed the girl, no body was found, so it is probable that she recovered and said nothing about her experience.

Now followed several short prison sentences for various offences, including lying in wait for a girl and attempting to shoot her with a rifle. He deliberately committed minor infringements of prison regulations so that he could get into solitary confinement and indulge himself in sadistic fantasies. In 1905 he was released, and discovered that setting fire to haystacks and barns excited him sexually. Now he had a "grudge against society" (and a certain amount of justification for it), and associated sexual pleasure and "getting his own back" on society. He even invented a notion of "compensative justice", by which the punishment for his crimes would be visited on people who had tormented him. Here, it can be seen, is the typical criminal rationalization; the life forces or forces of "individual destiny" are objectified as "society"; a failure of self-analysis leads deeper into crime.

After a further seven years in prison for theft (during which time he was temporarily insane, and – he claims – succeeded in murdering a fellow prisoner in the hospital without being

suspected), Kürten was released in 1913, and almost immediately committed his first sexual murder. The victim was a
thirteen-year-old girl. Kürten broke into a house in Köln-
Mulheim one evening; the family was away at some celebra-
tion, but the child was asleep in bed. Kürten strangled her, cut
her throat, and penetrated her genitals with his fingers. All
this gave him such intense pleasure that he was able to give
the most precise details sixteen years later. The girl's uncle was
falsely accused of the murder, but finally acquitted. Kürten
derived great pleasure from listening to people discussing the
crime and expressing horror. Kürten now began deliberately
to look for sadistic sensations during his burgling activities.
He used a hatchet, and procured an orgasm by knocking out a
man and a woman and seeing their blood. (For some reason
they never reported the attacks.) He was also interrupted
when he was about to strike a sleeping girl with a hatchet, and
ran away, leaving the hatchet behind. He burnt a hay wagon,
and attempted to strangle two women. Undoubtedly he was
now prepared to embark on a career of rape and murder.
However, he was caught thieving again, and this time sentenced to eight years in prison.

Released in 1921, Kürten returned to Altenberg, claiming
that he had been a prisoner of war in Russia. There he met the
woman who became Frau Kürten. She was older than Kürten,
and had spent time in jail for shooting her lover, a gardener
who promised to marry her and then changed his mind after
she had lived with him. Kürten was almost certainly attracted
by her gentle and inoffensive nature; it would have been impossible for a man like Kürten to feel attracted to a woman
whom he could not dominate and bully. His attitude towards
her was based on pity and protectiveness. She married him
only after he threatened to murder her. However, it soon
emerged that he had made an excellent choice. Although he
never treated her with cruelty (Kürten, oddly enough, was not
a cruel man except in sexual perversion), she had to put up
with a great many infidelities; on one occasion she even discovered her husband in bed with another woman. For some

curious reason Kürten was very attractive to women. He was not bad-looking, certainly had none of Lombroso's criminal characteristics, was quietly spoken, and obviously intelligent, and dressed as well as he could afford, taking care to keep his shoes well shined and his hair brushed. He philandered as much as possible, and found it easy to pick up girls. (At his trial he declared that his crimes were partly the fault of the women who were all so easy to pick up.) He did not always kill his victims, or even harm them. Some girls found his manner of love-making slightly rough, but did not object to being throttled a little. To one girl who protested, Kürten explained that "love was like that". At least one of them was in love with him and hoped to marry him; when she accidentally discovered that her "fiancé" was already married, she was inconsolable.

Kürten's marriage seems to have been a good influence. For several years he worked as a moulder in Altenberg, became an active trade-unionist, and committed no murders. He was twice charged with maltreating servant girls, and on one occasion his wife saved him from prison by begging the girl to drop the case. His sadistic fantasies continued, however. Finally he decided to return to Düsseldorf – perhaps because the larger city would permit him more anonymity. On the evening he returned – in 1925 – he was delighted that the sunset was blood-red.

Now began Düsseldorf's "reign of terror", which has very few parallels in criminal history. He began to indulge his sadistic propensity with a few attacks on women, none of them fatal. These became steadily more frequent. His wife worked as a waitress at night; Kürten would escort her to work, and then go out looking for a victim. Until 1927 there were only three cases of attempted strangulation of young women. Then Kürten took up arson again, and burned haystacks and barns. He hoped that he would incinerate some tramp sleeping in the hay. He committed eighteen cases of arson during the next two years. His appetite for blood was also developing, and he was no longer satisfied with strangling women. On one occasion, when he could find no victim, he cut off the head of a sleeping swan and drank some of its blood. One day he saw a horse in the street involved in an accident; the sight caused a sexual orgasm.

In 1929 he began using various cutting weapons in his attacks – knives, scissors, a hatchet. In this year he committed eight murders, and committed about fourteen attacks, many of them involving serious wounding. The first victim was a Frau Kuhn, who was set upon in the dark and stabbed twenty-four times. She recovered after many months in hospital. He stabbed and killed a drunken workman, and then an eight-year-old child, Rose Ohliger. He left the child behind a fence, and returned early the next morning with paraffin with which he made an attempt to burn the body. His sole motive, he explained later, was to increase the horror felt about the crime. He joined the crowds standing at the murder-site the next day and experienced a sexual orgasm listening to their horrified comments. During the next few months there were only four cases of attempted strangulation. Then he killed a servant girl called Maria Hahn in the meadows near Papendelle and buried her. Later he returned to change the site of her grave, had anal intercourse with the corpse, and considered crucifying it on two trees. The body was too heavy to lift. Later, Kürten wrote to the police, telling them where to look for the body. In the meantime he frequently returned to the grave and masturbated on it.

It would be pointless to detail the other cases.* Three more children were murdered, and two servant girls were killed with hammer blows, and found in positions indicating sexual assault, although intercourse did not appear to have been completed. The police were baffled by the crimes, and assumed that there were several murderers. The day after the murder of two children, a servant girl was stabbed several times; it seemed inconceivable that a man could satisfy an urge to kill on Saturday night and then commit another attempted murder on Sunday afternoon.

*An account will be found in *Encyclopaedia of Murder*.

Although Kürten was not arrested until May 1930, he committed no more murders, and went back to attempted strangulation to satisfy his sadistic appetites. It is possible that he was now experiencing a certain disgust over the murders; he was by no means as completely degenerate as Heath and Christie; he took a considerable interest in his own "case", tried hard to rationalize his sadism, and read various psychologists. So it is remotely possible that, even at this late date, he was succeeding in salvaging something from the wreck of his own being.

The attacks produced a frenzy of activity on the part of the police. The police received 13,000 letters denouncing the murderer; they interviewed 900,000 people, and followed up 2,650 clues. One of the denunciations was from a girl who had been assaulted by Kürten; the police fined her for "gross nonsense".

The net finally closed around Kürten when he assaulted a servant girl named Maria Budlick. She was an ugly, bow-legged girl who came to work in Düsseldorf and was picked up by Kürten, taken to a lonely spot, and forced to submit to "mild throttling" and sexual intercourse. But Kürten had also taken her to his home in Mettmannerstrasse. She did not bother to report the incident to the police, but wrote about it in a letter to a friend that was sent to the wrong address. Someone else opened the letter, read it, and gave it to the police. One day in late May 1930, Kürten came out of his upstairs flat to see Maria Budlick pointing him out to a policeman. He was not arrested immediately, but realized that it was close. He now confessed his murders to his wife and advised her to give him up to the police and claim the reward. He took her out to a restaurant to complete the story of his crimes; she was so upset that she could not eat; Kürten ate her share as well as his own. The next day she went to the police, and her husband was arrested by a nervous detective. In due course she received the reward, which partly relieved her anxiety about starvation in old age. Kürten's workmates and neighbours would not believe that the police had arrested the "monster"; they all believed that it was a mistake.

During his trial, Kürten showed little concern. He ate and slept well – danger seemed to stimulate his appetite – took an obvious pleasure in recalling the details of his crimes (all with extraordinary accuracy), and talked frankly to Berg. One of his teenage girl friends gave evidence that he had stood in front of criminals in a waxwork exhibition and declared that one day he would be as famous as any of them. He was inspired by the case of Jack the Ripper (which took place when he was five). He told Berg of his interesting fantasies: how he would some-times dream of blowing up the whole city with dynamite, and at other times would dream of saving the city from "the monster" and being made chief of police by the grateful citizens. He talked a great deal about his "injustices", about revenge, and about how the prison system incubates "master criminals". He was completely frank with Berg; at a later interview he even admitted that he had been looking with professional interest at the slim white throat of Berg's secretary On the eve of his execution he ate a hearty meal, which he enjoyed so much that he asked for it a second time. He told Berg that his chief desire was to hear his own blood drip into the basket as his head fell. In spite of widespread protests (Germany had abolished the death penalty for all but extreme cases) he was guillotined on July 2, 1931.

There are very few cases in the annals of murder that are as horrifying as this one. England and America have perhaps one each – Jack the Ripper and Albert Fish.* But it would be too simple to say that Kürten was turned into a murderer by social conditions. It is very likely indeed that, under different social conditions, Kürten might have been only a "mental sadist" like Powys or "Mr. Evans". But somehow, the Freudian analysis of the "aggressive libido" is less convincing than

*Fish strangled and partly ate a child. Although the psychiatrist on the case – Frederic Wertham – described Fish as "the king of perverts", his published documentation of the case is by no means as full as Berg's. Fish was a sadist and masochist with religious delusions, who attacked only children. He undoubtedly committed more murders than the one for which he was executed. Wertham's brief account of Fish can be found in his book *The Show of Violence*.

Powys's idea of a man whose erotic nerve receives energies from the destructive side of the "First Cause". The Kürten who was elated by the sight of a blood-red sunset, the Kürten who walked through the streets of Düsseldorf dreaming of blowing up the whole city – and yet could take an intelligent interest in his own "case" – is somehow better understood in terms of a "dark energy" flowing from outside himself.

These various considerations lead the discussion into what is certainly its most difficult stage. It would seem that there is much evidence to support Freud's idea that sadism proceeds from a different source than the other sexual perversions. Freud's "special source" was explained at length in *Beyond the Pleasure Principle*; it was the "death wish", the Greek *thanatos*. Freud was puzzled by the problem of human aggression, and felt that Marx's theory of the class-war was superficial; he therefore produced this "new" concept of his own. (In fact, the concept was formulated by Schopenhauer, who was in turn inspired by certain Christian mystics and by Buddhism.) Human beings fought wars because they secretly wished to die; the need for self-preservation may be very deep, but a lust for death is even deeper. Sadism is therefore (according to Freud) a mixture of the two most potent impulses in the human being: sex and the death urge. Kürten would be understood to be committing suicide when he went out to kill; he had flung himself into a stream that would bear him to death, and allowed the need for sex and the need for death to mingle in a kind of delirium.

At first sight, this view is plausible. A Freudian might argue that Nietzsche had already postulated a kind of death wish in his "pale criminal". But this is only because we confuse the romantic wish for darkness, for "return to the womb", with the wish for death. The pale criminal did not actively want to die; he had only reached a point of fatigue and degradation where he did not actively want to live. Human beings sometimes think seriously of dying in the way that a hard-pressed business man thinks of bankruptcy; but the business man usually wants to start up in another business, without the burden of old debts. There is no desire to retire permanently from business. In the same way, the nineteenth-century romantics dreamed of a retreat to the womb, "half in love with easeful death"; but what they really wanted was a reduction in the difficulty of living, a time to rest and recuperate. Sometimes it seemed to them that *all* life is inevitably miserable, that it allows us to recuperate only in order to exploit us further. But such poets as Traherne, Blake, Wordsworth – even Shelley – had intuitions of a greater intensity of life, a power that would make all torments seem trivial. Towards the end of the century this question of "eternal yes" versus "eternal no" had been clearly formulated by a considerable number of poets and artists – Carlyle, Nietzsche, Van Gogh, and Rilke among them. And in many cases the answer was not simply a stoical "yea-saying", as in Carlyle, but a mystical affirmation. Freud went no deeper than his own sick romanticism, mistaking death for the dark womb of life. (Rilke was inclined to do the same kind of thing.) A healthier – and profounder – attitude towards death was stated by Camus, who wrote "For me, it is a closed door . . . a horrible and dirty adventure". Shaw also recognized this. In *The Domesticity of Franklin Barnabus* there is the following exchange:

"CONRAD: . . . Do you know what people really die of?

"IMMENSO: Of reasonableness. They do not want to live forever.

"CONRAD: Of laziness and want of conviction, and failure to make their lives worth living. That is why."

Even Dostoevsky, a confirmed romantic, disowned the "death wish", and stated that "eternal life" does not mean life in heaven, but physical life here on earth, in a state of intensity that is inconceivable to us at present.

If this view is preferred to Freud's neo-romanticism, then the death-wish explanation of sadism must be abandoned. Degeneration is not synonymous with the death wish; one is a state of neutrality; the other a positive downward-movement. Shaw doubted whether it is possible for living creatures to wish their own death on the deepest instinctive level, and there

is much evidence to support his view. Tolstoy's Anna Karen-
ina, on the point of committing suicide, when it is too late to
withdraw, realizes suddenly that death is the last thing in the
world that she wants. Tolstoy's intuition went deeper than
Freud's. Degeneration is the result of "nihilism".* All animals
are saved from such a peculiar condition by the strength of
their instincts, which give life a certain framework of "values".
But as brain increases, the instincts are weakened; and if
society suddenly becomes far more difficult and complex – as
it has over the past hundred years – men need to increase their
intellectual co-ordination to an enormous extent to survive.
To the average Elizabethan, even a stupid Londoner (or New
Yorker) of today would seem a highly remarkable example of
social co-ordination. The instincts are suddenly weakened.
The result is that man feels himself in a kind of "spiritual"
desert, not knowing what to do because his instincts no longer
tell him. In this state, he may well turn to pleasure as the only
positive value – as men have always turned in decadent civilizations. But the pleasure nerve is not strong enough to carry
the whole current of human evolutionary striving; it becomes
calloused and insensitive. Sexual perversions are an attempt to
stimulate the jaded pleasure nerve. Sex is used instinctively as a
safety valve, because it is a temporary reconnection with the
instinctive forces that are the source of all "values".

In *African Genesis,* Robert Ardrey has an interesting example
of this increase of sexual emphasis under conditions that
weaken the instincts. Sir Solly Zuckerman observed the behaviour of a group of baboons in the London Zoo, upon
which he based the generalization that sex is the great motive
force in animal society. Baboons, like many animals and birds,
have a strict hierarchy of rank, and the "aristocratic" baboon
is likely to get a sizeable harem (which chooses him) while his
proletarian colleagues remain sex-starved. Zuckerman observed that this sometimes led to sexual battles. One of the
sexually underprivileged baboons would work himself up to

---

*I use the word in Nietzsche's sense: the total collapse of the sense of
values due to a poison in the social system, or to "decadence".

making an attempt to steal a member of the harem. Other baboons would join him, and the aristocrat would be forced to defend his rights. If he lost, he would become one of the "proletariat" of bachelors; another bachelor would take his place as aristocrat. This, and other incidents of the same type, led to Zuckerman's generalization. But, as Ardrey points out, zoo conditions are thoroughly artificial. When baboons are observed in their natural surroundings, such sexual battles are never seen. The "social order" is never challenged by the "proletariat"; the greatest force in baboon society is precedence, the "will to power". It becomes sex in captivity only because sex is the only outlet. (Ardrey offers an impressive array of examples to support his view.) "Sex is a side-show in the world of the animals, for the dominant colour of that world is fear", Ardrey writes. He also produces some interesting examples of the way in which the "natural instincts" of animals are weakened when they are thrown into strange social conditions (on board ship, for example). Transfer this to the human social context, and we begin to understand why the rate of sex crime rises steadily, and why various sexual abnormalities are on the increase. Animals and birds choose their sexual partner by social precedence. In this highly complex modern social machine, which can grind individuals to fragments in a completely impersonal manner, we have a large number of privileged individuals, who find no difficulty in obtaining sexual release, and an even larger number of "ciphers" who feel themselves to be sexually underprivileged. A famous film star can sleep with every hat-check girl in Hollywood; a moronic truck driver like Charles Floyd is forced to murder a young and pretty girl in order to possess her. A society like ours is the ideal incubator for all kinds of sexual abnormality.

But this does not explain the sadistic impulse. Charles Floyd battered women to death in order to rape them; but at least he felt no desire to torture them. Sadism leads into altogether deeper waters. Again, Robert Ardrey advances views of considerable interest. Ardrey quotes the theory of the South African anthropologist Raymond Dart, that humankind developed from a tribe of killer apes. The more flattering view – held by most anthropologists – is that "early man" possessed a larger brain than the ape, and so came to develop weapons and tools. Dart suggested that a tribe of killer apes branched off from the normal non-aggressive ape. These apes used weapons – rocks or heavy bones – and were forced to develop larger brains in order to co-ordinate muscles and senses. And so came man. Ardrey's somewhat depressing thesis is that since man developed as a killer, aggression is an ineradicable part of his nature. Preachers and humanistic sociologists continue to speak of universal peace, goodwill towards men; but the competition of weapons – in modern terms, the arms race – is too deeply ingrained in the human psyche. If the survival of the human species depends upon peace, then it is impossible that we should survive – this is Ardrey's thesis. And he points out that tribes of animals are naturally hostile to one another. A naturalist placed a number of monkeys on an island, and made sure that they had ample food and space for all. Instead of turning into an anarchist society, peaceably wandering over their domain, they separated into tribes, staked out territories, and expressed hostility to all other tribes.

This conclusion may be depressing – and perhaps not entirely accurate – but it only states the truth intuited by Nietzsche and stated repeatedly in modern culture: that "sweetness and light" is an excellent formula, but it is too far from the deep psychological reality of man to be a working rule for society. In his impatience with the "sweetness and light" school, Nietzsche went to extremes, declared that war is nobler than peace and that he preferred a warrior to a monk.* Bergson, Sorel, and Pareto went further, and built up a kind of rationale of the irrational.† T. E. Hulme declared

---

*I need hardly add that Nietzsche's final position by no means depends on these views, and that he himself frequently said things that are in opposition to them. The anti-humanist is frequently driven to overstate his position in sheer exasperation.

†See my *Religion and the Rebel*, Chapter Two.

that human nature is unchangeably corrupt, and that the dogma of original sin expresses a basic truth; he later wrote a series of articles against pacifism, and explaining why he was proud to fight in the 1914 war. Unfortunately destiny was on the side of his opponent (Bertrand Russell) and clinched the argument by killing Hulme, demonstrating that even if a man of intellect decides on a paradoxical defence of violence, he had better take care not to act according to his stated convictions. Ezra Pound continued the Nietzsche tradition, and wrote a poem in which he declared: "I have no life except where the swords clash." (Pound, however, was sensible enough to keep out of the war.) And finally, Ernest Hemingway provided the most powerful argument of all by demonstrating that a healthy and vigorous form of writing could have its roots in violence and the acceptance of death. Like Hulme, though, Hemingway soon took his convictions to the point of absurdity, created a kind of mystique of bull-fighting, big-game hunting, and death, and ended as a victim of his own cult of violence and anti-intellectualism.

But the fact that Hulme and Hemingway were almost as wrong as Matthew Arnold and William Morris does not mean that the "irrationalist" school must be abandoned. The nineteenth century grasped the basic truth that man's evolution has been due to his ability to analyse and use symbols.

This is a point of immense importance, and cannot be stated with too much emphasis. It is central to the argument of this book. There are two basic modes by which men "grasp" the outside world: intellect and intuition. But consider what meanings underlie this cliché. You recognize your brother's face by intuition, not by analysis; in other words, by a faculty involving "Gestalt". You *may* recognize a stranger by analytical perception, by saying "This man has red hair and a broken nose – therefore he *must* be X whom I met last week". But such a procedure would be unusual. All our basic recognitions come through this "Gestalt" intuition, in which is involved Husserl's factor of intentionality (i.e. subconsciously deciding which aspects of someone's face to *notice most*). In this, human beings are like animals.

It has been observed that certain birds and animals can "count" up to four or five; baboons (according to Ardrey) can count up to three; certain birds can count as high as six. This is determined by a simple experiment. Baboons are raiding an orchard; three farmers go out, and the baboons run away, but wait nearby. Two farmers emerge from the orchard while the third lies in ambush. But the baboons are too sensible to walk into the ambush. However, if the experiment is repeated with four men, and three of them leave the orchard, the baboons fail to notice that there must be a man lying in ambush, and return to the orchard – where, presumably, they meet with a blast from a shotgun. The English naturalist Lubbock tells a similar story about a crow that shows that it could count up to four. It is also generally known that if a bird's nest contains eggs, and one is taken, the bird fails to notice the loss; if two are taken, the bird will desert the nest.

But to say that birds and animals can "count" is misleading. Counting involves the use of number-words like one, two, and three. It also involves an *analytical* procedure, taking each unit on its own, rather like attaching a marked label to each object counted. An animal "counts" in the same way that it recognizes the face of its mate – by "grasping" the whole, and relying on its function of intentionality to retain a more or less accurate picture of that whole. This, of course, is also common with human beings. In Kipling's *Kim*, Kim is taught how to become an efficient secret-service agent by being shown a tray of assorted objects, and told to memorize them after a very brief glance. This involves additional training of the Gestalt faculty. The reader might try the experiment of glancing at a bookshelf of assorted books, and then seeing how many of them – in their proper order – are retained in the memory after a glance of two seconds. There is no time to count and apply special "labels" to each book. The work must be left entirely to the Gestalt faculty, the intuition of form. This intuition, within its limitations, is a great deal swifter and more efficient than the intellect. The intellect would require a five-minute contemplation of the bookshelf, and would need to apply names and numbers to the books. Nevertheless, for all its elephantine slowness, the intellect is more efficient in the long run; it can grasp huge tracts of strange material – whole libraries – where the Gestalt faculty is limited to a bookshelf. An animal would simply not see the sense in such ponderous human procedures as language and number symbolism, any more than a poor man sees the need for a bank account and life insurance. Human language is a tribute to our belief in our *endurance* and far-sightedness; its slow development is an indication of our basic animal mistrust of any but immediate and self-evident procedures.

But where does all this apply to sex theory, and particularly to sadism?

Its basic point is this: the Gestalt faculty (a more precise word than intuition) plays a tiny but nevertheless wholly indispensable part in human evolution. The intellect does all the real work. For thousands – perhaps millions – of years man used both these faculties about equally. Then, quite suddenly – within the past few thousand years – man decided to take the plunge and entrust his capital and his future to the intellect. Even so, the intellect's expansion was very slow; a man like Aristotle could make all kinds of extraordinary generalizations without bothering to test them by the "elephantine procedure" of experiment.

The sudden tremendous rise in the stock of intellect occurred less than four centuries ago, and is associated with names like Galileo, Kepler, and Newton. The stocks not merely doubled and trebled their value; they went on rising until they had increased a thousandfold. Throughout the eighteenth century they went on rising, until, in the nineteenth century, they reached a peak. Men like Comte, Mill, and Marx declared unbounded faith in the analytical procedure; their faith and optimism were so great, in fact, that they lost sight of the all-important "Gestalt faculty"; they declared that analysis was *everything*, that man needed nothing but analysis to increase his stature and improve his society indefinitely.

But this is like declaring that a country's economy can be built entirely on a paper currency, without gold in the banks. The roots are severed. It will not be surprising if a culture built on such foundations soon begins to show signs of serious illness. Before any improvement can take place, the notion of the Gestalt faculty, the intuition, must be restored to its small but rightful place. This, in fact, is the revolution that has been progressing slowly but steadily in many fields for the past hundred years.

Now it is unfortunate that sexual theory was almost wholly created by a man who was almost as analytic, as blind to Gestalt, as John Stuart Mill. Freud's achievement is incredible; but he is still, in many ways, the worst thing that ever happened to the new science of psychology.

These considerations make it possible to offer a basic and comprehensive definition of existentialism. Gestalt is the basis of our lives, and therefore of our evolution. Gestalt (or intuition) is the roots of the tree; analysis and intellect are the tree itself, the whole portion above ground. The nineteenth century declared that the tree does not need roots. The existentialists came back and declared defiantly that the roots do not need the tree. (So Kierkegaard attacked Hegel, and Heidegger declared that he is interested only in "pure being".) Yet these are absurd extreme positions. The greatest existential thinkers – Nietzsche, Whitehead, William James (John Dewey might also be added – with reservations – to this list) only took up the reasonable position that the tree needs its roots in their proper position – under the ground, in contact with the living soil, the vital forces. Each of them developed a different way of saying this, but the general intention was identical.

This, as I have suggested, is particularly true for sex, which remains incomprehensible without such an approach. In the early chapters of the book I have tried to demonstrate the use of such an approach. But the problem of sadism reveals that it is completely indispensable. Freud's need to invent the death wish reveals this inadequacy; he discovered the need to somehow deepen his concept to explain aggression, but was unwilling to attempt a general deepening of his theory; so his death wish remains the eagle in the flock of Freud's pigeons. This is usually the fate of the attempts to reduce complexities to one oversimplified concept. (Russell and Whitehead's attempt to reduce all mathematics to logic in *Principia Mathematica* is another example; their "system" was left uncompleted when the internal contradictions became obvious; but not before Russell had tried a few compromises of the same type as the death wish.)

What, then, is the existential alternative to the Freudian view? It is, to begin with, the need to recognize that the sexual impulse is not the basic human drive. It is no more "basic" than the urge to social reform or to doing mathematics. It may be *stronger*, but that is an entirely different thing. Freud declared, as it were, that sex is the universal power-house, and that all other lesser "currents" run off it. Adler tried to modify this view by asserting the importance of the will to power, the need for social orientation, self-respect. Ardrey's book indicates that this view is now becoming self-evident in zoology. But even this is not basic enough. Powys – for all his vagueness and obscure mysticism – is closer to a basic unifying view with his talk of a "first cause" with positive and negative poles. But even this must not be taken too literally. For the existential psychologist, the truth would seem to be something like this: the power-house is an evolutionary impulse of such enormous strength that it is almost impossible to make any basic assertions about it. T. E. Hulme wrote: "The process of evolution can only be described as the insertion of more and more freedom into matter. . . . In the amoeba, then, you might say that impulse has manufactured a small leak through which free activity could be inserted into the world, and the process of evolution has been the gradual enlargement of this leak" (*Speculations*, p. 208). But it is not merely a question of brute force enlarging the leak. The life urge is something of a bull in a china shop; or it could be described as an elephant trying to learn to crochet. And with remarkable delicacy for such an immense force, it has built up a careful series of valves and dams, rather like the fuses that prevent a faulty electric fire from burning down the house. Hence the nervous system which serves the double purpose of connecting hand and brain, and acting as a "fuse" that prevents too much life from blazing into the brain and creating a consciousness that is too intense for the menial tasks of evolution. It is rather as if a despot should place a certain limit on the rise in wages and prosperity because if we were all rich there would be nobody to clean out the sewers and empty the dustbins.

But what of sadism? Once the immense energy of this "powerhouse" is grasped, a plausible answer suggests itself. Our "values" (i.e. notions of right and wrong) are all connected with the instincts. And the instincts in turn are closely connected with the nervous system and the various valves for "keeping out" too much life force. Ardrey points out that the instinct of order is general in the animal world, even where there is no social need for precedence and hierarchy; it is a basic law of nature that must be unfair to the few if it is to be fair to the many. The nerves and the instincts are all directed towards maintaining order and preventing chaos. Yet it would be false to speak as if there were a fundamental opposition of purpose in the nerves and in the "life impulse", The whole system of "valves" is the creation of the life impulse.

And yet, as has been seen repeatedly in this study, these valves and repeating mechanisms frequently appear as tyrants where sex is concerned. So when the instincts are weakened by a sudden increase in the complexity of a civilization it becomes possible to revolt against the "valves". Where the instincts are weakened, the living creature turns naturally to the source of values, the life impulse itself. The tired nerves are asked to ease their restrictions on life impulse.

But if the nerves and instincts are our "policemen" they are also our law-givers of right and wrong. The life force itself is not in the least concerned with our social rights and wrongs. Like Caesar, it is above the law; it leaves it to its policemen to see that its minions obey the law. And if these policemen are weakened or by-passed, anything can happen. The astonished minion discovers abruptly that the life impulse is not interested in social taboos and "ideas of good and evil". This is expressed perfectly by Nietzsche in a letter; he tells his friend how he went to a nearby hilltop as a storm approached, and took shelter in a hut where a man was killing two kids. Normally, blood would have revolted him; at this moment, the storm broke. Nietzsche writes: ". . . I had an indescribable feeling of well-being and zest. . . . *Lightning and tempest are different worlds' free powers' without morality* Pure will, without the confusions of intellect – how happy, how free." For a moment the Dionysian element in life has outrun the Apollonian; the water has spilled over the vessel.

These, of course, are all images, and have the usual advantages and disadvantages of images. And yet they explain the nature of sadism more directly than any amount of analytical language. The nerves and instincts are like guardians who set up a qualified prohibition on alcohol. The sadist is the man who has found a source of bootleg alcohol. But unlike the usual alcohol, it comes without "moral" taxation. All the guilt mechanisms – associated with the instincts – are by-passed. But like most bootleg liquor, this is far more poisonous than the legitimate article. Hence the degeneration of the Heaths and Christies.

What of the suggestion – made by Powys and Boehme – that there are two types of energy that emanate from the "powerhouse"? In fact, such a hypothesis is unnecessary to explain sadism. The nerves make up the "legitimate" electrical circuit. The power flows in one direction, from positive to negative. If this is by-passed, there is no telling what can happen. Our notion of good and evil is associated with this one-way flow of power. If the power piles up and flows back on itself like a tide, good and evil will seem to be reversed.

Powys, then, is both right and wrong in his attribution of a "duality" to the life impulse. Our Western religious tradition insists that "God is good". This may be true – but certainly not in the sense that "God is moral". What is "good" for the life impulse is completely beyond our comprehension, and is only vaguely related to our ideas of good and evil.

But in another sense Powys is wrong. For why is it necessary to posit two types of energy in the life impulse that account for altruism and cruelty? The energy of malice is usually vital energy gone rotten. We have only to think of the malice and petty-mindedness that are often associated with small communities to realize that "evil" is often another name for frustration or boredom. It is what Blake meant in writing: "When thought is closed in caves, then love shall show its root in deepest hell." Did not the cruelty of Eastern despots spring from the boredom of having too much power and no particular purpose? Sexual habits, like other habits, are often a matter of *faute de mieux*.

An example might make this clearer. Paul de River cites a curious case of bestiality that concerned a girl and an Alsatian dog. The girl was a healthy but "highly sexed" teenager who had frequently been excited by the sight of mating stallions on a farm. One night her Alsatian dog came into the bedroom and showed curiosity about her genitals (she was wearing a nightdress) and she allowed him to lick her, and finally helped the dog to have sexual intercourse with her. It became a habit; some time later, when she was caught, she admitted that men had now lost all attraction for her. Only an animal could excite her sexually.

And yet it would clearly be innaccurate to say that there is a certain sexual impulse in women that is directed to animals rather than to men, and that under certain circumstances this impulse may develop to the point of abnormality. The girl's normal sexual impulse had been "hypnotized" at an early stage by the sight of a stallion mounting a mare. The size of its sexual organ impressed her. She admitted to having fantasies about sexual intercourse with a stallion while she was actually having it with a dog. The dog's sexual member, of course, is a great deal smaller than that of most men. But the chain of association was welded by repetition: stallion, sexual intercourse, dog. The dog may have been a "second-best" compared to a stallion, but it was closer to a stallion than a man. Hence a second-best in the sexual act became a habit and a necessity. It is rather as if a very poor man should drink methylated spirit until he is so used to its taste that he finds whisky insipid. But methylated spirit, like whisky, is alcohol; a preference for methylated spirit would be a preference for its *impurities*, not for its alcohol content.

The same is surely true of sadism. The reasons for the addiction to "bootleg liquor" are multifold. In most cases, "poverty" is an important part; this certainly accounts for a great deal of criminal sadism. But how does a man develop a sadistic impulse in the first place? Why was Kürten the only sadist in a family of thirteen? Hereditary degeneracy plays an important part, of course. But this would only ensure a certain feebleness of the life impulses, not a desire for cruelty. Sadism springs from the reaction of the Dionysiac impulse on an enfeebled nervous system. And as far as we can determine, the men who are born with the ability to receive sudden "tides" of undiluted life impulse are freaks in the same sense as Siamese twins. If Kürten's excess vitality could have been carefully channelled, and kept clear of too much association with sex, there is no reason why he should not have ended as famous instead of infamous. The degenerate impulse has been present in many creative men. De Sade is, of course, a border-line case, who might be dismissed as wholly criminal. But Isidore Ducasse, who wrote under the name of Lautréamont, is already halfway to the major poet. His "Chants de Maldoror", a long prose poem put into the mouth of an arche-typal "romantic outsider", are full of sadistic fantasies that cannot be excused as "art". They are simply degenerate and nasty. If you read Ducasse, it is impossible to swallow him whole and approve of all, unless you can enjoy descriptions of tearing out a baby's eyes with fingernails. And yet parts of the "Chants de Maldoror" rank with Rimbaud's "Illuminations" as the greatest prose poetry to come out of France in the late nineteenth century.

This is the distinction between the criminal and the creative mentality. There is an element in the criminal mentality that must be rejected, even if it is part of the expression of unusual vitality. We can accept the indecencies of Rabelais or the obscenity of Joyce as a "digestible" part of their creation. But we do not accept the blunders and mistakes made by a man of genius early in his writing career; we merely separate them from the better passages in his juvenilia; or we may ignore the juvenilia completely because it reduces our pleasure in the mature achievement. We make a clear distinction between what is creative and what is *accidental*. Now the genuinely criminal – the degenerative – is wholly accidental. It is not vital power flowing, for some reason, counter to our usual social notions of right and wrong. It is usually characterized by a pathetic sense of boredom and *waste*. And if it circulates in living systems, waste is synonymous with poison. Sadism is a poison, not a separate part of the vital energies. It is, as Freud stated, different from the other "perversions" for obvious reasons. Homosexuality is only a misdirection of the sexual impulses, probably based largely upon physical factors such as hormones. Fetichism and necrophily are also misdirections, but also have mild justification as attempts to pursue a "pure" sexual experience, free of the usual dilutions by personal and social factors. Their degenerative influence may be no larger than in masturbation. But sadism is quite simply a poison of the sexual impulses, a habit-forming poison of immense degenerative influence. The failure, in a man like Powys, to eliminate it from his system, is an unfortunate proof of an immaturity that is frequently apparent in his early work. (A volume of essays like *The Pleasures of Literature* reveals a dilettantism that is characterized by imprecision of thought and language, a tendency to wallow in vaguely literary moods.) Both sadism and masochism are illnesses of childhood, a way of intensifying a life impulse that will be strengthened by other transformers in later life.

And yet the breakdown in "values" in our society, analysed so penetratingly by Nietzsche, must inevitably lead to an increase in sadism as well as in all other sexual abnormalities, from masturbation to necrophily. And it should be recognized that this breakdown is largely a *cultural breakdown*. A society's culture is a kind of counterweight to its social pressures. The Middle Ages achieved something close to perfect equilibrium, with a simple, agrarian society and a powerful Church. Since then, the balance has been changed to an extent where a mere revival of "religion" would be no advantage. We live in an industrial civilization with a basically materialistic culture. It might be objected that our culture – with its roots in Newton, Marx, and Freud – is hardly closely connected with the rising rate of sex crime and perversion. This is untrue. Improved social conditions allow more freedom than ever before to the play of human intelligence. Any man or woman of reasonable intelligence can obtain an education. Naturally, the man with an active intelligence feels more interest in the contemporary "monuments" than in older "monuments of unageing intellect". And the number of contemporary "monuments" who influence most of these prehensive intelligences is very small indeed. Twenty-five years ago the magic names were all to be found in the works of T. S. Eliot, Hulme, Baudelaire, Dante, Laforgue, Newman, etc. Add Joyce, Yeats, and Proust, and the list is almost complete. A generation earlier, the magic names were all contemporary: Freud, Einstein, Wells, Shaw – and possibly Nietzsche. Fifty years before that it would have been Carlyle and Ruskin. And these groups of names are usually connected, welded together into some attitude which may not represent any one of them. Twenty years after Newman entered the Roman Catholic Church, England had a wave of Catholic conversion. Twenty years after Shaw and his friends founded the Fabian Society, England had its first socialist government. The consequences of "cultural changes" can be far greater than might seem at first sight.

No matter how great or small the degree of truth contained in these generalizations, one thing is certain, a major social change must be preceded by a major change in "values" – that is to say, by a cultural change. If one of the major problems is a rise in sex crime, then the whole problem of sex must be discussed in a more precise and more flexible language.

Note: The Problem of the Prevention of Sex Crime

The steady rise in the number of sex crimes in Europe and America has occasioned a great deal of disquiet. It is true that all classes of crime have increased; nevertheless, sex crime and violence against the person has shown the steepest rate of increase. The figures are as follows: In England in 1938 there were 5,018 sex crimes; in 1951 the number had increased to 14,633; in 1955 this had again increased to 17,078. Since then, the figure has been fairly constant. This shows an increase of more than 300 per cent. Larceny and breaking and entry have also increased, but only by 50 per cent. But crimes of violence have also trebled.* In the United States there are more than 15,000 sexual assaults per year.

The reason is undoubtedly the increasing social tensions of our highly mechanized civilization, the constant threat of atomic war, and the tendency to increased centralization that has the effect of increasing the individual's sense of "insignificance". The "emotionally disabled" are the first to respond to these pressures. And since criminality is essentially a matter of social immaturity, the immediate result is an increase in crime. It is also notable that the number of juvenile criminals has increased. In speaking of this rise in crimes of violence among juveniles, Reinhardt points out that "where *lust* appears as a factor, it seems to have entered as a subordinate component to the dominating lust for the thrill of a cruel murder".† The Leopold and Loeb case is an obvious example, and Reinhardt cites many more.

The problem is a complicated one, and must be considered in parts.

*These figures are quoted from the *Encyclopedia Britannica* Yearbook for 1956. American figures are unfortunately not available, but have shown a comparable rate of increase. Latest figures for British crime (1961) show a further 26 per cent increase.

†*Sex Perversions and Sex Crimes*, p. 200.

The simple view of crime, fashionable at the beginning of the century, was that it is an outcome of poverty; improve social conditions, improve education, and crime will disappear. Undoubtedly this is partially true, as can be seen from the case of Kürten. But improvement of social conditions is by no means the whole solution, if the improvement is accompanied by increased industrialization, and its various pressures that make for the "insignificance" of the individual. While social improvement may cause a decrease in crimes involving larceny, it may have the opposite effect on sex crime. In eighteenth-century England, when poverty was widespread, the modern sex crime was almost unknown, as can be seen from the *Newgate Calendar* or Pelham's *Chronicles of Crime*. Vidocq, the first chief of the Paris Sûreté, mentions in his Memoirs hundreds of cases of murder and robbery that he solved, but not (as far as I can recall) a single sex crime. And it might be pointed out that the notorious degenerates of history – Tiberius, Gilles de Rais, De Sade – were the over-privileged rather than the underprivileged. Most of the recorded sex crimes of the eighteenth century were rapes and abductions committed by noblemen. In our own time the typical psychopathic crime is often the "crime of boredom", the crime that appears to have no particular motive, but to spring out of "too much freedom" and total lack of a sense of purpose.

In *Crime and the Sexual Psychopath* de River suggests that "we should have laws to prevent the spread of various hereditary tainted diseases". Sex criminals are often found to have descended from a line of alcoholics, epileptics, etc. A family history of insanity or congenital feeble-mindedness is not unusual. Professor Julian Huxley has recently suggested that society will soon have to come to terms with the idea of selective breeding to produce a higher level of administrators. De River's idea might be taken as a natural corollary of this suggestion; if "desirable" unions are to be encouraged, then obviously undesirable ones should also be discouraged.

In the meantime it is obvious that more time and attention must be devoted to the study of the criminal mentality. Case studies like the one Berg made on Kürten are far too rare. It may also be that the old principles of Freudian analysis obstruct a fuller knowledge of the world of the criminal, and that some revision of principles may be necessary. (This is discussed more fully in the following two chapters.)

The problem of sex crime has so far been complicated by the horror it arouses. It is surely greatly to the credit of the Germans that there was a widespread appeal to save Kürten's life in 1930, in spite of the terrible nature of his crimes; this is surely a civilized recognition that murdering the murderer is no solution. He might still be "useful" to society if his mentality is carefully studied to determine the psychological and social causes of the crime. In America particularly, a pointless and unreflecting puritanism complicates the problem of sexual deviation. (This can be observed in the priggish moral tone of certain books about sexual offenders, which occasionally suggests that the author wishes to convince his readers that he is not writing out of any kind of morbid fascination with the subject.) This may lead the sexual offender to think of himself as a dangerous criminal with insoluble moral problems. The following quotation from Reinhardt illustrates this point; it concerns a thirty-four-year-old man who was sentenced to four years in jail for sodomy with a ten-year-old boy.

"Dale is still seeking a way out of his dilemma. He is now completely preoccupied with finding his salvation in the religious sphere. He is being aided in this endeavour by family and church members on the outside, who are assisting him in planning for his preparation for the ministry after his release. While Dale has no hope of ever achieving a 'normal' heterosexual adjustment, he does hope to live a happy and useful life as a 'saintly celibate'. But he is fearful that his sexual fixation on adolescent boys and his inability to sublimate his sexual energies through 'socially acceptable channels' will be a source of severe personal conflict to him all his life."

Although it is impossible to judge such a case without more

detailed knowledge of its problems, it sounds as if Dale has chosen a solution that may be more disastrous than the original offence. The result of such repressions can frequently be appalling.* If, on the other hand, Dale should learn to accept his homosexuality as "normal" for himself, and seek out circles where it is also regarded as "normal", the personal conflict might well disappear, and the possibility of further offences against minors be removed.

Under the circumstances it is not surprising that most of America's homosexuals prefer to congregate in the large cities – New York, Washington, Chicago, Los Angeles – where the sense of belonging to a group helps to relieve some of the social strain.

Reinhardt cites several cases of sexual offences where the sentence seems to be out of all proportion to the crime. There is, for example, the case of Glen, who went to a dance hall in the hope of picking up a girl who would be willing to permit him sexual satisfaction; he soon found a girl whose manner suggested that she might. After an evening spent in drinking and dancing, during which time his excitement mounted, the girl announced that she would allow him no sexual liberties, and that she intended to walk home alone. He followed her, choked her into submission, and raped her. For this offence he was sentenced to fifteen years in prison. This was his first sexual offence, although he had been sentenced to a reformatory twenty years earlier for burglary. Under the circumstances the sentence seems barbarous. The prosecuting attorney described Glen as a "vicious man who ... would not hesitate to commit the crime again", while the prison administrators, on the contrary, describe him as "amenable to discipline, intelligent, co-operative, and trustworthy", and of

*In a recent case in Plymouth (England), a Church of England clergyman was restored to his place in the church after serving a prison sentence for a sexual assault on a young boy. He then started a sodomy club for choirboys, presenting each qualified member with a rabbit; he was finally charged with committing sodomy on 107 choirboys, all members of the "rabbit club".

"superior mental ability". Plainly, this is the kind of treatment that incubated a Kürten.

Another case where excessive moral indignation seems to have led to a savage sentence is that of a forty-two-year-old man serving a sentence of twenty years for incest with his fifteen-year-old daughter. The arresting sheriff describes the case as "one of the worst on record". Luke, the offender, was described by the prison psychologist as "slightly antagonistic", but otherwise lacking in "abnormal personality traits". Reinhardt remarks that Luke seems to regard the whole business as an unjustified interference with his personal affairs. From the details he then offers, it would appear that Luke is partly in the right. He was on bad terms with his wife, who had refused him sexual satisfaction for a long period. They had six children, and were extremely poor; Luke remarked: "We didn't go nowhere hardly at all; we were too poor and had too many kids."

He was aware that his two elder daughters were leading "fast sexual lives"; the fifteen-year-old worked in a cheap eating place as a waitress and prostituted herself to the customers for money; the eldest daughter worked in a factory and also had many lovers. Luke decided to approach his daughters sexually; they were willing, and intercourse with them took place frequently. The mother suspected, and reported it to the police, who extorted confessions from the daughters by threats of a reformatory (for their general promiscuity). The upshot was Luke's twenty-year-sentence.

It could be argued here that the only real offence was having intercourse with a minor. He could not be accused of impairing morals that were already past recovery. (In Cornwall, England, where this kind of offence is very frequent, the sentence would probably have been from three months to five years in jail; possibly it might have amounted only to probation.) Under the circumstances, Luke's attitude of "slight antagonism" seems justified, and his comments can hardly be judged as revealing incorrigible moral obliquity: "I can't see what business it was of anyone else's – we weren't hurting nobody. . . . I ain't done no worse than lots of other people, and I don't know why people had to make so much of it." He declared his belief that incest was common, only "others is smart enough not to get caught". Reinhardt remarks that the other prisoners treat him with contemptuous tolerance (apparently the normal attitude of prisoners to sexual offenders), and that he is accorded only "minimum social acceptance" by his fellow prisoners. His prison record was good. (He had no previous convictions.) The prison chaplain noted his indifference to religion, and Luke himself commented that, while he is willing to do whatever is expected of him in jail, he does not "want anyone preaching to him about what he should do or what he shouldn't have done".

Reinhardt mentions two other cases of incest in which the sentence might seem excessive (in one case twenty, in the other, thirty years), although the daughter involved in each case was only eight years old. In one case – the man who received thirty years – intercourse had been taking place, with the daughter's willing consent, from the age of eight to the age of fifteen (when she discovered herself to be pregnant). In the other case the man seduced two of his daughters when his wife refused to have intercourse with him, but after his arrest (following his wife's denunciation), his wife pleaded for his release, while the daughters wrote letters asking for the return of their "dear Daddy". Obviously his wife had not expected the sentence to be so savage. This leads to the supposition that, if she had realized the results of her denunciation, she would not have gone to the police, and her husband would have escaped all punishment. It follows that these excessive punishments may sometimes defeat their own end.

The whole problem, then, is complicated (in America more than in Europe) by the attitude of the legal authorities to sex crime, and by a certain amount of moral cant. Frederic Wertham has devoted a powerful and convincing little book, *The Show of Violence*, to pleading that it is more important to study crime than to punish it. The problem, of course, is not as simple as that. There are not enough psychiatric clinics or

enough qualified psychologists to carry out a useful and con-
certed programme of criminological study. Nevertheless, like
the similar problem of lack of schools and qualified teachers,
this could be overcome as soon as its necessity had been clearly
recognized.

To summarize: the rise in sex crime is one of the great
problems of our time. It is a result of the pressures that are
inevitable in an industralized society; it is characteristic, moreover, of a time of intellectual and moral nihilism. On the
intellectual and social level, "society" can do nothing about it,
for the intellectual and moral wellbeing of society has always
been in the hands of a relatively small number of highly
talented and responsible individuals – its originators of new
thought and new directions. But on the social level a great deal
can be done about it, solely by treating the problem as immediate and urgent, and recognizing the need for a far deeper study
of the subject.

* * * *

*Robert Ardrey has drawn my attention to an experiment that
throws some fascinating light on this section. It was an experiment on
the effect of overpopulation among rats, and was conducted at the
National Institute for Mental Health by Calhoun.*

*The rats were placed in a room that contained four pens. After a
short time, two male rats emerged as "leader-rats", rodine dictators,
and each of these two selected a cage for itself, and set up a harem in it.
All the other rats were driven to find themselves living-space in the
other two cages. However, there was plenty of room and plenty of food,
so there were no immediate ill-effects. But after a short time, it became
obvious that the two cages containing the "dictator" rats were becoming healthy and normal communities, while the two "left-over" cages
were developing all the characteristics of slums. Infant mortality was
fantastically high among the left-overs; 80 per cent. in one cage and
96 per cent. in the other.*

*But most amazing – and relevant to this chapter – is the develop-
ment of a* criminal class *among the uprooted rats. The uprooted males
divided into three types: leaders, who kept up a more-or-less normal
life, dominated males, who sank out of sight and displayed no sex-
drive, and the "criminal class", which "Calhoun called probers". I
quote Ardrey: "These weren't dominant. Neither did they accept
subordination. They chased the females in packs, ate abandoned in-
fants. (Though as I say, there was plenty of food.) Most interesting, in
the sex life of rats there is normally a considerable period of courting
before copulation. The dominant males kept this custom up, even in the
crowded pens. But not the criminals. They never challenged the status
of the dominant ones, but despite all pursuit, never resigned like the
submissive ones. Calhoun calls them hyperactive, hypersexual, and also
homosexual. They became rape artists, violating every sexual ritual.
. . . ."*

*Here is a remarkable parallel with Carpenter's case of the rhesus
monkeys. Zoologists have known for some time now that the "land-
owning instinct" is one of the most powerful of all animal instincts,
deeper even than sex. The zoologist C. R. Carpenter observed this
when he shipped a boatload of monkeys to an island off Puerto Rico.
Deprived of their natural territory on the ship, the monkeys seemed to
become "morally bankrupt"; mothers fought their children for scraps
of food, husbands ceased to defend their wives. Once on the island, they
quickly staked out areas of "territory" and separated into tribes, and
their instincts again reverted to normal.*

Both cases might be taken as a fair parallel of present-day society.

The important thing to note is that the rats had plenty *of food
and space; this was no case of a revolt of the underprivileged. The rats
had only been deprived of the dominance-drive, the drive for self-respect;
they felt themselves to be totally unimportant. Plainly, as a class they
stand one stage below the leader-rats but one stage above the dominated
rats.*

*The disturbing footnote to all this is provided by a speech given by
Aldous Huxley to a congress of scientists and intellectuals on December 2, 1962, in Santa Barbara. Huxley pointed out that while it previously took 1,600 years for the world to double its population of 250
millions, the world population at present stands at 3,000 millions,*

and will have doubled by the end of the present century. The United States will probably be one "vast continental city" by the year 2,000. The poorer countries increase their population at a greater rate than their prosperous neighbours, so the threat of war becomes obvious. Under the circumstances, it would seem to be impossible to hope for any fall in the rate of sex crime.

Equally interesting is Calhoun's observation that a percentage of the "prober rats" became homosexuals. This might also suggest a line of thought to explain why homosexuality increases in "decadent civilizations".

CHAPTER VIII

EXISTENTIAL PSYCHOLOGY

Summary of history of psychology. Freud, Jung and Rank. Existential psychology: its history and development. Case of illegitimate girl. Medard Boss's case of compulsive patient. Von Gebsattel's case of compulsive. Fellini's La Dolce Vita; *Steiner's* Angst. *Dostoevsky and Briussov. Summary.*

SOMETHING must now be said about the methods and ideas of existential psychology. This is of central importance to the thesis of this book; in fact, it could almost be said that existential psychology is its main topic, and sex only the avenue through which it happens to have been approached. The method of discussing sex in this book will have prepared the reader for the completely new conception of psychology developed by Minkowski, Straus, von Gebsattel, Binswanger, Storch, Boss, Kuhn, and many others in Germany, Switzerland, France, and America.

Psychology, as it is known today, is a development of the past hundred years. Significantly its rise paralleled the rise of industrial society. An inadequate response to an increasingly complex environment is called neurosis. This is not to suggest that "neuroses" first appeared in the nineteenth century; a neurosis is a relation of the subject's vitality to the complexity of his environment; it is a degree of success or failure of prehension. Therefore, in theory, *any* living being can experience a neurosis at any time – from the amoeba upward.

In England, the psychologist James Ward saved the subject from the mechanism and associationism of the older schools, and developed a more individual approach, allied to the approach of Brentano, Husserl's teacher. Men like George Frederick Stout and William McDougall continued his work.

In an essay, *The Present Chaos in Psychology*, McDougall made a useful distinction, which can be taken as the basis of existential psychology. He pointed out that there have been two major schools of psychological thought, which he calls the Apollonian and Dionysian (borrowing from Nietzsche) – that is to say, the mechanistic and the vitalist. In modern times the mechanistic current starts with Descartes, continues through Spinoza, Locke, Hume, Hartley, the Mills, Spencer, and Bain, down to Russell's Behaviourism. Russell comes in for a particularly spirited attack; Russell reduced Behaviourism ("a poor misshapen and beggarly dwarf") to "the lowest level of banality". The vitalistic or organic current is romantic in origin, beginning with Pascal and Boehme, and coming down through Goethe, Schopenhauer, Nietzsche, Bergson, William James, Freud, and Husserl.

Although Freud, Jung, Adler, and Rank would be automatically included in this second group, it can be seen that they represent a minority, for a dozen other important names could be added, none of them in the psychoanalytical movement (for example, those of Koffka, Wertheimer, and Köhler, the founders of Gestalt theory). The modern educated man tends to identify psychology with Freud and his followers; in fact, Freud owes his pre-eminence to the spectacular nature of his theories and the attendant publicity; he has gained credit for "inventing" a great deal that is actually the common property of modern psychology. (I have even seen it stated in print that Freud first produced the concept of the "subconscious".) This is not to belittle Freud's achievement, which is vast, nor to deny his genius. Freud was as startling an originator as Aristotle; unfortunately, his work must be sifted as carefully as Aristotle's for truth and error. He was, after all, a doctor, concerned with the "epidemic" of neurosis brought about by the abrupt social changes of the early twentieth century. The fact that his premises were false makes no difference to the value of many of his conclusions, or to the over-all importance of his achievement. William Rowan Hamilton discovered that a completely consistent mathematics can be constructed upon certain false or inverted premises. Strangely enough, where science is concerned, the foundation does not matter; what matters is the structure reared on it. For science is unlike a building in that its foundations can be altered at a later date without causing any damage to the building. Mathematicians will explain about the use of imaginary numbers (like the square root of minus one) that can be introduced into a mathematical structure – like invisible bricks – and made to support it until it is time for them to be removed; when the imaginary "bricks" are removed, the structure is unaltered; it certainly does not collapse.

What Freud failed to realize is that if a patient is suffering from neurosis, almost any intelligent analysis, under any theory, will solve his problems. Often, the patient only needs a "psychological boost" to enable him to make a new effort of prehension, and to solve his own problems. Neurosis might be likened to debts that have been allowed to pile up; too many of them result in the bankruptcy of insanity. The patient then slips into a passive attitude towards these "debts". The life energy fails; "discouragement" sets in. Then almost anything can happen.

Like most early psychologists, Freud failed to recognize the importance of "intentionality", of the immense rôle played by the will-power of the patient. He looked for mechanical causes for the effects, underestimating the freedom and power of human intentionality. It has taken fifty years of Gestalt psychology and phenomenology to reveal some of the truth about the mind's ability to turn its preconceptions into realities.

Freud immediately grasped the negative side of this ability: for example, the patient's power to induce illness to escape some onerous responsibility. But he views the person's neurosis against the background of some "social norm" or ideal of perfect "adjustment" to life or society. It never seemed to strike him that, since there is no upward limit to evolution, there can be no final adjustment – although a creative person might discover an unusual degree of health and balance in a flow of creative energy. This curious piece of blindness on Freud's part led him to undertake preposterous psychoanalytical study of various men of genius – Leonardo and Dostoevsky, for example – always with the idea of "cutting them down to size", of iconoclasm (Freud's habit of iconoclasm, like Shaw's, became ingrained and a little tiresome). This was the triumph of abstraction over common sense.

One of the earliest criticisms of psychoanalysis illustrates this humourless and abstract approach: writers on the subject would ask how it is possible to be sure that the psychoanalyst himself is perfectly "normal". It never seemed to strike these critics (a) that a one-eyed oculist or one-legged doctor may be as efficient as a "normal" man, and (b) that the relation of the neurotic patient to the analyst is far more *active* than the relation of a doctor to a tuberculosis patient. There was an underlying assumption that a psychoanalyst ought to be somehow infallible, just as a priest ought to be, on the whole, free of mortal sin. Already Freud was assuming the status of a Pope; his disciples were priests, carrying the infallible word. All this is inherent in the criticism.

These various cricisms were first developed by Adler and Jung. They felt that Freud's outlook was far too "intellectual", with a naïve, nineteenth-century faith in the power of reason and experimental method. Adler declared that Freud's insistence on tracing back the patient's sexual history was only another opportunity for the patient to escape the reality of his present problems; he insisted that the job of the psychologist is to give the patient a kind of "mental charge" so that he makes a new attempt to overcome his problems and his desire to escape. Adler's view pays more respect to the freedom of the individual than Freud's – and at the same time, to the hidden forces of intentionality that could allow the patient to cure himself.

Adler then made an immense step in the direction of an existential psychology. He declared that man is driven onwards by his sense of inferiority (the same inferiority that led the earliest men to develop weapons and form society) towards some state of final perfection, "as by a blind teleology". For Adler, man's health is connected with the "law of overcoming" – as in Nietzsche – and neuroses are not of sexual origins, but connected with the will to power, to overcome inferiority. Adler's doctrine of the inferiority complex has become as famous as Freud's libido; in fact, it is frequently attributed to Freud.

Jung's break with Freud started when he published his book *Transformations and Symbols of Libido* in 1912. In this work, Jung showed that his mind was of a different quality from Freud's. He could not be content with the atmosphere of the consulting-room and the case-record; he was equally interested in literature, history, and mythology. Freud's mother fixation has to be given new depth by relating it to the Earth Mother, Kali, and so on. In his later work it became apparent that Jung was less a psychologist than an anthropologist with a deep religious impulse.

For Freud and Freudians, these new emphases were only a departure from scientific rigour, an admission of weakness.* On the whole, their attitude was wise. Intuition is important, but it has no value for the "analytical" scientist unless it can be supported analytically. This kind of support was developed slowly and painfully by Koffka, Wertheimer, and Husserl.

The third important revolt from Freudian method was made by Otto Rank. First of all Rank developed Adler's idea that therapy should be a "conscious" affair, not a groping around with dubious dream symbols and childhood influences. Rank anticipated the discoveries of modern anthropology and zoology in declaring that sex is *not* the basic animal drive, nor was it the basic drive in our distant ancestors. Rank later developed a theory of unconscious will that is close to Husserl's later views. Ira Progoff summarizes the net result of the "revolution": ". . . the emergence of a new kind of psy-

*For example, the late Ernest Jones, Freud's biographer, borrowed my copy of Ira Progoff's *Death and Rebirth of Psychology*. He returned it to me with a letter admitting that it is, on the whole, fair and accurate. But his annotations reveal that he is completely unreconciled to the new approach. For example, where Progoff has written: "Freud's most obvious weakness lies in the determinism that underlies his work", Jones has underlined "weakness" and written in the margin "Strength".

chology that no longer seeks to diagnose modern man and reduce him to 'normality'. It attempts instead to provide a means by which the modern person can experience the larger meanings of life and participate in them with all his faculties." This revolution "reaffirms man's experience of himself as a spiritual being".

While it is impossible to deny the immense value of the later work of Jung and Rank, the old objection remains open: it is too unscientific, too much a matter of intuitions and inspired guesses. It is important that the gap between scientific method and "poetic insights" should not be overlooked. Mary Baker Eddy's ideas about the relation of the "power of mind" to the human body may well prove to have a basis in fact; they already anticipate the later development of the theory of intentionality. But they cannot be regarded as scientific until Gestalt theory and phenomenology have been taken to a point where controlled experiments can show them to have some foundation. Even when (and if) this happens, however, Mrs. Eddy's *Science and Health* will still be nothing more than sloppily written and badly constructed rambling.

Jung saw, rightly, that the development of such a consciousness would involve nothing less than the re-creation of the "religious approach" to life. The priest, for example, feels that he, as well as his penitent, is involved in the universal problem of original sin; yet his attitude is not therefore pessimistic. But Jung turned too easily to the old "religious truths", and to re-interpreting them in the modern manner; this might have been very useful in its way, but it did not advance the science of psychology.

At this point, there sprang up in various parts of Europe the school that has since been labelled "Existential psychology", and which is considered by many to be the most revolutionary advance in psycho-therapy since the days of William James. According to Rollo May, the school sprang up "spontaneously" – that is, no single thinker was responsible for its basic ideas – unless, perhaps, we take the view that Kierkegaard or Nietzsche was its real founder. The psychologists involved in this revolution were Eugene Minkowski in Paris, Erwin Straus in Germany (and later in America), and V. E. von Gebsattel, also in Germany. These three represent the "phenomenological stage" of the movement. Then came Ludwig Binswanger, A. Storch, Medard Boss, G. Bally, Roland Kuhn, J. H. Van Den Berg, and F. J. Buytendijk, and certain others, who represent the "existential stage" of the movement.

I have already spoken of phenomenology. It could be defined simply as "an attempt to be scientific about feelings". The whole method of this present book has been phenomenological – that is to say, has tried to confine itself to a steady contemplation of "the facts" about sex, without theoretical preconceptions like "conscious and unconscious", the death wish, race-consciousness, etc. Herbert Spiegelberg, in his brilliant and comprehensive book *The Phenomenological Movement* (Martinus Nijhoff, The Hague, 1961), says: "Phenomenology is the systematic exploration of phenomena not only in the sense of *what* appears . . . but also of *the way* in which things appear . . ." and again, even more simply, defines phenomenology as "the ways of given-ness". Again, he speaks of the aim of phenomenology as "to detach the phenomena of our everyday experience from the context of our naïve or natural living, while preserving their content as fully as possible". Spiegelberg devotes an interesting section to an attempt at a phenomenological description of the idea of "force". He points out that the aim of phenomenological description is to convey a certain sensation to a person who has never felt it. (Example: try to describe to someone what it feels like to get an electric shock, and how it differs from plunging into cold water on a hot day; if you can do this convincingly, you are a good phenomenologist!) And the most interesting point that emerges from Spiegelberg's account is that such an attempt *makes for increased precision of language*; it helps to destroy linguistic vagueness. It serves the function that Eliot claimed was the aim of poetry: "to purify the dialect of the tribe".

Now it will be seen immediately that such a method is a revolution in psycho-therapy. Because all psychology so far has begun with a set of *preconceptions*, and has made its solution dependent on making the "facts" fit in. Consequently its effect on language and precision has been poisonous. It has introduced lots of new words and terms, thereby greatly confusing the issues; but it has done little to explore and clarify our simple concepts.

This is a point of considerable importance, and perhaps I might be forgiven for dwelling on it. The difference between the old approach and the phenomenological approach might be made clearer by a comparison with literature. When you read a great novelist of the nineteenth century – Dickens or Dostoevsky, for example – your world may be *transformed* by it. You walk around and see things as Dickens or Dostoevsky would have seen them. Their vision has been temporarily imposed on your own, like putting on an extra pair of spectacles.

Consider, on the other hand, the effect of reading certain pages in Proust or Joyce. When Proust devotes half a page to describing the sound of the beginning of a shower, he is not imposing his vision on the reader; he is only sharpening the reader's ability to observe the same thing. Instead of handing the reader a pair of coloured spectacles, he hands him a microscope. The same is true of James Joyce; his minute descriptions of Dublin only make the reader's observation of his own town more minute and precise.

Freud is like Dickens and Dostoevsky. In his story *Childhood of a Leader*, Sartre has an interesting description of the effect of reading Freud on an innocent young provincial; the boy is shattered; he sees things in a new light. *But he does not observe them more precisely*. Many readers will bear witness to this effect of a first reading of Freud, and the way that it "changes the colour" of the world.

Phenomenology is not interested in painting the world a new colour; it wants to get the world as colourless as possible *to begin with*. It does not want to introduce new concepts, but to refine the old ones, and to reveal subtleties and inner-contradictions by careful analysis.

All this, then, explains the revolution brought about in psychology when Minkowski, Straus, and von Gebsattel introduced the methods of Husserl. Its effect was essentially to refine the language, to increase the subtlety of concepts.

The "existential stage" then followed. We might almost say that it is the inevitable response to the type of problem encountered by psychiatrists in the twentieth century. Freud's psychology developed in an age of security and optimism, an age dominated by "convention" and taboo; it is, in effect, an attack on convention and taboo. The intellectual climate of the nineteenth century tended to be insular and self-satisfied. This was the age when Herbert Spencer and Max Muller explained away "myths" as an outcome of man's misunderstanding of language. Psycho-analysis dynamited this complacent world by declaring that sex and violence and irrationality are the basis of all society and all human behaviour – respectable or otherwise.

The world of the mid-twentieth century is an entirely different affair. No one could accuse us of feeling too much security; wars and revolutions seem to have broken every window in the house of man's complacency. Consequently the typical neurosis has changed. It is no longer a question of people being driven into neurosis by too many taboos and conventions, but by the pervading "anxiety" of the twentieth century. And this social anxiety produces the state of mind in which man becomes aware of the basic problem of the human condition, and in which we are all slightly closer to "the pain threshold" – the border line between health and sickness. Freud aimed to cure his patients by bringing their subconscious repressions to light – perhaps by demonstrating that a certain man had always had a fear of castration, and felt guilty about wanting to murder his father and rape his mother. But for men living in the shadow of the hydrogen bomb the idea that anyone might be "cured" and "reconciled to society" by such a revelation is laughable. We fear the outer-violence as much as the inner-violence. So it is no longer permissible to assume, like Freud that all neurosis has a sexual basis, and disappears when man is adjusted to society. Society is no longer stable, so adjustment to it is no longer the wholly satisfactory solution.

Existential psychology may be defined in this way: It is a recognition that man's problem of adjustment is *to life itself*, not merely to society. For Freud and the nineteenth century there was no huge question mark behind life. Religions were a response to man's need for a father figure, an outcome of his gullibility and ignorance, not a genuine response to a real mystery. There was no real mystery.

Existential psychology is a response to the need for a less materialistic vision. Its aim might be expressed simply like this: If God existed, then he would be the ideal psychiatrist, since he would say to his patients: "*This* is why you are alive, *this* is your aim and purpose, and this is how you've got yourself into such a mess." For the basis of the prevalent twentieth-century neurosis (if the generalization might, for the moment, be allowed to pass) is not man's fear of his own irrationality, but a deeper fear that all life is futile, is a horrible joke. We might say that only religious faith could meet such a situation, but this is not necessarily true. Edmund Wilson once remarked: "The answer to Mr. Eliot's assertion that 'it is doubtful whether civilization can endure without religion' is that we have got to make it endure". And this is also the answer to the assertion that the "angst" of modern man can only find its cure in religion. Most religious revivalism of the twentieth century has been a step backwards into the dark ages. Religion *imposes* its answer, and always has done. A religious man might retort that science will never be able to answer the "riddle of human existence". The answer is that we might give it a try. And where do we start? We might try interrogating the sexual impulse, using the phenomenological method – this, at all events, is a beginning.

In short, existential psychology is a psychology whose basic preoccupations and premises are the same as those of Nietzsche and Kierkegaard, instead of those of nineteenth-century materialism. Of necessity, the relation of the psychiatrist to patient is different. In psycho-analysis the analyst is assumed to be somehow "outside" his patients' problems. In existential psychology the analyst knows perfectly well that he himself is involved in the same riddle that is imposing strain on his patient. He can help the patient to help to sort out "inessential" neuroses from the basic "angst", and, depending upon his own inner resources, powers, and insights, might even suggest a more fruitful approach to the basic problems. But the relation is different; they are like two soldiers on a march, the stronger helping the weaker. But both are in enemy territory, and a stray bullet might kill either of them at any moment.

An example cited by Rollo May demonstrates the existential method. The patient was an intelligent woman of twenty eight, who had fits of uncontrollable rage, acute anxieties, and various other minor symptoms. She was an illegitimate child, who had been made to feel unwanted; her mother had even told her that she had tried to abort her.

One day, after some months of treatment in which the analyst attempted to deepen her awareness of her relation to existence, she had an experience that might have come from James's *Varieties of Religious Experience:*

"I remember walking that day under the elevated tracks in a slum area, feeling the thought: 'I am an illegitimate child'. I recall the sweat pouring forth in my anguish in trying to accept the fact. Then I understood what it must feel like to accept: 'I am a Negro in the midst of privileged whites' or 'I am blind in the midst of people who see'. Later on that day, I woke up and it came to me in this way: 'I accept the fact that I am an illegitimate child'. *But,* 'I am not a child any more'. So it is, 'I am illegitimate'. Then what is left? What is left is this: 'I *am.*' This act of contact and acceptance with 'I am', once gotten hold of me, gave me (what I think was for me the first time) the experience: 'Since I am, I have the right to be'.*

*Existence, p. 43.

What has happened here is the dawning of an *awareness* in an area for which, so far, we have no terminology. We can perhaps say vaguely that the patient had lost her basic self-respect, her sense of the necessity of her existence, and that the neuroses that developed were rather like the noise made by the engine of a car when it is disengaged from the gears and then revved. The loss of contact with reality leads to a kind of hysteria. The discussions with the psychologist evidently restored the patient's sense of self-respect, her ability to take herself seriously. (She had received little conventional schooling, but was highly intelligent and had educated herself; this reveals a basic sense of purpose, with which she was again placed in contact by the analysis.)

Plainly this is simple "outsider-psychology". When the talented person feels that his (or her) powers are being wasted, neurosis is inevitable. The more talented the person, the more powerful the need for "friction with reality". A cow can graze quietly in a field all its life without becoming neurotic; it needs very little friction. Shaw expressed his sense of dislike of the Dublin society described in *Ulysses*:

". . . the life that Dublin offers to its young men. No doubt it is much like the life of young men everywhere in modern urban civilization. A certain flippant futile derision and belittlement that confuses the noble and serious with the base and ludicrous. . . . When I left my native city I left that phase behind me, and associated no more with men of my age until . . . I was drawn into the Socialist revival of the early eighties, among Englishmen intensely serious, and burning with indignation at the very real and fundamental evils that affected all the world." (Preface to *Immaturity*.)

Shaw might easily have developed a neurosis like the one cited above if he had been artificially confined to Dublin society, and denied access to the "serious men" in London.

But in the case of the young woman, the task of the therapist was simplified by her intelligence, and by her previous training in self-education. Long discussions with any serious and intelligent person could have affected the cure.

Nevertheless, this, in general, is the approach of existential psychology. Neurosis is assumed to be the sign of "the engine revving in a void", out of touch with the gears.

It can now be seen, perhaps, why the movement decided to ally itself with existentialism in the form created by Kierkegaard and Heidegger. For existentialism attempted to develop a terminology that would distinguish "degrees of existence". It is true that certain existential psychologists have taken over Heidegger's obscurities and dark metaphysical incantations a little too enthusiastically,* without realizing the shallow nature of some of his generalizations. But on the whole, the language is made an instrument of the psychological insight, and is not allowed to become its tyrant.

It is also true that the existential interpretations sound occasionally as far-fetched as anything in Jung or Freud. Medard Boss, for example, cites a case of a patient who suffered from handwashing and cleaning compulsions. He had dreams of church steeples which had been interpreted by Freudian analysts as phallic symbols, and by a Jungian analyst as a religious archetype symbol. One day this patient had a dream in which he entered a locked lavatory, plunged waist-deep in ordure, and tried to pull himself out by a bell rope leading up to a

---

*It should be mentioned, for those unacquainted with the existential movement, that for some years now Heidegger's position has been held to be extremely dubious. Certain aspects of his achievement are unassailable. Yet it is hard to think of Heidegger as a truly disinterested philosopher. Hulme once said that philosophers clothe themselves in armour to impress the gullible, but that the illusion vanishes when you see the armour-clad figure in the pantry stealing tarts. This is specially true of Heidegger. Although his bearing is as ponderous and obscure as that of any German philosopher, the reader feels occasionally that one of Heidegger's fundamental preoccupations is to "put himself across" as a profound thinker. Professor Kaufmann's brilliant attacks on him are slightly unfair; after all, it is hardly to the point that Heidegger became a Nazi supporter and disowned his old teacher Husserl (who was Jewish), and then, after the war, took care to disclaim all enthusiasm for the Nazis. But Kaufmann's observation of the *theatrical* nature of much of Heidegger's thinking is devastatingly accurate. Heidegger's showmanship is insidious because, unlike Sartre's, it is carefully concealed.

church steeple. Boss interpreted all this as meaning that the patient had locked up certain vital potentialities within himself and was unconsciously refusing to develop himself; this caused guilt feelings. He failed to face and absorb the two opposed aspects of himself: the spiritual and the lower physical. The analysis was brought to a successful conclusion after the patient had a psychotic relapse due to the dream.

Boss may be right in his analysis; without a personal acquaintance with the patient it is impossible to say. But on the surface, the talk about "locking up spiritual and physical potentialities" sounds as unlikely as the Freudian interpretation of phallic symbols or the Jungian idea of religious archetypes.

Nevertheless it must be admitted that existential psychology brings a new approach to such problems as the world of the compulsive. Von Gebsattel quotes a case in which a seventeen-year-old boy was governed wholly by compulsive behaviour. The boy seemed to live off the edge of his nerves. He would sit on the lavatory for hours waiting for his penis to stop dripping because he believed that the least drop of urine would make him smell offensively; he would wrap the end of his sexual member in toilet paper, and even this would seem ineffectual. He could not continue reading, if he decided to do so, because he would find himself staring at every word separately. All his movements, from getting up in the morning, were rigorously ordered, and he found himself observing himself in the tiniest action. He had an obsession about dirt, and would not go through a door without carefully avoiding the door supports in case he dirtied his clothes. He was able to read occasionally if he accidentally came upon something readable, but not otherwise.

The case sounds bizarre to the layman; but it is not unlike the "case" described by Sartre in *La Nausée*. Roquentin also analyses experiences down to such minute particulars that they lose meaning. The operative word for this case is *meaning*. The analytical faculty has somehow got out of hand; this is by no means unusual in adolescence, particularly if the adolescent is intelligent and cut off from social intercourse. Gurdjieff would declare simply that the patient's intellectual centre was doing the work of his moving centre. A man learning to type has to keep his critical sense awake to observe the position of the keys and to make sure that he hits the right one. As he becomes skilled in typing, the moving centre takes over the work, and he types "automatically".* If he tries to allow the intellect to interfere in the typing, total confusion results. It is significant that the compulsive patient in question could only read when he accidentally came upon something readable. Then the intellect ceased to interfere with the other centres.

This case, cited by Gebsattel, has its roots in frustration and the unbalance of a developing adolescent with no outlet for the sexual and social impulses. A milder form of the same problem occurs to many teenagers. It is the outcome of inactivity and too much self-analysis; all the sexual and emotional energies pour into the intellect, with an effect like that of driving a car at fifty miles an hour in low gear. The engine heats up; the resultant sense of strain develops into an anxiety neurosis. An effective cure depends only upon somehow passing the work back to the moving centre, and somehow persuading the intellect to relax and to cease to play the dictator. This requires an inner co-ordination that may be beyond the powers of most adolescents. But it *could* be effected by solutions as simple as getting drunk, having a love affair (a consummated one, that is), or joining the army. James Joyce, who appears to have experienced something of the same problem in his teens, solved it adequately by spending most of his money on prostitutes and beer. It is hard to say whether these had any permanently harmful effect on him, but it seems doubtful.

*I have observed an interesting example of the sort recently – of a kind that must be common experience. A particularly good dart-player of my acquaintance throws his dart only after many hesitations. He explained that he used to throw the dart quickly and easily. One day, someone asked him: "How do you throw a dart?" He began to observe himself throwing the dart, with the consequence that he found it extremely difficult to *let go* of the dart when preparing to throw it. This is obviously a mild example of "compulsive behaviour".

In Federico Fellini's remarkable film *La Dolce Vita* there is an episode that bears all the signs of being a true case history.* The hero of the film is the young journalist Marcello – honest, but unsure of himself, caught in the corruption of Roman society life and inclined to drift. His friend Steiner seems at first to be one of the film's few symbols of meaningful living. Kind, serious, a scholar, he is not unlike some of Aldous Huxley's symbols of warmth and humanity in the later novels – Propter in *After Many a Summer*, for example. He is happily married, with two young children, a beautiful wife, brilliant friends, and an apparently ideal home life. One night Marcello attends a party at Steiner's home; when the friends stand alone in the bedroom of the children, Steiner expresses his basic fear, the Kierkegaardian *angst*:

"Any life, even the most miserable, is worth more than a sheltered existence in a world where everything is organized, where everything is practical, everything has its place. . . . Sometimes the night, this darkness, this calm, weighs on me. It is peace that makes me afraid. Perhaps only because I distrust it above everything. I feel that it's only an appearance, that it hides a danger. Sometimes, too, I think of the world my children will know. They say that the world of the future will be wonderful. But what does that mean? It needs only the gesture of a madman to destroy everything."

And later in the film Steiner murders his two children and then shoots himself. Marcello's last symbol of strength and decency has crumbled.

A Freudian, even a Jungian, would be baffled by such a case, and would spend time investigating Steiner's past for guilt feelings and complexes. These might, of course, exist, and contribute to the breakdown. But the basic causes of the breakdown can only be grasped through existential psychology. The characteristic of Kierkegaard's "anguish" is that it is not anxiety *about* some specific threat; it need not even be a general anxiety about the cruelty of life, like Ivan Karamazov's; it is a

*The film script – by Fellini – has been published in the United States by Ballantyne Books.

recognition that man is a sleepwalker, preoccupied by his little problems, and that he is actually walking with complete unawareness along the narrow top of a wall a thousand feet high. When Sartre speaks of "the basic horror of existence", he is being unnecessarily melodramatic. There is certainly immense *danger*, but that is a different thing. Man is alone in a universe of which he knows nothing except his own corner. As a child, he accepted the benevolence of the adult world; as an adult, he tends to accept the benevolence of the universe at large; but there are moments, confronting death or pain, when this seems to have been a comfortable illusion. Every morning the newspaper brings new evidence of man's cruelty and indifference to the suffering of others, murder of children, and torture of animals; and there are times when nature seems a malignant force taking pleasure in natural disasters. A man who became sensitive to all this would then be in a position to appreciate the finer "metaphysical evil" of the universe: the ravages of time, man's ultimate death and the illusions that keep him from being aware of it, the possibility that life is a trap, that man is a victim being fattened by a butcher.

Are these ultimate horrors? Is there no escape from them? This question cannot be answered, for we have not yet made a start on the real problems. There are times when life burns in us with such certainty that the unknown landscape seems to be revealed by a lightning flash, and we become convinced that whether or not *we* can know the answer, "Life" knows perfectly well where it is leading us; if we could deepen our understanding and conscious grasp by immense effort, we might ourselves be slightly more capable of grasping the purpose. But since our everyday life is a stumbling match, with blinkers on our eyes, it is impossible to know whether the vision of horror or the vision of meaning is "deeper".

But it is important not to confuse "angst" with human weakness, and to assume that every fool who blows out his brains has been involved in a wrestling match between Ultimate Yes and Ultimate No. Most neurosis is a result of human intentionality. As children, we think of "punishing" our parents, if they make life too difficult for us, by becoming ill or feigning weakness; the habit is ingrained, and in adulthood we may want to "punish" life for not treating us with the consideration we deserve. It is a conscious – or almost conscious – decision: "No, I *won't* go on under these conditions; if Destiny wants me to go on, it had better make me a better offer. Otherwise I'll lie down and kick". This childish element can be present in the strongest of human beings, to be evoked by some particularly difficult circumstances.

Now although existential psychology can do nothing about the real "angst" – which must always remain unless man can turn himself into a god – it can, to some extent, deal with this weakness. And it is important to realize that the weakness acts as an amplifier of the "metaphysical angst". There is no earthly reason why an intelligent man, with a fairly firm grasp on "reality", should decide to kill himself because of the "horror of life". To begin with, he may only be jumping out of the frying-pan into the fire. When man is "balanced" – when the centres are working reasonably – he can achieve a balance between his perception of "danger" and his knowledge of the potential strength of human beings.

These considerations should make it apparent that "Steiner" might have been helped by an unusually authoritative existential psychologist, but would have little to hope for from any of the Freudian schools.

It is of interest that Steiner remarks that "Any life, even the most miserable, is worth more than a sheltered existence in a world where everything is organized". To begin with, the remark betrays immaturity; a few months under really difficult conditions would soon make him grateful for what he has. This problem must be further considered in a moment. But the second half of his remark – about organization – reflects a current of thought that is of some importance in modern Western culture, a tendency to anti-rationalism. It appears first in Dostoevsky's novel *Notes from under the Floorboards*, where the "beetle man" explains to the reader that he is a man without will-power or self-respect; he is too intelligent to admire himself. But he goes on to speak of the ideal scientific millennium, when human beings will all be healthy, rational and happy (something like the unattractive state that Wells portrays in *Men Like Gods*), and says that when this great day dawns, there will still be a little man with bad teeth who will leap up and reject the "happiness" in the name of some strange freedom.*

Aldous Huxley later took up the social aspect of this subject in his *Brave New World*. Perhaps its most powerful expression is in Valery Briussov's story *The City of the Southern Cross*. Briussov's city of the future is at the South Pole, under a huge glass dome that keeps the weather temperate all the year round. It is run by a few capitalists, with hordes of "happy" workers, all made to live and dress in exactly the same manner in their ideal "Welfare State". There is no apparent discontent, until one day a strange disease breaks out called "contradiction mania". When a man intends to do something, he finds himself compelled to do the opposite; when he is about to kiss his wife, he is forced to bite her; if he wants to turn right, he feels forced to go left, and so on. When the disease spreads, the whole city is thrown into an uproar, until the victims of the mania destroy it completely and leave it a heap of ruins. The picture of its destruction is particularly powerful.

This is the same insistence on the need for "freedom" rather than mere "order". A great deal of this tendency can be found in twentieth-century literature. *But*, it should be recognized, this rejection of "order" may be only a form of immaturity, like Steiner's suicide. When a human being loses his subjectivity, his sense that "he exists" (like Rollo May's "illegitimate" woman patient), all order becomes intolerable. The

---

*The beetle man, like Steiner, is an interesting mixture of weakness and strength, and should be the subject of a paper by an existential psychologist. The characteristic of his type is their tendency to confuse their weakness with their strength and to insist that they are interdependent. Dostovesky himself was of this type.

fault may not lie in the social order, but in the patient's relation to his own "being".

This raises again the question inherent in the first part of Steiner's remark: "Any life, even the most miserable, is worth more than a sheltered existence". The human tendency not to appreciate what one has has already been discussed; it is bound up with the "repeating mechanism", and life's tendency never to allow man to retain more than one per cent of his gains. The purpose of this mechanism is to act as an evolutionary spur, to prevent laziness and relaxation. It is symbolized in the story of the old woman in the vinegar bottle who found it impossible to stop complaining, no matter how much a good fairy improved her condition; so in the end the fairy transferred the old woman from a palace back to her vinegar bottle.

But if this mechanism was too strong, human beings would simply die of boredom or frustration. Consequently , it would seem, we have another psychological mechanism – this time connected directly to the will – for absorbing the poisons deposited in us by boredom and frustration. When the fairy transferred the old woman back to her vinegar bottle she was implying that it was partly the old woman's fault that she continued to be querulous and unhappy. It is true that the repeating mechanism sees to it that our sense of achievement is kept trimmed low; yet even so, we are allowed to retain enough of the sense of achievement to keep us optimistic. If boredom succeeds in destroying *all* sense of achievement, then it is because the will has gone to sleep. And it is a sign of immaturity – or of degeneration. In Steiner's case it would seem to be immaturity; in the old woman's, degeneration that springs from a long-established habit of self-pity.

I have elsewhere suggested that we require a new concept in existential psychology – the concept of "the indifference threshold".* It would seem that there is a psychological state in which human beings have become indifferent to pleasure, but can still be stimulated by pain. No doubt the old woman

*See *Beyond the Outsider: An Outline of a New Existentialism.*

who failed to learn gratitude when she was transported into a
palace learned it retrospectively when she was put back in her
vinegar bottle. This occurs when, out of annoyance at having
our experience so heavily taxed, we fall into complete apathy,
and refuse to cheer up for any pleasure. In *Six Characters*
Pirandello remarked that unhappiness drives us to ask questions, while we accept happiness as our right. Since it is in the
interest of evolution that we should be kept asking questions,
it is understandable that some biological mechanism should
try to prevent us from becoming too happy. Nevertheless, by a
difficult process of compensation it *is* possible to defeat the
repeating mechanism occasionally, and to benefit from a new
intensity of experience. (The easier methods of defeating the
mechanism – drugs, alcohol, etc. – are self-defeating, since the
mechanism increases its strength to combat them – as resistance to a disease increases as its germs are absorbed – and only
makes it more difficult for the drug-taker when the effects have
worn off.) If human beings could develop a tendency to question their happiness as vigorously as their unhappiness, no
doubt the repeating mechanism would be discarded as bio-
logically unnecessary.

But already it is becoming apparent that the problem of sex
crime – and of sexual perversion – is one of the characteristic
problems of our time. It would not be too inaccurate to say
that we live in a schizophrenic society. The chief problem in
Freud's day – the early twentieth century – was hysteria, the
patient's first reaction to the increasing difficulties and complexities of existence. An attempt at adjustment is made, but an
inadequate attempt that adjusts only the surface of the being.
The result is the split between "mature" surface and adolescent depths. Schizophrenia might be considered as a slightly
"maturer" ailment than hysteria; the shift from hysteria to
schizophrenia indicates that society has made some slight progress in adjustment to the new conditions.

The rise in sex crime and sexual perversion requires a new
examination of the origins of the sexual impulse. In *Caste and
Class in a Southern Town*, John Dollard observes: "Sexual per-

versions are said to be less frequent among Negroes, masturbation rarer, and smearings and self-mutilations less common than among white patients. The reason alleged is that the direct genital expression of Negro sexuality is less prohibited, and the inner pressures which might drive Negroes to substitutive forms of sexual gratification do not exist." He also observes that the white man tends to envy the Negro his sexual freedom.* But Dollard's book was first published in 1937. It would be interesting to discover the statistics of today, a quarter of a century later. A superficial glance at the *True Detective* magazines of the 1950's reveals a steep increase in the number of Negroes involved in sexual crimes – particularly against white women; it seems probable that sexual perversion would also show an increase.

An existential examination of the sexual impulse reveals that the inability of the older psychology to deal with the problem of sexual perversion sprang from its assumption that there is a basic energy called the libido, and that the impulses of the libido are the deepest known to psychology. This conclusion was buttressed by the findings of Darwinian biologists, who declared that sex is the driving impulse in animal society. Since then, zoology has modified its conclusions, and it is becoming widely recognized that the will to precedence and the need for territory are even more "basic" than the sexual drive.

*"The other said that a Negro man always has about ten women beside his wife on the string – one never satisfies him." (*Op. cit.*, p. 398.) Dollard's analysis makes it clear that in some respects Negro society comes close to Blake's idea of complete sexual freedom. A Negro school teacher remarked that most of her girls had had sexual experience at an early age.

CHAPTER IX

THE THEORY OF SYMBOLIC RESPONSE

Conclusion.

Is it possible, then, to move from the consideration of sexual abnormality to any more general statements about "man" of "the nature of human intelligence"? Maurice Merleau-Ponty, the French phenomenologist and follower of Husserl, considered the problem in his book *The Phenomenology of Perception*. Merleau-Ponty was mainly concerned to attack certain "materialistic psychologies", particularly behaviourism (to which he devoted most of his earlier book, *The Structure of Behaviour*, published in 1942). On a severely scientific level, he attempts to undermine Watsonian behaviourism and Pavlov's "reflexology", and proves that only a Gestalt theory can fully account for human behaviour and responses. Merleau-Ponty's interest, in the present context, lies in his use of sexual perversions to refute "mechanistic physiology".

The present book has ignored total materialism as a possible solution of the origins of the sexual impulse, since it cannot even begin to explain sexual perversion. The leader of the behaviourist school, J. B. Watson, once wrote that no behaviourist had ever observed "anything that he can call consciousness, sensation, imagery, perception, or will". Since Watson was presumably conscious when he wrote these words, it is hard to see exactly what he meant; at all events, we may assume that no one nowadays would take seriously his assertion that man is wholly a machine. Nevertheless, the Freudian view implies that man *is* a kind of machine in that his "fuel" is a power called the libido, and that a man whose libido is healthy and unadulterated will be somehow a well-adjusted machine.

The conclusion to be drawn from a careful study of sexual perversion is that the libido, as such, does not exist.

An analogy might make clear exactly what I mean by this. To the Freudian, a "sexually abnormal" person is somehow "wrongly orientated". We might picture man's "psyche" as a large circle. In the centre of the circle – at the centre of man's being – is a fire called the libido. At various distances from the centre of the circle are points labelled "perversions". Fellatio and cunnilingus are fairly close to the centre; further out lies homosexuality and fetichism; further out still lies sadism and somewhere near the circumference is sexual murder. "Curing" a pervert would mean persuading his sexual inclinations to move back towards that centre.

Existential psychology rejects this picture. If man's total "psyche" is again represented by a circle, then "sexual normality" is not at the centre of the circle, but somewhere midway between the centre and the circumference. Beyond "normality" – closer still to the circumference – lie various perversions.

But the significance of this new picture can be immediately seen. In the Freudian picture a man has achieved a kind of stability once he has been pushed back to the centre of the circle (unless he goes on through it towards the other side). In the existentialist picture a "pervert" could be pushed back to "normality" – *but he could then go on through normality, beyond sex, closer still to the centre.* He could, in short, lose the sexual impulse altogether, and be even more "normal" than the most sexually normal person.

An immediate difference from Freudian psychology becomes apparent. In Freud, sex is a kind of Nirvana. Somerset Maugham's story *Rain* is the perfect Freudian parable. The missionary who was trying to convert Sadie Thompson was really a sexually frustrated and twisted old man, as he revealed by his final attempt to rape her. He had made an unsuccessful attempt to "sublimate" his sexual frustration, but he was not strong enough. He would have been better off if he had acknowledged that his religion was a cover-up for sexual desire. Sublimation is a second best, a poor substitute for the real thing, the proper expression of the libido.

The existential psychologist finds this view unnecessarily dogmatic. Imagine a potential Peter Kürten who falls into the hands of an expert existential psychologist. With careful re-conditioning, a re-channelling of the desires, stimulation of the intellect and sense of beauty, he might be weaned away from his sadism and turned into a normal man. But "normal man", as we know him to day, has no particular need of intellect, sense of beauty, enthusiasm; with a comfortable job and a television set he can get through life without any discomfort. A man like Kürten, who had learned to abandon the infliction of pain as a means of sexual expression, would also come to realize that the same energy of idealism could lead him to become altogether independent of sex. History is full of such men and women – the saints, artists, social reformers, scientists – men and women whom Freud would regard somehow as "unfulfilled". It has often been said that Freud has taught us to face unpleasant truths about ourselves; this may be so; but in this case he has taught us to face an unpleasant lie.

What then are the ultimate conclusions of existential psychology on the subject of human nature? This question takes us beyond psychology and into the realm of philosophy. To begin with, the study of sexual perversion makes it apparent that man can be conditioned to respond sexually to almost anything. What he responds to is a "Gestalt", a set of relations, rather than a definite object. After reading about various cases of fetichism, it is easy to imagine a man having an orgasm at the sight of a cube or a triangle. Sex is subjective. By this I mean that there is no necessary relation between the sexual energy and an object. If you are hungry, a meal will satisfy you. If you pick up a live coal, it will burn you. There is a real relation between your stomach and food, between your hand and a coal We think of the relation between male and female sexual organs as being the same kind of thing. Observation of perversion disproves this; what happens is that the mind bestows a kind of approval on certain objects or symbols, and "permits" an orgasm when these appear in conjunction. In *Crime and the Sexual Psychopath*, de River cites a case of a fetichist who became uncontrollable if he saw bras and panties in conjunction; one day when he was out driving with his wife he saw these objects on a line, and stopped the car down the block, telling his wife he wanted to call at a house they had passed. He then went into the garden, placed the undergarments on the ground in the position they would have have been on a woman's body, and was "copulating" with them when he was arrested. Plainly, his instincts had bestowed so much "approval" on these symbols of woman that he was affected by them as a "normal" man would be affected by the sight of a naked woman in the garden, to such an extent that he even went through the action of copulating with them. Such cases as this dispose of the notion that sexual response is any kind of a subject-object relation. It is a response to *symbols*.

Bearing this in mind, then, let us attempt a "phenomenological study" of man, attempting to consider only what we have been "given" (remembering the definition of phenomenology as "the study of the given"). We are "given", then, an animal walking on two legs, with a known "case history" dating back fourteen million years (if one of Leakey's estimates is accepted). This creature is largely a machine, and we know something about the way the machine operates. He can only act when he has a motive. Robbed of motive and purpose, his energy and his will die away, leaving him a kind of "Oblomov", melting away like a snowman in the sun.

He cannot act without energy, and energy is partly physical in origin. But it is also dependent on the will. This can easily be observed when a man has to respond to a new stimulus – let us say increased hardship in his living conditions. The stimulus causes him to *concentrate his will*, and after a time his body begins to develop more energy by burning up surplus fat. Action depends on energy. Energy depends on concentration of the will. But the will also needs a stimulus – purpose.

It is at this point that the mechanists and materialists say: "Precisely. And purpose *must* come in the form of a stimulus from the outside world, like dropping a penny into a slot machine." Now this is certainly true up to a point. But a simple stimulus could only elicit a simple response. And the strange thing about man is that his whole inner world adjusts itself to the stimulus, reacting in any number of ways that have come into being by some previous activity of the will.

It is on this point that behaviourism must be attacked, for it is here, and only here, that it can be refuted scientifically. The behaviourist argues Man draws his energy from food – from the outside world. He also draws his sense of purpose from the outside world. So what is to distinguish him from a kind of self-winding machine? To say that his responses are usually more "complicated" than the stimulus is only to say that he is a complicated machine.

And yet quite beyond these physical considerations his basic motive seems to be a will to increased complexity. How can we account for this in terms of mechanism? Any machine can be complex. A machine might conceivably react to certain threatening situations by striving to become more complex. But why should a machine possess a desire to become more complex without any kind of stimulus?

Let us concentrate, for a moment, on the notion of "purpose", which appears to be the ultimate link in the chain. My sense of purpose can be increased or decreased by external stimulus. "Damn braces; bless relaxes", says Blake. This is true; but to some extent I can choose whether I allow blessings to relax me. In other words, "stimulus" and "purpose" are by no means the same thing.

At this point the mechanist interposes: "But you have not demonstrated that any real inner-chose exists. Neither *can* you demonstrate such a thing, for once you have done a thing, it is done, and your assertion that you did it by choice has no ad-

---

*See Teilhard de Chardin's *The Phenomenon of Man*. Teilhard has invented the term "complexification" to describe the basic "symptom" of evolution.

vantage over my assertion that you did it for various *reasons*, all of which are to do with your inner mechanism."

And yet this is the point where I am able, to my own satisfaction, to refute the mechanistic psychologists and to go beyond them. For example, as I write this page, I am aware of my mind hovering over a large expanse of "facts" and ideas, as an owl hovers over a field looking for mice. I am aware of being able to choose any number of these to illustrate my point and shape my argument. I am also aware, to some extent, of being able to choose the words in which I express these ideas. (For example, in the last sentence I might have written "the words in which I clothe these thoughts", but my mind rejected the metaphor automatically.) No, to some extent, I am continually aware of my freedom. I may also drive myself to go on working long after my mind is tired of "flying", and it takes me longer to write half a page than it took me to write the previous three pages. This is again an act of choice, no matter how far it may depend on stimuli.

But at this point I become aware of a response that is not a part of the simple action-energy-will-purpose-stimulus chain. Although I am aware that my will is a passive quantity, dependent on purpose, I am also aware that my will possesses a curious tiny purpose of its own to *look for purpose*, in fact to scrutinize my own inner being for purpose. This purpose is quite dinstinct from external stimulus. It is as if my will attempted to become quiescent, to become a kind of radio-set to pick up some inner-vibration of purpose. Will is not only capable of responding to purpose; some second level of purpose drives the will to seek to re-establish communication with the primary level of purpose. But what is this primary level? What can we learn about it by the use of the phenomenological method?

At this point we can turn back again to sexual perversion and the sexual impulse. For the study of this inner-purpose leads to questions on the nature of the imagination. For again, three are assumptions here that will be seen to be unjustified. The mouth of a hungry man will water at the sight of a good meal. But his mouth will also water if he imagines a good meal with sufficient intensity. We say that the imagined meal evokes a milder response because it is *not* real. Imagination is "counterfeiting" what is "external". The naïve theory of sexual perversion runs along the same lines. The "real" object is an attractive member of the opposite sex. A man who masturbates using a picture of a naked woman, or a fetich, can expect a milder response since the object is not real. But we have seen that this is not true. If Sergeant Bertrand preferred a dead woman to a living one, it was because the living woman was too "real" and provided too many distractions and irrelevancies to the sexual impulse; he preferred his imagination and a dead body. In the same way it will be remembered that the officer "M" declared that masturbation can be more satisfying than actual intercourse because it can be controlled and "graded" more precisely.

Plainly the "inner purpose" *grants reality* to sexual objects and permits a response. There is no external reality, independent of the energy of imagination. A man whose imagination has lost its vitality might lose interest in a woman in the very act of making love to her. Where sex is concerned, there is no "object"; only a symbol clothed with reality by some innerpurpose; when this symbol corresponds to a living woman we call the desire "normal".

But the "inner-purpose" has constructed a sexual mechanism on the idea of alien-ness. Satisfactory sex is the invasion of the other's "alien-ness". This is why we call the sexual parts our "private parts". All depends upon the idea of violating strangeness. For the most part this mechanism works well enough. But unfortunately the "inner-purpose" failed to place enough checks and guards on the mechanism. When the intensity of sexual response depends on the alien-ness that has been invaded, it follows that men will try to intensify the response still further by going further afield in alien-ness. Since their enjoyment of "normal" sex depends on the sense of violating a taboo, it follows that they will try to increase their satisfaction by including as many taboos as possible in the sexual object. In a simple form, this can be found in German romanticism – in Wagner and Mann, for example – in the preoccupation with incest. If, on the contrary, we lived in a civilization in which you were expected to have sexual intercourse with parents or siblings, the idea of sleeping with one's mother or sister would be incredibly tedious ("but we see them all the time!"), and the thought of "violating" an alien girl correspondingly exciting. All sexual perversions, from mere adultery to necrophily, can be seen as attempts to increase the alien-ness of the act by increasing the number of taboos involved. Sex can never, on any level, be "healthy" or "normal". It always depends on the violating of taboos – or, as Baudelaire would have said, on the sense of sin. If the "evolutionary force" was ever examined by a panel of biologists and psychologists, they would be justified in demanding why the propagation of the race was made dependent upon a sense of sin, and in pointing out that this piece of incompetence has led to the downfall of many civilizations through sexual decadence.

By a phenomenological observation of ourselves and our sexual responses, we can, then, arrive at a theory of "symbolic response", in which the symbol is invested with meaning by a kind of "grace" of the inner-purpose. The next stage is to observe that "symbolic response" is not confined to our sexual activities. All "aesthetic appreciation" is symbolic response. Yeats has a moving poem, "Towards Break of Day", in which he talks about a waterfall "that all my childhood counted dear", and goes on:

> I would have touched it like a child
> But knew my finger could but have touched
> Cold stone and water. I grew wild
> Even accusing heaven because
> It had set down among its laws:
> Nothing that we love over-much
> Is ponderable to our touch.

These last lines are only a statement of the theory of symbolic response. Why is a waterfall beautiful when it is only cold stone and water? Why could Wordsworth see "unknown modes of being" in a hill above Windermere when the hill was made of ordinary earth and grass? Why do mountain ranges strike us as sublime, when they are made of the same materials we can find in the back garden, only piled higher? Poets and philosophers have been pointing out for hundreds of years that beauty is not a subject-object relation, but is "in the eye of the beholder". But there has to be something "out there" to produce an aesthetic response. But, as with sex, the "inner-purpose" is tolerant; it does not insist on the reality; it will permit the same pleasure response to a painting, or even a description in a book.

At this point speculation might run wildly afield for a moment and consider whether there is any true subject-object response, or whether it is *all* symbolic. When you feel sick, a certain psychological adjustment can defeat the sickness. The exact nature of this adjustment is difficult to define; it is not simply an act of will, but a kind of act of self-persuasion. It is only a few steps from this realization to the assertion of certain mystics that there is no "external reality". Whitehead wrote: "People make the mistake of talking about 'natural laws'. There *are* no natural laws. There are only temporary habits of nature." Mrs. Baker Eddy claimed that all illness is "symbolic response", or rather a failure of symbolic response, that can be defeated by renewed contact with the "inner purpose". Saints and fakirs claim that even the contact between the subject and the physical world is an illusion, and hold lighted coals to prove it. The scientific study of "extra-sensory perception" even seems to indicate that the future is already "present" in some sense, and can occasionally be predicted with fair accuracy.

This is only to suggest that the theory of symbolic response *may* possess a relevancy outside the field of sex and aesthetics. But how is it possible to investigate the nature of the relation between "mind" and "external reality" when mind is the investigator, and the unknown relationship also intrudes into the investigation? It can be done, of course, just as any un-known "x" can be discovered if there is enough data for a series of comparisons. Human beings have always found it simpler to negate "mind" and search for objective laws of nature. Science likes neat equations, where everything can be accounted for. And on the whole, it has been successful in constructing its equations, and ignoring the facts that refuse to fit in. And the idea of "life" or "purpose" is one of the elements that the science of the past two hundred years has preferred to leave out of its equations. So in Darwinism we have a "mechanical" evolution, and in Watson we have a mechanical psychology, just as Newton and Descartes provided us with a mechanical universe. Watson, of course, did not mean to imply that consciousness does not exist; this would have been an absurdity. But he implied that consciousness is a *passive spectator* of the universe, a mere "witness" of what goes on.

Gestalt theory and phenomenology assert that, on the contrary, consciousness is *always* interfering. The mechanistic theories – from Newton to Freud – assert that something is happening "out there", and that all responses depend on what is out there. Responses *happen*, and they are as "physical" as throwing a match into gunpowder.

The theory of symbolic response denies this, and asserts that, except for "consciousness", *the response would not happen at all*. Science continues to investigate the world "out there", and believes that one day, when it has enough facts and formulae, the universe will be "explained". The theory of symbolic response declares that even when every inch of the universe "out there" has been mapped and compressed into formulae, the key will still be missing, for the key is "in here"; is an inner-purpose that imposes responses on the outside world.

Recapitulation

These conclusions are so important, and their implications so immense, that it may be as well to pause before pursuing this argument to its final stages, and re-state them in a manner that will leave no room for misunderstanding. For what is now appearing is nothing less than a completely new mode of thinking which may very well mark a definite stage in the evolution of the creature called man.

Let us consider first of all the basic *données* of the argument. On the one hand we have a creature called man, whose life-span is less than a hundred years. Man is surrounded by "nature" – which outlasts him and dwarfs him, but which is not as "alive" as man.

The question: what is man's place in nature? How important is he? What does it all mean?

Man has existed for many millions of years. It is only in the past few thousands of years that he has become a "question-asking" creature.

But when we consider human culture – man's responses to the question: "Who am I?" – we notice an interesting thing. *Man has always taken himself for granted.* He has tried to scrutinize God and Nature, but he has always assumed that he can leave the subject of himself until later. He "is". That is enough to be going on with.

When we examine human thought from its earliest origins – in the Vedas or ancient myths – down to the nineteenth century, we notice that man always thinks of himself as a "creature in an inferior position – like a boy in school under the eye of a schoolmaster, or a son under the eye of a despotic father. There have been many "revolutions" in thought; but they have always been revolutions against other men – that is, against the other schoolboys in the class. Never against the teacher.

For example, we think of religious rebels like Luther and Calvin as men who stood out for more freedom, who defied the authority of the Church. It is startling to examine these men more closely, and to find that, in all essentials, they were "more conservative than the conservatives", that Calvin had Servetus burned for denying the Trinity, and that Luther's major tenet was that every word of the Bible is literally true. They were, in many ways, far more reactionary and old fashioned than the Church they were attacking. Luther set Christianity back a thousand years.

It may seem startling to us that all great thinkers of the past were so blind in matters of religion, but we should remember that to our nineteenth-century ancestors it was not at all startling. What *was* startling to them – indeed, terrifying – was the new wave of thought called "romanticism", that shook its fist at God and declared that man ought to be "free", ought to be his own judge of right and wrong.

Many of them blamed this revolt on to "science". But they were wrong. For the great founders of modern science – Galileo, Kepler, Newton, Descartes – were all profoundly religious men, *and they incorporated their religious views in the foundations of their science*. This last statement may seem surprising; after all, none of these men ever mention "God" or Christ in their scientific works. But God was implied in their vision of science. For in their picture the universe is "out-there", waiting for man to investigate it. God does not actually interfere in its workings; all that is attended to by "natural laws". But God made these laws, and he set the machinery going in the first place. God "wound up the clock". And here is man, on earth, a tiny ant of a creature, peering at the universe through a telescope, doing his best to understand why God made it the way it is. "God is a mathematician" said Newton. The important thing about this picture is that *man is an ant*. He can "understnd" nature by using his intelligence, but he is still a very tiny creature, and very unimportant.

The greatest of all revolts – probably the greatest single revolt in the history of human thought – was that change of attitude that occurred around the beginning of the nineteenth century: the change that was expressed by Dostoevsky and Nietzsche in the statement: "All things are lawful"; i.e. there is no God up in the sky, and man is his own judge of right and wrong.

What exactly does this mean? Remember that, according to the "new science", man is still taking himself for granted, just as he did when the Church was at the height of its power. As an analogy, I might say that "Man" is playing a game of hunt-the-thimble, searching every corner of the room, but taking it for granted that the thimble is not in his own pocket. The "thimble" is the question: "What are the laws of the universe?", and man continued to rummage around the universe, lifting mountains, peering at stars, making endless calculations, and still not finding his thimble. The Catholic Church declared: "The thimble is hidden in St. Peter's pocket; you must accept his word for it". Luther declared: "No, the thimble is hidden in the Bible". Newton came along and declared in the most demure way possible: "You can forget St. Peter and the Bible". (In fact, Newton wrote a vast commentary on the Bible – but he did not look there for the "secret of the universe" – only for a few minor details in God's chronology.) The "secret", for Newton, was out there, in the universe, and with enough science and mathematics, it could be discovered.

Now the full – and most fascinating – implications of that statement: "All things are lawful" can be seen. It boils down to three statements, two of them correct, and one wrong. (a) We cannot discover the meaning of right and wrong by looking through a telescope; no amount of scrutiny will reveal God's Purpose inherent in Nature. (b) This is because there is no God "out there", who is in control of right and wrong. (c) But man is only a small, miserable creature, who also has no ultimate ideas on right and wrong. Therefore, all things are lawful.

This statement summarizes the intellectual position of romanticism for a hundred and fifty years. It is as true of Goethe's *Faust* and Schiller's *Robbers* as of the works of Camus and Sartre. Sartre has only added a pendant to (c), declaring that although man *is* a miserable creature, he can at least dignify himself by recognizing that he has to choose right and wrong, that he can add slightly to his stature by "committing" himself.

It will now be seen what an extraordinary revolution has been brought about by these two apparently academic and highly technical theories, phenomenology and Gestalt psychology. For what they have done is to substitute a quite different clause in (c). They have suggested that man tries looking in his own pocket for the thimble. The ground was prepared for them of course, by Freud, with his insistence on the "subconscious". For although Freud was not the inventor of the idea of the unconscious mind, he emphasized it in a way that gave it new importance. The clause (c) began to change when Freud said: "Man is not the small, simple creature he appears to be. That is only his conscious mind. Beneath this is an immense ocean of subconscious, of instinctive 'mind', about which he knows very little". Man thereby became something altogether bigger and deeper.

But for Freud, the unconscious is in some way "inferior" to the conscious mind. It is as if man kept an immense herd of elephants in his back garden; they are frightening and powerful; they might even trample his house down; but they are still elephants, mere animals.

Phenomenology and Gestalt psychology together created a new concept of the subconscious. Unknown it is; here they agree with Freud. But it contains some strange principle of value and meaning that is greatly superior to anything in the conscious mind.

It will be seen that Dostoevsky's "All things are lawful" immediately vanishes. This was based on a misunderstanding: the idea that *if* there is meaning and value, it is "out there"; and if it is not out there, then it doesn't exist.

This idea of a source of values inside man is both new and old. The concept of the inner-light has been familiar since Peter Waldo, the twelfth-century founder of the Waldenses, and has been a commonplace since the days of George Fox. But although the Quakers recognized the "inner light", God was still an external reality, communicating with men by means of a kind of internal telephone. This was the God whose death was announced by Zarathustra.

I doubt whether Husserl or the Gestalt psychologists intended anything as general and metaphysical as the statement I have made here. Their disciplines were only a new and interesting way of studying the subject–object relation and attacking the problems of perception. It is only in the "moral" light of existentialism that their value can be fully seen. But in their quiet statement that there is something "in there", that imposes form on our perceptions, they had reversed the whole current of human thought of two thousand years. The only great modern thinker to reach similar conclusions by following an independent line of thought was Alfred North Whitehead, whose importance in twentieth-century thought is still not even suspected.

The theory of symbolic response is only a single logical step from the conclusions of Gestalt and phenomenology. If a hidden "intentionality" imposes forms on our perceptions, presumably it also projects the values that we "see" in nature. These values reflect the "aim" of "intentionality".

Nowhere is this more clear than in the regions of sex and aesthetics. A non-phenomenological psychology would like to explain sexual perversion in terms of a basic, external sexual "reality", and the deviations from this reality. If, for example, some physiologist could discover that men and women carry magnets in their genitals, and that the male magnet has the North Pole pointing outwards while the female magnet has its South Pole outwards, this would provide the perfect "scientific" and objective basis for all perversion. Homosexuals would be men whose magnet has accidentally got turned the other way. A little ingenuity could easily explain other perversions in terms of induced magnetism.

Unfortunately there are no such "objective facts" to explain why male animals experience the urge to bring their genitals into contact with the female organs. It is true that, among the lower animals, the smell of oestrum plays a part. But this only moves the problem next door; why does oestrum excite the male?

We can explain many human "habits" in terms of social conditioning – conditioning from "outside", and Robert Ardrey has pointed out how important a part this conditioning plays. But the sexual urge is deeper than any social urge. It cannot be explained in terms of externals. Any attempt to "explain" it has to proceed synthetically, not analytically: that is, it cannot start with simple "facts" and build up from there; it has to begin with some idea involving *value* or "perfection" (they imply one another) and work inward. Hence both the Garden of Eden legend and Plato's legend of "spherical men" begin with the idea of an earlier perfection – a value – which is the driving force behind sex. They begin with the idea of an interior purpose, not a response to something "out there". What is "out there" does not explain the response; the only plausible explanation is of an interior drive – an evolutionary drive – that *orders* the response. We must suppose the evolutionary nature of the drive since it is impossible otherwise to account for the "direction" of the drive, which appears to make for increasing complexity. Our aesthetic responses, for example, appear to have no physical or social *raison d'être*. If the "inner-purpose" aimed at nothing beyond "civilization", there would be no reason why a landscape should strike us as beautiful; on the contrary, the "purpose" might prefer to condition us to loathe nature, like the children in Aldous Huxley's *Brave New World*. But the beauty of nature is associated in our minds with the ideas of solitude and of freedom, both important to evolution. Man in a city with a million other men is an ant; man alone with mountains and lakes is aware of the challenge to be a god.

Again, the whole question of colour is connected with this problem of evolution. Colour is a "residue" of sense that is unexplainable to science; we can understand about the eye responding to the wave-length of red light, but no amount of explaining can get beyond our knowledge of the difference between green and red. The same is true of our knowledge of the difference between the smell of eau-de-cologne and beer, or the taste of tomatoes and eggs, or the sound of a violin and a bird. When the scientist analyses the physical world he tries to examine the "bricks" that constitute the house, and he finds wave-lengths, relative densities, volatility, etc. But when we look at the universe we are not aware of these bricks. And this is not because *our* universe is not also made of bricks. But our bricks are colours, scents, sounds, and tastes, and feelings. And these are the "bricks" of intentionality, the bricks with which the "inner-purpose" builds its structures. The interest of colour in particular lies in the uselessness of the colour sense from the point of view of survival. In most animals, colour sense is undeveloped, while hearing and smell are more acute than in human beings. Experiments indicate that very young children have no colour sense. It seems probable that our ancestors of a thousand years ago had far less sense of colour than we have; there are very few references to colour in the ancient poets. Homer did not even notice that the sky was blue, and his colour sense was so poor that he could compare the sea to wine simply because both are dark in colour. If there is any truth in the legend that the authors of the *Iliad* and *Odyssey* were both blind from birth, this would be understandable, but it would not explain why all the other ancient poets seem as blind to colour. What seems more likely is that the colour sense is a luxury that has developed with civilization for no practical reason, but because the sense of beauty is an important spur to evolution. In so far as our attention is required for the details of survival, we cannot afford a sense of beauty. Aldous Huxley has described the intensification of his sense of colour under mescalin, and explained that this intensification was accompanied by a pleasant lethargy, a positive disinclination to act or think. But it is not improbable that human beings in a thousand years from now will all see things with this intensity.

It is important that this point should be understood. Beauty *is* meaning, although it is not the only kind of meaning. I may enjoy the sound of rain because I am a gardener, and my plants need rain. So my enjoyment, my perception of meaning, is a subject–object relation, the object being my garden. But I may enjoy the sound of rain for no reason at all – or for the same reason I enjoy a landscape. In this case it is useless for me to look *outside* for the cause of my enoyment; like Yeats, I shall only be aware of "cold stone and water". The pleasure is a kind of bonus from my intentionality, and is not supposed to lead me to *do* anything; it is a demonstration of affection, like stroking a cat, intended to intensify my vitality and sense of purpose.

There are, then, two kinds of meaning. One is a subject–object relation, and a call to action, a call for a definite response. The other is a "bonus", and demands no kind of response except pleasure. It is curious that the life-force has decided to make our sexual relations an exception to this rule.

It should be noted that Huxley declared that the world became far more meaningful under mescalin, although he could not describe its meaning, except by talking about the "is-ness" of a chair. Again, we are faced with the fundamental religious question. Men have always scrutinized nature for the subject–object meaning, the meaning put there "by God", in the way that they might stare at a coded message, to try to penetrate its secret. They wanted a meaning about which they could *do* something. The increased meaning that Huxley saw under mescalin did not inspire him to do anything; it was pure "bonus".

Now it would appear that the life-force offers this bonus unwillingly. It is important that men should keep their wits about them and build civilization; their attention must be confined to necessities. Beauty makes for sitting still. Conversely, a lack of beauty and meaning engenders a desire for movement. Ideally, then, a man's sense of beauty and meaning should increase when he has earned the right to sit still. Consequently the nineteenth century was full of artists and poets who felt that they had *earned* a right to see meaning in nature, but whose "intentionality" declined to pay them their wages. It was a century of boredom, a century whose symbol is Faust, aware that he will not discover meaning in books, and Oblomov, lying in bed because there is nothing else to do. Both Faust and Oblomov think back longingly on their childhood, when "meaning" and beauty were given in abundance.

This is obviously a revolutionary concept: this "meaning" which is not a subject–object relation. "Meaning" means a *relation*, not a thing in itself. It was Gestalt psychology and phenomenology that pointed out that you cannot build a science on this definition of "meaning"; you must allow that there is another kind of meaning, coming from inside and working outwards.

This inner-meaning could also be defined as a "grip on life", or as a grip on the external world, for it is a projection of the life-force into the external world. For a dying man, the world is drained of meaning.

This analysis of sexual perversion has, then, isolated a new concept in psychology; the concept of meaning that is not external, but is "projected" from a subconscious intentionality. Plainly, then, here is a new field for investigation. Writers on sex in the past have confused the two types of meaning. Sex happens to be an ideal subject for the study of this "intentional meaning" because sex is *nothing but* intentional meaning. It has no objective component. We are then inclined to ask the question: How about other human activities? How about art, for example? The art of the twentieth century could almost be called a defeatist art. Our literature is full of defeated heroes, men who are crushed by society, who feel perpetually inadequate, while painting and music have developed an aesthetic counterpart of the "Everything is lawful" idea to cover their lack of "anything to say". This comes of identifying meaning with "external meaning" and an undiscriminating acceptance of the old psychology. The artist has come to neglect the "meaning projected from intentionality" because he does not know of its existence; an awareness of its existence could lead to a revitalization of art and literature in our time.

This, then, seems to me the answer to the question posed at the beginning of this book. The "origin of the sexual impulse" is not the "libido"; it is an intentionality that is not confined to sex alone, but that also projects the "meaning" of man's aesthetic and religious activities. Its mode of operation might be suggested by an analogy. Imagine an officer riding in the depth of a tank, with an observer looking out of the gun-turret. The officer cannot see what is going on outside the tank; he has to rely on the descriptions of the observer, who may say: "Suspicious looking house with something that might be a machine-gun behind its chimney stack". The officer would then give the order to the gunner: "Open fire on it". The officer is completely dependent on the temperament of his observer, and if the observer is a neurotic who sees enemies everywhere, then the officer is in the position of the "intentionality" centre in man when the senses are "neurotic".

This image should not be examined too closely; but, taken superficially, it does offer a basically accurate picture of the workings of "symbolic response".

But what is most important in the "theory of symbolic response" is the idea of intentionality as a "meaning projector".

As I have already pointed out, this view raises questions that have so far been ignored as lying outside the field of science. Nineteenth-century science thought of "meaning" as something inherent in the world, to be discovered by scrutiny. The idealists – from Locke to Hegel – questioned this view in a rather abstract way, suggesting that some of the "meaning" is added by the senses. Berkeley went farthest in claiming that the world is entirely a projection of the mind, that ceases to exist when there is no one to observe it – at least, that *would* cease to exist, if God were not everlastingly present to observe it. In a way, Berkeley came closest to the concepts of phenomenology, in allowing man's mind the same kind of power as God. Now phenomenology seems to take a similar position. There *is* such a thing as "objective meaning", but it is not the only kind of meaning that colours the world.

All the same, such a simple dualism is not entirely satisfactory; it almost suggests the God-and-devil dualism of naïve Christianity. H. G. Wells expressed a sense of horror at this kind of dualism in *Mind at the End of Its Tether*, his pessimistic last book, when he suggested that "mind" and "nature" were like two railway lines that had been accidentally running parallel for millions of years, but are now casually separating.

In short, no one wants to believe that there is a meaning in the world which is totally independent of man and of mind. It was this view that led to the despair and nihilism of the late nineteenth century. Since phenomenology has succeeded in resolving this ancient problem and overcoming the "bifurcation of nature", it seems absurd that phenomenology should only have produced another kind of bifurcation, another dichotomy. The question we now wish to ask is: how far is intentionality connected with nature and time? Our senses are "intentional", projected out into the world of objects by the inner-will. That is to say, they are a "connection" between the "inner-will" and nature. Is it not possible that other connections exist? Rhine's studies of extra-sensory-perception over the past quarter of a century support the view that the "five senses" may not be the *only* projections of the hidden intentionality. It seems remotely possible that there may be "other senses" that are, at present, as unnecessary to man as the colour sense was unnecessary to the men of Homer's time. In fact, man has always possessed another "sense" that distinguishes him from the animals – imagination, the power of anticipating events. All the senses possess an "anticipatory" function; a shepherd can tell tomorrow's weather from the appearance of the sunset. No animal possesses such anticipatory powers. But imagination not only increases the strength of man's anticipatory powers; it can also be used as an instrument of "maturity", making certain experiences unnecessary because they be anticipated with such fullness, and thereby weakening the tyranny of the instinct that drives us to "fullness of experience". Imagination has increased man's autonomy more than any of the other senses.

But if we possess these anticipatory powers, how far does "intentionality" steer us according to anticipations of which we are not consciously aware?

These are questions that, for the moment, I raise and leave unanswered. They are clearly implied in the theory of symbolic response, but "speculation" would be a pointless procedure. What is needed is a scientific method of investigation, possibly along the same lines as the method of Gestalt psychology or the study of extra-sensory-perception. What is very clear is that the investigator's most valuable guinea pig would be himself.

But what of experiment? Phenomenology can suggest methods of observation, but can go no further. And here it seems possible that the field of aesthetics – particularly the procedure of the creative mind – might be ideal for the purpose. The great artist, after all, creates "in the service" of his intentionality, and the greatest art has always been a collaboration between the conscious will and the hidden intentionality. When the artist loses his belief in purpose and meaning, he tends to throw the burden of creation entirely upon intentionality. Tachist painting is an example of this kind of creation; certain kinds of electronic music another. All creation might be called an act of faith in intentionality; these forms of "abstract" art require a minimum of faith. We might borrow one of David Riesman's sociological terms, and say that this "faith in intentionality" is another name for inner-direction. (Riesman opposes this to "other-direction" – too much concern for what the Joneses say and do.) This failure of inner-direction is, as I have pointed out elsewhere,* the chief characteristic of twentieth-century art and literature. Many writers on aesthetics have blamed this loss of confidence and purpose on the failure of religion; they point out that great art has usually been religious art. But the theory of intentionality is nothing less than a reinstatement of the central idea of religion – the notion of a purpose that is somehow both personal and impersonal, beyond man (as a conscious being) and yet "inside" him. It remains to be seen, then, how far the scientific study of intentionality in art can make the artist aware of these drives that are at once personal and impersonal, and that, translated into consciousness, are the main constituent of great art. The ideal subject for such an investigation would be a creator who is also an intelligent phenomenologist.

Conclusion

One of the aims of this book has been to suggest a method of psychological investigation that has so far been neglected – the existential method. But its main purpose has been to argue

*The Age of Defeat.

that all writers on sex have so far looked in the wrong place for their "norm". "Natural" and "normal" are used as synonymous; this is to say that the norm is objective, is a part of nature, one of the laws of "Mother Nature". My purpose has been to attempt to show that nature has no preferences. Sex is a projection of the evolutionary intentionality. While this intentionality certainly has preferences regarding "normality", it takes no very efficient measures for enforcing them. In so far as a "libido" exists, it is *not* the origin of the sexual impulse, but a projection of intentionality – like the aesthetic impulse, the religious impulse and the social impulse. It is possible to be "sexually normal", but to be sexually supernormal would be to lose interest in sex altogether, except, as Tolstoy says, with the conscious purpose of begetting children. I have no doubt that Shaw is also right when he suggests that human beings, in the course of their evolution, will lose interest in sex in the sense of having instinctive sexual urges. Our first reaction to such an idea is dismay, the feeling "What a dull world it would be". But this is to forget that dullness is synonymous with lack of meaning, and that the intentionality which at present clothes the symbols of sex with apparent reality is in itself the organ of meaning.

It is true that this theory of evolutionary intentionality conflicts with most present schools of psychology, but the major objection is to an "evolutionary force" that is simultaneously conscious (in the sense of possessing purposes and drives) and unconscious. But the apparent contradiction arises from the Freudian habit of using unconscious (i.e. not conscious) as a synonym for sub-conscious (below consciousness). But if the mind has a basement, why should it not also have an upstairs, equally beyond the knowledge of consciousness? Since there can be no doubt of the existence of an extra-conscious intentionality, would it not be more reasonable to describe it as super-conscious rather than subconscious?

This, however, is unimportant; it might even be contended that the word "superconsciousness" is undesirable, since it suggests that it is in some way preferable to consciousness. In fact, the aim is and must always be *increase of consciousness*. The immediate problem is the development of methods for extending consciousness into the realms of intentionality.

APPENDIX

THE CRIMINAL MENTALITY

THE problem of the criminal mentality has been touched upon several times in the course of this book; it is dealt with at length in the essay "The Study of Murder". The interesting problem, for the existential psychologist, is to sort out the "creative" elements in the criminal mentality from the degenerative.

Shaw on Crime

But now an interesting question arises: is there *ever* a "positive" element in the criminal mentality? Shaw's Andrew Undershaft declares: "I moralized and starved until one day I swore I would be a full-fed free man at all costs; that nothing should stop me except a bullet, neither reason nor morals nor the lives of other men. . . . I was a dangerous man until I had my will: now I am a useful, beneficent, kindly person". Here, Shaw states the case for a certain amount of "criminality" to achieve self-expression, and justifies it by pointing out that Undershaft is now a philanthropist and model employer. It would be interesting to look up "criminal" in a concordance of Shaw's work. There is the important statement: "We judge an artist by his highest moments, a criminal by his lowest". Apart from a brief reference to Jack the Ripper in a preface (where he speaks of "poor Jack's horrible neurosis") Shaw's attitude towards criminals is, on the whole, sympathetic. (See the long dissertation on them in the stage direction of Act 3 of *Man and Superman*, the "scum and the dregs of society" – those who are too good for ordinary social employment, and those who are not good enough.) Shaw obviously believed that a good deal of crime is a justified protest against society. But Shaw enjoyed stating things in blacks and whites, and he liked the idea that a burglar may be a better man than an honest grocer. Admittedly, he agreed that it would be wiser to kill certain criminals "in a friendly and frank manner, without malice" because they are too dangerous to be left unchained, and they cannot expect to waste the lives of other men in watching them. In the *Imprisonment* preface he develops this idea interestingly, suggesting that we should destroy all prisons as breeding grounds for crime, and encouragers of all kinds of vices in the warders as well as the prisoners. The habitual criminals should be killed "without malice" as incorrigible wasters of society's time; but most criminals are "first-timers" anyway, and could be easily kept in line by social ostracism.

The theory is plausible and very attractive; but unfortunately, at the moment, any truth it contains is "poetic truth". Josephine Bell's book *Crime in Our Time* explains why. Miss Bell begins her book with a chapter on a day of crime in London – February 6, 1960, the day of the PEN Club murder, and lists the number of calls that the London police had to answer in twenty-four hours. The list would have jarred Shaw; it includes innumerable assaults, thefts, burglaries, a kidnapped baby (it was recovered in an hour, slightly bruised), and a few attempted murders. Shaw's idea that we could do without the police force is not supported by Miss Bell's chapter.

And what of Shaw's feeling that the criminal may be the man who is "too good" to accept a menial position in society? Again, the study of murder offers very little support for the view. In the preface to *Encyclopaedia of Murder* I quoted a number of typical murder cases; they were typical in that they all revealed the same slavery to the trivial. The central statement of the preface is the following: "Belief in the abnormality of the murderer is a part of the delusion of normality on which society is based. The murderer is different from other human beings in degree, not in kind. *All our values are makeshift*; the murderer simply goes further than most people in substituting his own convenience for absolute values". I cited the case of

Winford Smith, who raped and then murdered a girl in Sagi-
naw in 1941; the judge who sentenced Smith said that it was
one of the most cold-blooded murders in his experience. In
fact, Smith attempted to kiss the girl; she slapped him, and he
punched her and knocked her half-unconscious. Smith's confession contained the words: "Then I had to have her". He
killed her after the rape, when she threatened to tell about it.
"Cold-blooded" is hardly an apt term to apply to such a
murder. But it serves the purpose of erecting a barrier between
society and the criminal; he becomes an animal in a cage instead of a rather ordinary, frustrated, frightened human being.

Metaphysics of Murder

Most murders seem to have a curious quality of *miscalculation* about them. James Joyce writes of an eccentric who insists
on tapping every lamp-post with his cane as he passes. Many
people we would consider perfectly sane have similar foibles –
taking care not to walk on the cracks between paving stones,
for example. But why? It serves no practical purpose. It is a
strange result of boredom. Kierkegaard points out that we are
all more or less bored most of the time, and says that civilization was built out of boredom rather than the urge for progress. He also points out that men possess the power of dis-
ciplining themselves out of their usual state of unfulfilment;
a schoolboy who is bored by a dull lesson can provide himself
with endless amusement if he has a beetle under a nutshell. The
answer to boredom is a kind of internal pressure within man.
It cannot be called exactly "purpose"; is it purpose that keeps
the schoolboy amused with his beetle? It is rather a form of
concentration, of direction of the attention. The attention longs
to be directed in the way that a masochistic woman longs
to be dominated. A man feels strangely uncomfortable if his
attention is spread and diffused. Hence the stepping on paving
stones and tapping lamp-posts by people who have nothing
more important to "overcome", no other obstacle to concentrate the will.

This is plainly a question of "values". Let us have a working definition of the word "values". Values are what determine an act of choice. They need not be "metaphysical" or religious values. They can be simply the factor that makes a donkey choose one bundle of hay rather than another. A man who "chooses" to tap every lamp-post with his stick feels that there are no bigger issues that he prefers to choose at present.

These considerations are the basis of criminal psychology. It is as if a man lived half a mile from his work and could get to work by a direct route, but felt *compelled* to take a ten-mile detour to get to work. His workmates might reach one of two conclusions: either that he suffers from a compulsion psychosis, or that he has not yet discovered that a direct route exists. A study of most crimes produces the same feeling. They give the impression that the "values" that led the murderer to make his act of choice were based upon absurd miscalculation. The murderer is usually absurdly confused about the pressures of life in society, about the meaning of his own life and in general. He is probably more confused than most of us; but it should be recognized that he only suffers from a more acute form of the bewilderment that we all feel in the face of existence.

In studying the problem of the criminal mentality we run into a fallacy that resembles the Freudian fallacy of "normality" and perversion; we assume that there is a real dividing line between sanity and insanity. In 1812 the British Prime Minister, Spencer Perceval, was murdered by a lunatic who believed that he was the victim of a persecution plot. The lunatic was executed for murder. In 1843 another lunatic named MacNaghton (or McNaughten) shot the secretary of the Prime Minister; he also believed that people were plotting to kill him. His trial established the McNaghten rules to determine criminal insanity; these state that a criminal must be aware of the nature of his act, or that he is doing wrong, before he can be rightfully convicted. But we can only say that the "values" that led Daniel McNaghten to murder were based entirely on delusions, while the values that led Seddon to poison his lodger for her money were based upon a more complicated illusion, and upon a meanness that springs from the same psychological root as tapping lamp-posts with a stick.

When we call a man "insane", we mean that he makes his acts of choice according to a system of values that is palpably false; they may, for example, be based on the assumption that he is Napoleon. Benjamin Haydon, the painter and friend of Keats, based his life's work on the assumption that he was a man of genius. He was not; to that extent he was "insane". T. E. Lawrence based his life on the conviction that he was not a man of genius, and hid himself away as an aircraftman in the R.A.F. to escape the need to live up to his celebrity. But he was a genius; therefore his later conduct was based on an illusion; Lawrence was also, by definition, slightly insane. But all of us live on certain assumptions about what we are and what we are not, what we can contribute to civilization and what we cannot.

It may seem to us that there is a very clear distinction between our "reasonable assumptions" about our capabilities and the assumptions of a madman who thinks he is Jesus Christ. The more we limit our perceptions to a narrow, "reasonable" present and its needs, the more apparent this distinction will become. Broaden the perceptions to take in man's total ignorance of himself and his nature, and the line blurs. This ignorance does not constitute insanity; but insanity is only an extreme and distorted form of this ignorance. Crime can hardly be understood until this is grasped. How, for example, can one reach any conclusion on the case of Leopold and Loeb, or Leonard Mills? Mills was a nineteen-year-old Nottingham clerk who one day decided that he would commit "the perfect murder"; he picked up a harmless woman in the cinema – a forty-eight-year-old mother of a family – took her to a lonely spot and strangled her. He then phoned the newspapers and offered to sell the story, claiming he had found the body when looking for a quiet spot to write a sonnet. Goat fibres under the victim's nails established Mills as the killer, and he was executed a few months later. But why did he murder? He wanted to be "different"; he was always trying to impress his friends at work with schemes for winning on the football pools and with his abilities as a poet. The murder was an expression of boredom, like tapping lamp-posts.

The same, in a more complicated sense, is true of the "crime of the century", the Leopold–Loeb murder case. This is the kind of case that might have inspired Dostoevsky. In spite of the number of words that have been written about it, the definitive work still remains to be written. Nathan Leopold and Richard Loeb were homosexual students of Chicago university, both sons of millionaires. Leopold, the more interesting and intelligent of the two, suffered from various glandular disorders that caused him to be easily bored or fatigued; his blood pressure and metabolism were low; he was anaemic and easily depressed. When he was fourteen a perverted governess had committed various sexual malpractices on him and taught him to perform cunnilingus on her. This developed his latent masochism. Richard Loeb, a year older than Leopold, was a heavily built, good-looking youth, a habitual liar and petty criminal. Leopold became his slave and pathic. The murder of fourteen-year-old Bobby Franks was Loeb's idea; probably he saw in it the first step in the career of two "master criminals". Their heads were full of the idea of the Nietzschean superman. But the prosecution declared bluntly that it was a sex crime pure and simple. The two youths showed no regret at the trial; it was obvious that somehow *all this was not real to them*. Both received life imprisonment.

The key to the murder is money – the immense fortunes of their parents. (Both were allowed to write cheques for any amount they wanted without question.) So much money meant that there were no "pressures" on them. There could be no "challenge and response" in their lives. Freedom was unlimited – and therefore boring. Because there had never been any social pressure on them they had never needed to develop any kind of strength of character. To bring out all the implications of their murder would need a psychologist of the stature of Nietzsche or Pascal. For the real "criminal" in the case was freedom – a metaphysical freedom. The importance of this lesson for modern society cannot be exaggerated; it was "the crime of the century" in more senses than one.

I have pointed out in *The Study of Murder* that the "crime of boredom" is peculiar to the twentieth century, and cited the strange cases of Edgar Edwards and Norman Smith. The Edwards case seems to be a case of murder as a protest against the meaninglessness of life; in some ways it anticipates Camus's novel *L'Étranger*. Norman Smith took a pistol and shot a woman through a window. He had been watching a television programme called "The Sniper", and thought he would like to try it. He was unacquainted with his victim.

The point I am trying to make is that our complex social system has kicked away the "values" from under most people's feet. Once upon a time there were religious imperatives as well as the instinctive revulsion from crime. Nowadays, most of us instinctively shy from murder or violent crime, but could not argue at length upon the "wrongness" of crime as our ancestors of the eighteenth century could. And when the instinct against murder fails we can do little but execute the criminal. Human beings living in a huge and complex society might well feel "negated" by it. In James Jones's novel *From Here to Eternity* there is a passage in which the hero sits among his fellow soldiers drinking beer, and suddenly experiences a feeling of great happiness – of solidarity with "the army", in spite of its brutality and discomforts. But most city dwellers never experience an analogous feeling about the city and civilization. The peasant or worker of the eighteenth century could recognize that life is "unfair", that some are born rich and privileged and some poor; nevertheless, he could accept this and feel a "solidarity" with society. The social order of today is altogether less satisfying. "Life" seems to bestow fame and fortune in the oddest ways, and the "average citizen" finds it harder to accept. The juvenile delinquent can feel "Why not me?" when watching a film of James Dean or Elvis Presley; the workman feels "Why not me?" when he reads of someone winning ten thousand pounds on the football pools. Crime may only be a response to this intelligent perception of the unfairness of life in modern society. The amoral attitude of the "Beats" as portrayed by Jack Kerouac is only one stage from criminality. What is surprising is not the rising crime rate, but that so many people do *not* commit crimes in a civilization in which they feel completely negated.

The paradox remains. Civilization was created when men decided to form into groups for self-protection. The high degree of comfort and of culture in modern civilization is the outcome of an immense, large-scale co-operation that would have been beyond the imagination of a man of five hundred years ago. But the sheer size of the operation negates its individual members; in less than a century, small towns have changed into cities, and groups of town have coalesced into giants like London and Los Angeles. Civilization and comfort mean increasing negation of the individual, and a rising rate of neurosis and crime. If the trend continues, and the over-population problem increases, we can only reckon on a crime rate that increases by arithmetical progression.

Expressed in this way, the problem may seem beyond our solution. Occasionally a religious reformer announces that all our evils will increase until we learn to worship together as Christians. The basic perception is correct, but the solution is wrong. They think of Christianity as an "idea" or a force, outside the limits of space and time. But a study of the history of the Church will show that this is untrue. The Church was not held together by an idea, but by historical circumstances and social forces. As these forces vanished, and some of the basic dogmas were overthrown, the Church ceased to be a binding force in society. The idea itself is a great one, but society cannot be held together by an idea, independent of other forces; and to hope for a revival of the Church is only muddle-headed thinking, a desire to put back the clock.

Can nothing then be done? There is no one alive who can answer this question; it would require a monstrous electronic brain into which was fed all the statistics about the increase in sizes of cities and populations, and all the relevant facts about the rise of neurosis and mental disease in general. It may be that society is about to blow apart like an overstrained boiler; it may equally well be that the pressure could go on rising steadily for another hundred years without danger.

But our lack of a super-electronic brain and the necessary statistics need be no cause for despair. There are simpler measures that can be taken. We can at least recognize that the tendency to negate the individual is aggravated by our cultural assumptions, by all kinds of legacies from the nineteenth century, from John Stuart Mill, from Marx and Freud and T. H. Huxley and a dozen others, and by the way that some of the subtler of these misconceptions have been propagated by the "fashionable" thinkers of today, from Bertrand Russell to Heidegger. A sociologist of the future might do valuable work by studying a broad cross-section of criminals, and determining how far purely social influences (slum-conditions, etc.) and how far subtler cultural influences have contributed to the mentality of the criminal. This would be a logical extension of existential techniques into sociology.

PHENOMENOLOGY

Ideas, by Edmund Husserl. Allen and Unwin.

The Phenomenology of Perception, by Maurice Merleau-Ponty. Routledge. (Chapter 5 of Part One, "The Body in Its Sexual Being", is of particular importance in this context.)

The Phenomenological Movement, by Herbert Spiegelberg (2 vols.). Martinus Nijhoff, The Hague.

Being and Time, by Martin Heidegger. S.C.M. Press, Bloomsbury.

Being and Nothingness, by Jean Paul Sartre. Methuen.

SEXUAL PERVERSION AND SEX CRIME

Corydon, by André Gide. Secker and Warburg.

120 Days of Sodom, by De Sade. Olympia Press. 3 vols.

The Marquis De Sade, A Biography, by Gilbert Lely. Elek Books.

Must We Burn De Sade? by Simone de Beauvoir. Grove Press.

The Second Sex, by Simone de Beauvoir. Methuen.

The Psychology of Sex Offenders, by Albert Ellis and Ralph Brancale. Charles C. Thomas, Illinois.

The Sexual Criminal, by Paul de River. Charles C. Thomas.

Crime and the Sexual Psychopath, by Paul de River. Charles C. Thomas.

Sex Perversions and Sex Crimes, by James Melvin Reinhardt. Charles C. Thomas.

Homosexuality, Transvestitism and Change of Sex, by Eugene de Savitsch. Charles C. Thomas.

Psychopathia Sexualis, by R. von Krafft-Ebing. Rebman Ltd., 1899.

Sexual Anomalies and Perversions, drawn from the works of Magnus Hirschfeld by Norman Haire. London Encyclopedic Press.

Encyclopedia of Sex Practice, by Norman Haire. London Encyclopedic Press.

Woman's Experience of the Male, by Sophie Lazarfeld. London Encyclopedic Press.

The Psychology of Sex, by Havelock Ellis. Heinemann Medical Books.

The Sadist, A Study of Kürten, by Karl Berg. Heinemann Medical Books.

Sexual Aberrations, by Wilhelm Stekel. 2 vols. Vision.

Antisocial or Criminal Acts and Hypnosis, by Paul J. Reiter. Munksgaard.

The Homosexual Community, by Evelyn Hooker. Munksgaard.

Murder For Sex, by Robert Traini. William Kimber.

Medical and Scientific Investigations in the Christie Case, by Francis E. Camps. Medical Publications Ltd.

Ten Rillington Place, by Ludovic Kennedy. Victor Gollancz.

The Offenders, by Giles Playfair and Derek Sington. Secker and Warburg.

The Violators, by Israel Beckhardt and Wenzell Brown. Harcourt Brace and Co.

Ninth Life, A study of Chessman, by Milton Machlin and William Read Woodfield. Putnams, New York.

The Basic Writings of Sigmund Freud. Modern Library Giant.

Murder, Madness and the Law, by Louis H. Cohen. World Publishing Co., New York.

PSYCHOLOGY

Existence, A New Dimension in Psychiatry and Psychology, edited by Rollo May. Basic Books, New York.

The Phenomenon of Man, by Teilhard de Chardin. Harpers, New York.

Psychoanalysis and Existential Philosophy, edited by Hendrik M. Ruitenbeek. Dutton Paperback Original.

Psychoanalysis and Social Science, edited by Hendrik M. Ruitenbeek. Dutton Paperback Original.

Battle for the Mind, by William Sargent. Heinemann.

The Death and Rebirth of Psychology by, Ira Progoff. Routledge.

Jung's Psychology and Its Social Meaning, Ira Progoff. Grove Press.

Basic Writings of C. G. Jung, edited by Violet de Laszlo.
Modern Library.

Psyche and Symbol, Selections from Jung, edited by Violet de Laszlo.
Anchor Books.

Beyond Psychology, by Otto Rank. Dover.

INDEX

Great Life Stories in Panther Books

Fascinating Non-fiction Reading in Panther Books

Real-life Adventure and Violence in Panther Books

All-action Fiction from Panther

SPY STORY	Len Deighton	60p	☐
THE IPCRESS FILE	Len Deighton	60p	☐
AN EXPENSIVE PLACE TO DIE	Len Deighton	50p	☐
DECLARATIONS OF WAR	Len Deighton	60p	☐
A GAME FOR HEROES	James Graham*	40p	☐
THE WRATH OF GOD	James Graham*	40p	☐
THE KHUFRA RUN	James Graham*	40p	☐
THE SCARLATTI INHERITANCE	Robert Ludlum	75p	☐
THE OSTERMAN WEEKEND	Robert Ludlum	60p	☐
THE MATLOCK PAPER	Robert Ludlum	75p	☐
THE BERIA PAPERS	Alan Williams†	60p	☐
THE TALE OF THE LAZY DOG	Alan Williams†	60p	☐
THE PURITY LEAGUE	Alan Williams†	50p	☐
SNAKE WATER	Alan Williams†	50p	☐
LONG RUN SOUTH	Alan Williams†	50p	☐
BARBOUZE	Alan Williams†	50p	☐
FIGURES IN A LANDSCAPE	Barry England	50p	☐
LORD TYGER	Philip José Farmer	50p	☐

*The author who 'makes Alistair Maclean look like a beginner'
(*Sunday Express*)
†'The natural successor to Ian Fleming' (*Books & Bookmen*)

All these books are available at your local bookshop or newsagent, or can be ordered direct from the publisher. Just tick the titles you want and fill in the form below.

Name ....

Address ....

....

Write to Panther Cash Sales, PO Box 11, Falmouth, Cornwall TR10 9EN. Please enclose remittance to the value of the cover price plus:
UK: 18p for the first book plus 8p per copy for each additional book ordered to a maximum charge of 66p. BFPO and EIRE: 18p for the first book plus 8p per copy for the next 6 books, thereafter 3p per book. OVERSEAS: 20p for the first book and 10p for each additional book.
Granada Publishing reserve the right to show new retail prices on covers, which may differ from those previously advertised in the text or elsewhere.